WOW! Roger Andersen has captured the truth and inside story for executives of faith! He will give you the insights, wisdom, and personal experiences that will change you forever without compromising your values.

—JOHN F. BEEHNER
FOUNDER, WISE COUNSEL

The Executive Calling is a complete handbook for an executive who wants to model his or her faith in their secular workplace. These practical topics will help you balance biblical values with the pressures of public companies. This is thorough, practical, challenging, and encouraging. Use this for small groups, your reference library, or for everyday guidance. Become a Daniel or an Esther in your workplace.

—KENT HUMPHREYS
PRESIDENT, FCCI/CHRIST@WORK

Roger Andersen brings to the table a background of experience that should be communicated to any Christian going out to make their mark for Christ in the real world of corporate reality. His practical yet biblical insight flows out of a well of wisdom only achieved by living in the tension between internal spiritual values and the external materialistic environment that demands "results" at almost any moral price. Thank you Roger, for paying the price!

—DENNIS PEACOCKE
PRESIDENT, STRATEGIC CHRISTIAN SERVICES

This book did two significant things for me. It crystallized the nonnegotiable principles for effective transformational leadership, and it profoundly increased my understanding of the unique call and role of high capacity leaders. I will be a more relevant teacher to my working congregation because of the words on these pages.

—JOEL JOHNSON
SENIOR PASTOR, WESTWOOD COMMUNITY CHURCH

The Executive Calling is excellent. There were times when I have wondered if any more books on Christian leadership could be written. Your book shows it can! It shines new light on many issues for the Christian businessperson. It's a "must read" for Christians in the corporate world.

—PAUL HORGEN
PRESIDENT/CEO, THINK MUTUAL BANK

I was astonished to find myself completely engrossed! This book is an excellent blend of personal experiences and good references, all woven into a fabric of scriptural principles. I particularly enjoyed the revealing survey from which a person could locate himself/herself. Had I seen this years ago, I could have made some needed self-corrections in my own career. This is a good reference book for executives who desire to be godly in business without being religious. Secular executives will also derive benefits from the content.

—ROBERT O. NAEGELE JR.
FOUNDER OF THE MINNESOTA WILD NHL FRANCHISE

You will find that *The Executive Calling* provides an excellent bridge between the church and workplace, a path that Christians can follow to demonstrate excellence in their marketplace.

—STEVE MARR
AUTHOR OF *PROVERBS FOR BUSINESS* AND HOST OF THE ONE-MINUTE RADIO
FEATURE *BUSINESS PROVERBS*

It is an interesting phenomenon that while working in the corporate world with hundreds, even thousands, of people, you can feel that you are isolated and alone, particularly when faced with demanding requirements and difficult decisions. *The Executive Calling* is a great companion to help the corporate leader navigate the challenges of leading in the corporate environment while growing in your relationship with Jesus Christ.

—DAVID BROOKS
EXECUTIVE PASTOR, LIQUID CHURCH
(FORMERLY VICE PRESIDENT GLOBAL FINANCIAL SERVICES, BOC GROUP LTD.)

Roger Andersen has the experience and faith to explain what it takes to authentically walk out your faith in the marketplace. Roger's experience in how to be true to your faith in large companies, when times are good and when they are bad, needs to be heard by Christian business leaders. Thank you, Roger, for sharing your story.

—DENNIS DOYLE
CEO OF THE WELSH COMPANIES

ROGER D. ANDERSEN

THE
EXECUTIVE
CALLING

CREATION
HOUSE
A STRANG COMPANY

THE EXECUTIVE CALLING by Roger D. Andersen
Published by Creation House
A Strang Company
600 Rinehart Road
Lake Mary, Florida 32746
www.creationhouse.com

Unless otherwise noted, all Scripture quotations are from the Holy Bible, New International Version of the Bible. Copyright © 1973, 1978, 1984, International Bible Society. Used by permission.

Unless otherwise noted, all definitions come from *Merriam-Webster's Collegiate Dictionary, 10th Edition* (Springfield, Massachusetts: Merriam-Webster Inc., 1999).

Cover design by Amanda Potter

Library of Congress Control Number: 2008921644
International Standard Book Number: 978-1-59979-346-7

First Edition

08 09 10 11 12 — 9 8 7 6 5 4 3 2 1
Printed in the United States of America

DEDICATION

THIS BOOK IS dedicated to my wife, Beti, and daughters, Katie and Robin, who endured long work hours in my occupation as a corporate executive. As Leo Hindrey Jr., former CEO of AT&T Broadband said, "What does it take to be a CEO? A lot." Thank you for your love and patience when I was so often absorbed with my job.

I also dedicate this book to the employees who worked with me and for me. I pray that my work had a positive impact on your efforts in life.

Third, this is dedicated to the clients and vendors with whom I dealt. My goal was to associate with you honestly and fairly.

Finally, but not least, this book is dedicated to the owners of the companies that bestowed responsibility on me. I always endeavored to make your ventures successful. I hope I contributed along the way.

God blessed me. I thank God most of all.

ACKNOWLEDGMENTS

I WISH TO THANK the many friends who encouraged and helped me through the writing and publishing process. Special thanks to Ray Hagelman, Warren Serrenbetz, Connie and Mark Zurcher, Joel Johnson, Paul Horgen, Kent Humphries, John Beehner, Dave Brooks, Kathy Viscardi Martin, and Denny Loving, each of whom read various editions of the manuscript and offered combinations of criticism, praise, and good advice.

I would also like to thank Dennis Doyle, CEO of The Welsh Companies, who invited me to speak at a prayer group—at which I met Steve Strang (CEO of Strang Communications) and had the opportunity to leave him with a copy of my manuscript.

Finally, my greatest thanks go to Paul Teeter, my roommate from Wheaton College and good friend. He spent many hours reviewing and editing early versions of *The Executive Calling*. It is impossible to adequately describe how important his help was.

CONTENTS

Introduction..ix

Part I: Christian Perspectives on Business Leadership

Chapter 1 The Need for Christian Executives.............. 1

Chapter 2 Answering the Call......................... 23

Chapter 3 Understanding the Responsibilities.............. 33

Part II: Christian Leaders in the Corporate World

Chapter 4 Corporate Leadership Qualifications 55

Chapter 5 The Christian Advantage 64

Chapter 6 Perceived Christian Weaknesses 93

Part III: Managing Righteously—The Apostle Paul's Example

Chapter 7 Motivating the Team 125

Chapter 8 Setting Expectations....................... 143

Part IV: Dangers and Blessings

Chapter 9 Executive Dangers......................... 165

Chapter 10 Executive Blessings 188

The Christian Executive's Study Guide 197

Notes 217

About the Author................................... 227

INTRODUCTION

G OD DESIGNED YOU. He gives each of us gifts and talents that are designed for what He calls us to do. He calls some of us to be ministers; others to be lawyers, carpenters, caregivers, mechanics, or artists. He may have designed you to be a corporate leader.

Corporations, however, have been plagued by scandals—Enron, Tyco, WorldCom, and many others. Corporate leaders are distrusted and corporations are widely viewed as greedy and uncompassionate. The corporate world *needs* honest leaders of the highest character and integrity. God may have called you to be one of them.

As a Christian, integrity and a spirit of servanthood provide a strong basis for leadership. Christians, however, are sometimes perceived as lacking important qualities for leadership, such as decisiveness, toughness, courage, a willingness to take risks, vision, or charisma. Much of this is misunderstanding and secular bias, but in some cases it reflects our own misunderstanding of Scripture.

The church has largely been silent on many of the difficult practical matters that executives (and others in secular vocations) encounter in the business world. Certainly, we hear how we should treat others with love and forgiveness and to always act with integrity, but what advice does God have for handling a lazy employee, driving hard to improve profitability, the "problem" of wealth, being decisive and bold, holding people accountable, or the importance of your work to God?

Laura Nash, author of *Believers in Business* writes:

> Even business writing by evangelical authors tends to sidestep concrete problems in business such as choosing a product, being effectively shrewd without compromising Christian ideals, dealing with underperforming businesses, and making hard choices about benefits and salaries in the face of performance expectations from shareholders.[1]

As a Christian, you may have guilt about firing an employee instead of forgiving him; you may believe that profit doesn't really matter in the eternal scheme of things; that employees should always be shown compassion rather than be held accountable; that you should be prayerful and patient, not bold and decisive; or that you aren't as important to God in your work as are people in the ministry. Misconceptions such as these may have two results:

- The Christian may be seen as not having "the right stuff" because of struggles with handling many of these problems. Therefore, he or she is not selected for leadership roles.

- Or, a Christian may avoid a leadership role because of fears that, with such responsibility, he or she will face too many conflicts with a Christian life. Hence, he or she does not even enter the job race.

I believe both situations are unfortunate, unnecessary, and misguided. We need Christian corporate executives, and this may be God's greatest calling for you. If you were designed to be a business leader, He wants you to be a bold and effective one. There are dangers for Christians who seek the corner office, but God can help guide you on the right path.

I hope this book challenges your thinking. It is my prayer that this book will help guide you on the path to becoming a corporate leader or, if you are already there, that it will strengthen your belief that you are doing exactly what God called you to do.

PART I

CHRISTIAN PERSPECTIVES ON BUSINESS LEADERSHIP

— Chapter 1 —
THE NEED FOR
CHRISTIAN EXECUTIVES

WHY WOULD GOD call us to be an executive in a secular corporation? The business world is full of immorality, and Christians are bashed regularly. Those in prominent positions are especially subject to the microscope.

God, however, designed us for work, whether in the ministry or a secular career. We should thank God for missionaries who answered the call to take on challenging or dangerous missions, but we also have a mission field right here at home that needs Christian leadership—corporate America.

Why then wouldn't God also call you to be a leader in the business world? If God designed you for this, it may be your calling.

God's First Commandment

The LORD God took the man and put him in the Garden of Eden to work it and take care of it.
—GENESIS 2:15

A week contains 168 hours. A typical breakdown of the week might include:

- fifty-five hours involved with work (at work, commuting, dressing, etc.),
- fifty hours sleeping,
- ten hours spent with family,

- five hours doing home chores,
- five hours of recreation and community activities, and
- three hours related to religious activities (church attendance, Bible study, etc.).

Work, in this example, involves 71 percent of your *waking* day, yet how much time do church leaders spend teaching or talking about Christian life in the workplace? Doug Sherman and William Hendricks, in their book *Your Work Matters to God,* refer to a study done with two thousand people who regularly attend church. They asked them, "Have you ever in your life heard a sermon that applied biblical principles to everyday work issues?" More than 90 percent replied, No.[1]

Your church probably has support groups for unemployed members or holds retreats, which are also useful for networking among fellow Christians; however, it probably devotes little time to instruction and discussion about practical matters related to being both a Christian *and* a success in your job. A great deal of church effort is placed on your role as a husband, wife, or parent; your relations with neighbors; helping the needy; and evangelizing. These all are correct and important messages—but what about the other 70 percent of your life?

I attended and received my undergraduate degree from Wheaton College, a highly respected evangelical Christian college. I and fellow students received a strong liberal arts education and excellent scriptural instruction. However, might we also have been better prepared if there were greater focus on preparing us more specifically for living as a Christian in the careers we chose? Instead, the majority of us who chose secular careers went to a corporate world for which we were ill-prepared and one about which our churches said little. After college, our counselors were secular bosses on the job.

Christian institutions need to be far more active in preparing Christians to integrate faith with their secular careers. God wishes us to be a success at work: "Walk in all the way that the LORD your God has commanded you, so that you may live and prosper and prolong your days in the land that you will possess" (Deut. 5:33). My definition of the word *success* is doing our job well to glorify Him and receiving His blessing for performing well. He blesses us by meeting our needs.

God's very first command to Adam was to work and care for the earth (Gen. 2:15), and it was given as a blessing. Although the labor of work became more difficult after original sin, God reiterated his commandment: "So the LORD

God banished him from the Garden of Eden *to work* the ground" (Gen. 3:23, emphasis added). God did not make work a curse; he had already commanded it and blessed it in Genesis 2. God also made childbirth painful and more difficult (Gen. 3:16), but we still believe the birth of a child is a blessing!

Numerous passages later in the Bible refer to the blessing of work:

> The sleep of a laborer is sweet.
> —ECCLESIASTES 5:12

> He who works his land will have abundant food.
> —PROVERBS 28:19

> The hardworking farmer should be the first to receive a share.
> —2 TIMOTHY 2:6

In April 1942 Dorothy Sayers, an acclaimed mystery novelist, professor, and a devout Anglican, delivered this address:

> In nothing has the church so lost Her hold on reality as in Her failure to understand and respect the secular vocation. She has allowed work and religion to become separate departments, and is astonished to find that, as a result, the secular work of the world is turned to purely selfish and destructive ends, and that the greater part of the world's intelligent workers have become irreligious, or at least, uninterested in religion.
>
> But is it astonishing? How can one remain interested in a religion which seems to have no concern with nine-tenths of life? The church's approach to an intelligent carpenter is usually confined to exhorting him not to be drunk and disorderly in his leisure hours, and to come to church on Sundays. What the church should be telling him is this: that the very first demand that his religion makes upon him is that *he should make good tables*.
>
> Church by all means, and decent forms of amusement, certainly—but what use is all that if in the very center of life and occupation he is insulting God with bad carpentry? No crooked table legs or ill-fitting drawers, I dare swear, came out of the carpenter's shop in Nazareth. Nor, if they had, could anyone believe they were made by the same hand that made heaven and earth. No piety in the worker will compensate for work that is not true to itself; for any work that is untrue to its own technique is a living lie.[2]

Doing your job well is God's first calling to you. In response to this, God promises "sweet sleep," "abundant food," and "the first share." So why doesn't the church talk more about this and provide more practical advice on your life as a Christian who does his job well?

Sherman and Hendricks believe the silence of the church can result in three possible responses:

1. **Your work does not matter to God**. This destroys the dignity of what you spend 70 percent of your time on and, therefore, you are less likely to do your job well.

2. **Religion is irrelevant** because it doesn't speak to you about the activity you predominantly spend your time in. Therefore, you reject religion.

3. **You live like a schizophrenic**, in "God's world" part of the time and in a separate work world most of the time. As such, you can never fully be a Christian, nor can you fully receive God's blessing for your work. I think more of us have fallen into this third category.[3]

The Bible has a great deal to say about your life in the business world.

Work is the Bible's first commandment and God blesses it. Your Christian life and work life are meant to be integrated. Although evil is rampant in the corporate world, this is not God's curse on work but instead a reflection of man's sin. There are challenges, but there is no fatal clash between the corporate world and your faith. And doing your job well results in blessings from our Lord.

> I suggest that we have come to the day of the layperson, the day when the key operative in the Church is not a pope or a saint or a monk or an evangelist or a missionary or even a "highly committed" churchman—but the everyday worker who simply puts Christ first in his or her career, as in the rest of his life.[4]
>
> —DOUG SHERMAN and WILLIAM HENDRICKS

The Most Important Vocation

We have different gifts, according to the grace given us. If a man's gift is prophesying, let him use it in proportion to his faith. If it is serving, let him serve; if it is teaching, let him teach; if it is encouraging, let him encourage; if it is contributing to the needs of others, let him give generously; if it is leadership, let him govern diligently; if it is showing mercy, let him do it cheerfully.

—ROMANS 12:6–8

In Romans 12, Paul instructs Christians to participate in the church in ways that best use the gifts that God gave them. But what about God's calling in your vocation?

Sherman and Hendricks make this observation:

> …many workers feel that while it is easy to see how a missionary or preacher might be called, it is much less certain whether God's call extends to a plumber, a doctor, or a salesperson. Of course, this has unfortunate implications for the dignity of everyday work and workers. For if only clergy are called, that implies that "secular" workers are not called— that somehow they did not make God's "first team."[5]

Perhaps there is even a second string, junior varsity, and a scrub league. I wonder if there isn't an implicit hierarchy among Christians relating to their vocation:

- The Ministry (First String)—Those called to be ministers, missionaries, or evangelists are answering God's "highest calling" because they are saving souls and equipping other Christians to do God's work.

- Caregivers (Second String)—Physicians, nurses, social workers, and people working for charities are second in the hierarchy because they are working to heal suffering, meet the needs of people, protect the earth, or do other good deeds.

- Honest Laborers (Junior Varsity)—Farmers, people in trades, factory workers, and others who work with their hands and the sweat of the brow are respected for their hard work and the struggle to provide for their families. There are several verses in the Bible where God blesses the honest laborer.

- Management (Scrub League)—Many corporate managers and leaders are seen as oppressors of honest laborers. They are often thought to fire good people, make them work too hard, treat them disrespectfully, and are generally greedy in their efforts to gather wealth at the expense of others.

The purpose of this book is to show that if God designed you to be an executive, this is God's highest calling for you. If you have tremendous compassion for the sick and strong science acumen, God's highest calling might be for you to be a doctor. If you are highly mechanical and interested in engines, God's highest calling might be for you to be an auto mechanic. Or, if you have extraordinary mathematical and design skills, maybe you have been called to be a car or airplane designer. You might even be called to be a lawyer—perhaps someone should write *The Lawyer Calling*.

Sherman and Hendricks put it very well:

> If you want to find God's will you should start by assessing what equipment He has sovereignly designed into you. That equipment is part of His will. Design reveals the Designer's will.[6]

Would God have been glorified more if Albert Einstein were a missionary instead of a mathematician? Did God design Rembrandt for the ministry? If your gift is leadership and you have other skills that enable you to be a strong corporate executive, is this not God's calling? If God designed your skills to be an outstanding executive, God can be glorified by this better than if you enter a ministry to which you are ill-designed.

As an example of God's grace in your life, your character can be a witness to hundreds in your organization and to your vendors and customers as well. The opportunities are tremendous. This is your ministry.

By running a company well you are caring for the livelihood and well being of hundreds or thousands of families. This is an awesome opportunity for stewardship. You are a caregiver.

Despite what some think, being an executive requires a huge commitment in time and emotion. As an executive, you likely invest as much honest labor and emotional sweat as any other vocation, so much so that handling burnout will be discussed in a later chapter. You are an honest laborer.

The rub, however, is that management is highly compensated, which to some makes them seem greedy and insensitive to the plight of the poor. None of this is necessarily true. Great good and generosity to support ministry, caregivers, or the poor also should come from responsibility and wealth.

If your vocation is integrated with God's calling, you will feel that what you are doing is serving His will. If not, you may feel guilt for not performing work of eternal value. I personally felt an increasing sense during the last ten years that I was a steward for the thousands of people that worked in my company. Each week I would strive to make the company successful in order to protect the livelihood of those employees and, by extension, their families. I also promised the Lord that I would do my best to run the company based on virtues such as total honesty, respect, and caring for the employees. I had other motivations, such as providing for my own family and honoring my commitment to the goals of the owners—both also blessed and honorable.

If, however, you do not connect with God's purpose in your vocation as an executive, you might feel that what you spend most of your life on has no eternal value. As such, you might feel the need to find purpose outside of work. Your church might organize a mission trip, building a home in a village in Central America or going to Romania to work for several days in an orphanage. Such missions are wonderful and helpful in expressing love for the needy. However, I wonder if some executives do this as a balm for feelings of guilt that they are not serving the Lord in their daily work.

Many Christians integrate faith and work very well but are led to do even more through personal service ministries. By all means, join in these church missions, but I hope you do not do so primarily because you feel that your career work is not God's work. If 70 to 80 percent of your waking concentration relates to your job and you do not see this as integrated with your faith, a week in Romania is not going to fix that.

Dorothy Sayers had something else to say on this subject:

> It is the business of the church to recognize that the secular vocation, as such, is sacred. Christian people and particularly the Christian clergy must get it firmly in their heads that when a man or woman is called to a particular job of secular work that is as true a vocation as though he or she were called to specifically religious work.
>
> Let the Church remember this: that every maker and worker is called to serve God in his profession or trade—not outside it. The apostles complained rightly when they said it was not meet they should leave the word of God and serve tables; their vocation was to preach the word. But the person whose vocation it is to prepare the meals beautifully might

with equal justice protest: It is not meet for us to leave the service of our tables to preach the word.[7]

Once again, design reveals the Designer's will. In this book we will explore the skills and characteristics required to be a successful executive. We will study the Bible and what other Christian authors have to say on practical matters of being an executive. Perhaps this will help you to determine if God designed you for this work and whether or not this is your calling. We will also explore misconceptions about what an executive is, things that might lead you as a Christian to believe that there are inherent conflicts with your faith. God gave you gifts. They can be used appropriately to glorify the Creator or they can be used to glorify self. There are choices but there are no conflicts.

> I now feel like I am fulfilling my mission, as I am able to influence many more people, of all ages, than I ever dreamed possible and understand what it is to serve others through your business.[8]
> —BILL GEORGE, FORMER MEDTRONICS CEO

The Morality Vacuum

> But mark this: There will be terrible times in the last days. People will be lovers of money, boastful, proud, abusive, disobedient to their parents, ungrateful, unholy, without love, unforgiving, slanderous, without self-control, brutal, not lovers of the good, treacherous, rash, conceited, lovers of pleasure rather than lovers of God.
> —2 TIMOTHY 3:1–4

Enron, Tyco, Arthur Andersen, WorldCom, Adelphia, AOL Time-Warner—we seem to read about corporate scandals all the time. The downfall of each CEO, CFO, or even the entire company is covered enthusiastically by the media. Some news anchors seemed to cover these stories with glee that "another evil CEO" was uncovered. Each is cast as an example of corporate greed and the injustice of capitalism.

The condemnation of Arthur Andersen by politicians and the media was so bloodthirsty that they were totally out of business before the investigation was completed. Do most people even know that the Supreme Court eventually ruled that they were not guilty? It is likely that there was wrongdoing at Arthur

Andersen, at the very least in connection with shredding documents, but the court could not determine that there was an intention of wrongdoing. It didn't matter. The company was executed in the court of public opinion well before the verdict came in. In a June 2005 *Washington Post* article, Charles Lane stated:

> Although a rebuke to the government, the court's decision is little comfort for Andersen and its former employees. The Chicago-based firm has a staff of only 200 left out of the 28,000 people who worked there.[9]

I recall little concern in the network media for the 27,800 people who were unemployed, had to relocate, lost pensions, or job seniority. Liberal media broadcasts often characterize corporations as evil entities. Simply the suggestion of corruption or even the idea that the company is making too much money brings forth condemnation from some media and the far left. Wayne Grudem wrote in *Business for the Glory of God*:

> Words like *profit, competition, money*, and even *business* carry negative moral connotations for many people today. And some people who work in the business world even labor under a faint cloud of guilt, thinking that their work may be necessary, but that from a moral perspective it is probably "neutral" at best.[10]

Last year, when my daughter was a junior in college, I asked her what she hoped to do after graduating. Her response was, "Whatever it is, I am not going to work for a *corporation*, like you did." She said this with an air of moral superiority. Corporate scandals—perfect examples for socialist-leaning professors to indoctrinate students about the evils of capitalism in general and corporations in particular—had infected my daughter's view of this free market system that made our country so prosperous.

My daughter's view is not totally without merit. John M. Huntsman, chairman and founder of Huntsman Corporation, a business with twelve billion dollars in revenue, wrote in his book *Winners Never Cheat*:

> Cooked ledgers, look-the-other-way auditors, kickbacks, flimflams of every sort have burrowed their way in today's corporate climate.[11]

He also writes:

> I have known enough business executives…who through greed, arrogance, an unhealthy devotion to Wall Street, or a perverted interpretation of capitalism, have chosen the dark side. Their numbers seem to be growing.[12]

Even 150 years ago Abraham Lincoln said:

> There is no more difficult a place to find an honest man than on Wall Street in New York City.[13]

There is a morality vacuum! I believe it has grown significantly in the last fifty years. In the fifties most people believed commonly in certain absolutes of right and wrong. As the decades progressed, so-called enlightened intellectuals taught philosophies of moral relativism and situational ethics. These doctrines grew into a culture that largely claims the pursuit of one's own gratification is the only real right and wrong.

Dennis Prager, a conservative radio talk show host, commented:

> For anyone who believes that nothing is objectively right or wrong or even true or false, moral clarity is impossible.[14]

Among many executives and aspiring young managers, the pursuit of wealth is the consuming religion. What is right in the context of their workplace is what drives wealth. Of course, if an action is illegal *and the likelihood of getting caught* makes it risky, then it is wrong since it could have negative consequences to their pursuit of wealth (consistent only with an economic evaluation of prudent risk-taking).

I believe the morality vacuum in business has progressively become worse as people who grew up in the sixties and seventies, many of which believe in moral relativism, assume leadership positions. Today, most university faculty, especially in the prestigious East and West Coast schools, are liberal-thinking atheists who further influence the current generation's view on situational ethics and personal gratification.

I noted this in particular the last twenty years. First, in my roles with Rollerblade and, later, at Young America, I spent a great deal of time with investment bankers who were potential buyers or sellers. Most of the investment bankers in their thirties and early forties struck me as fairly dishonest, devious, and untrustworthy; the "Do-whatever-it-takes-to-close-a-big-deal—or make partner" types.

I was also saddened by dealings in the last several years with my clients' vendor relation managers. Some lied, cheated, acted disrespectfully, and treated people in my company abusively, all because they felt it would accomplish their goal for the next promotion. Most of these companies had admirable Value Statements about dealing with vendors, but leaders clearly weren't in touch with whether or not these values were followed.

Yes, there is a morality vacuum. Ghandi listed "commerce without morality"[15] as one of the seven sins. Commerce itself, however, is not immoral. Only immoral people make commerce immoral. Capitalism has been the most powerful engine in history for creating progress, technology, jobs, and prosperity. Nearly all countries of some prosperity practice a form of capitalism or free trade. The system works and has been practiced informally since before biblical times. But, for all its good, it is often abused and controlled by people of ethical emptiness. This, unfortunately, is often used by the media and academics to paint all of corporate leadership with the same brush.

The Bible, however, blesses commerce.

> The craftsman encourages the goldsmith.
> —Isaiah 41:7

> She considers a field and buys it; out of her earnings she plants a vineyard.... She sees that her trading is profitable.... She makes linen garments and sells them.
> —Proverbs 31:16, 18, 24

The parable of the talents, told in Matthew 25:14–28, also illustrates commerce through the story of a wealthy man who entrusted three servants each with some of his wealth. Matthew 25:16 says, "The man who had received the five talents went at once and put his money to work and gained five more." Later, in verse 21, the master said, "Well done, good and faithful servant."

Commerce, as with work, is blessed by God. Commerce enables laborers to trade the fruit of their labor for goods that bring mutual benefit to the buyer and seller. If conducted fairly and honestly, both parties benefit and are pleased with their transaction.

As with many aspects of God's creation, commerce, which is intended to be of mutual benefit to all parties, often is perverted by godless or immoral executives. This is not a reason for Christians to avoid executive responsibilities. Rather, it may be a calling, as in a mission. Do we not, as Christians, admire and praise those missionaries who choose to spread the gospel in the most dangerous or inhospitable lands of the world? Similarly, since much of the executive community has eroded moral values, should this cause Christians to cautiously avoid the corporate arena, or could it be God's calling for some to join this community, influence it, and be an example to change it?

Do not be overcome by evil, but overcome evil with good.
—ROMANS 12:21

The Assault on Christianity

Blessed are you when people insult you, persecute you and falsely say all kinds of evil against you because of me.
—MATTHEW 5:11

Non-believers' attitudes towards Christians have changed a great deal in the last fifty years, more outwardly so in the last few decades. In the 1980s we were embarrassed by televangelist scandals like Jimmy Swaggart and Jim and Tammy Bakker. Other prominent Christian figures have been discredited since then: Ted Haggard, Robert Tilton, Peter Popoff, and Jim Whittington. Even worse, perhaps, have been the widely publicized examples of pedophilia among Catholic priests.

Just as a few corrupt executives have given corporations a tarnished image, the widely publicized headlines on flawed Christian leaders have harmed the image of Christianity. The media, the art world, academia, and liberal politicians, who twenty years ago were generally respectful or at least silent towards Christianity, have become bold in their assaults. Hollywood actors frequently describe Christians as dumb, dangerous, or even compare them to religious fundamentalists like Muslim terrorists. Liberal politicians use religious beliefs as a litmus test to disqualify judges.

A study published in 1999 by *Public Opinion Quarterly* found that 37 percent of highly educated white Americans hold, "intensely antagonistic feelings towards fundamentalists."[16] There is a clear agenda now by many of the intellectual elite to discredit Christians and to erase Christian influences. Here are several examples:

- The American Civil Liberties Union (ACLU) aggressively campaigns to remove symbols of Christianity such as the cross or the Ten Commandments from public places. Legal arguments to remove phrases like *under God* or *in God we trust* have been attempted in the courts. In 2000, the Sixth Circuit

Court of Appeals told the state of Ohio to remove from its motto "With God, all things are possible."

- A growing number of universities bar expressions of Christian belief from campuses, especially during Christmas, claiming they are offensive to others. Classes such as Introduction to Islam, however, are considered to be good instruction in diversity.

- Several popularly acclaimed theatrical plays have depicted Jesus, the Virgin Mary, and nuns in revolting stories masquerading as—and I use the term loosely—art.

- Retailers succumb to threats of lawsuits if they do not replace *Merry Christmas* with *Happy Holidays*.

- Politicians who profess to be Catholic, Episcopalian, or members of other denominations regularly condemn other politicians who actually support Christian values. Some Christians in these positions are even labeled as *evangelical* in a way designed to be a slur and suggest the person has weak judgment and intelligence.

- Although academics claim to worship diversity of thought, they act as thought police against widely held concepts, such as intelligent design.

- President Bush is deeply hated by many simply because he professes to be a Christian.

- Some liberals even defend Muslim terrorists as freedom fighters while attacking Christian views as hate speech.

- The Boy Scouts are prosecuted for their stand against gay troop leaders, even though their stance is supported by nearly all scout parents.

- High school valedictorians are barred from mentioning their faith in commencement addresses.

- The concept of separation of church and state has been corrupted from our founder's intent. Originally meant to protect the free expression of all religions, it has come to mean a concerted denial of any religious beliefs or values in the hope of driving every religious conviction—especially Christian faith—out of this country.

The Left's agenda is to stereotype Christians, evangelicals in particular, as dumb, narrow-minded, poor, easily led, and out-of-touch. Even non-Christians can often see this. Tammy Bruce, a former leader in the women's rights movement, is an atheist and a lesbian. Yet, in her book *The Death of Right and Wrong* she writes:

> When the bashing of Christian symbols is so prevalent, so mainstream, it effectively distorts our views of Christians and Christianity—arguably even Christians' view of themselves.[17]

Vincent Carroll and David Shiflett write in their book *Christianity on Trial*:

> Christians are regularly targeted for ridicule and vilification by a significant portion of America's cultural elite, a situation all the more striking in view of the prevailing hypersensitivity toward other religions, ethnic and lifestyle groups.[18]

There is a battle going on in the United States against Christianity. In David Limbaugh's book *Persecution: How Liberals Are Waging War Against Christianity*, the author describes how Christian beliefs are suppressed and attacked in education, in politics, and in the media. Churches and other Christian institutions are under fire—and corporations are also wandering into the crosshairs, as Limbaugh describes:

> Like their public sector counterparts, private sector employers are also guilty of anti-Christian discrimination. Moreover, many private corporations choose to police themselves by cleansing from their products and corporate culture anything that speaks of God.[19]

There is also an anti-Christian bias in corporate America because the image of an executive and that of a Christian are often depicted as being worlds apart. Imagine placing an ad for a CEO position and using 1 Timothy 3:2 as the basis for the qualifications:

> The overseer must be above reproach, the husband of but one wife, temperate, self-controlled, respectable, hospitable, not given to drunkenness, not violent but gentle, not quarrelsome, not a lover of money.

We probably see these as appropriate qualifications for a church leader, but they certainly do not fit with today's view of corporate leaders. The media, government, and nearly all citizens, however, say that they would like to see corporate executives of the highest moral character. One would think that a Christian would have a step up in this regard instead of being denigrated. But they don't.

Why then, should you as a Christian be called into a corporate executive career? There are six reasons:

- The corporate executive world is often a moral mess, and God might call you to shine a light in the darkness.

- A very activist segment of our population wishes to relegate Christians to unimportant roles befitting the stereotype of them as dumb, out-of-touch, and easily led astray. We know this stereotype is false. Those with God-given abilities and gifts for leadership in government, schools, and business are called to use them.

- With responsibility comes opportunity. A tremendous example is stewardship. You may find yourself responsible for the welfare of dozens, hundreds, or thousands of employees and their families. Your choices as a Christian may have a profound impact.

- As an executive you will be compensated relatively highly. Some Christians feel wealth is a problem, so I've also attempted to address this in a later section. However, wealth is clearly a blessing in that it allows you to give back generously towards your church, the poor, the ill, and other causes or charities.

- Your leadership can be a witness for Christ. It may create opportunities for you to influence the spiritual lives of many. The secular corporate world will put constraints on your freedom to witness in the workplace, but just the example of your actions can draw some to seek the truth.

- You may even be able to tip part of the cultural erosion back toward an environment that allows people to more openly declare their faith and others to seek it.

Christians are often attacked today in the media, in politics, in the judiciary, and even in business. The solution is not to withdraw from leadership challenges, but for more Christians to earn prominent positions where their views can have an influence.

> Religion must be destroyed among respectable people and left to the canaille [populace, riff-raff, scum] large and small, for whom it was made.[20]
>
> —Voltaire,
> eighteenth-century French philosopher

The Clergy Conundrum

> Now listen, you rich people, weep and wail because of the misery that is coming upon you. Your wealth has rotted, and moths have eaten your clothes. Your gold and silver are corroded. Their corrosion will testify against you and eat your flesh like fire. You have hoarded wealth in the last days. Look! The wages you failed to pay the workmen who mowed your fields are crying out against you. The cries of the harvesters have reached the ears of the Lord Almighty. You have lived on earth in luxury and self-indulgence. You have fattened yourself in the day of slaughter.
>
> —James 5:1–5

Your minister may not agree that God can call people into a corporate career. Many clergy are essentially anti-capitalistic, though they may not realize it. While businesspersons view capitalism as an engine that creates value, innovation, growth, great efforts, opportunities, and prosperity, some clergy see it predominantly as a system that creates great social and economic injustice.

Laura Nash and Scotty McLennan in *Church on Sunday, Work on Monday* describe the view of most clergy:

> One of the most disturbing findings in our interviews was the pervasive lack of awareness or interest among ecclesiastics in how deeply anticapitalist the message continues to be among many liberal and conservative clergy, however much they cultivate a warm relationship with members of their congregation.[21]

Business is regarded as the source of the economic injustice, not the cure. It is depicted as a negative force to be fought. The perceived injustices include underpaid laborers and overpaid executives, offshore outsourcing, corporate layoffs, lack of compassion for employees, corrupt cultures, and the so-called evil pursuit of corporate (and shareholder) wealth. If clergy feel that capitalism is a negative force to be fought, then you can see why it may be difficult for them to see how God could call you to make a corporation more successful.

Such views are hard to discern because, even if a minister views the corporate world as a negative force, he or she is careful to cultivate friendships with successful professionals because of the church's desire for financial support. The executives' vocations might be viewed as contaminated, but their contributions are more than welcome.

As a result, the clergy usually tend to stay on the periphery of our business lives. There is almost a wall that we pass through when we enter the corporate world. The church may not feel competent to comment on biblical teachings related to matters within our work life, but they usually don't make the effort to gain the competence or bring someone onto the church staff that has relevant experience to speak from. More likely, they feel our corporate world is in conflict with Christian salvation and consciously avoid deeper discussion about our lives at work. Therefore, the church rarely engages in instruction or discussion on how a person can be successful in the corporate world as a Christian. They could view this as aiding and abetting.

Paradoxically, clergy often believe that they *are* actively involved in addressing the needs of business people. Yet, if we look at the nature of this involvement, we see that the church most often skirts the challenges and issues pertaining to our work day, ministering primarily to the problems of disenfranchised workers. While they minister to the needs of those hurt by the corporate world, they invest little effort to provide biblical counsel on thriving as a Christian in the business world. This is another reflection of the view that corporations are the source of the problem and not a solution for it. I would categorize most of the church's focus relative to people's secular work into two categories:

- speaking against capitalism's social and economic injustices, or
- supporting members who are *casualties* of corporate life.

Speaking against injustices of capitalism

Corporations lack a social conscience and executives have insufficient compassion for the needy. This is largely the view of many clergy. The point of view is not altogether false, but it is also not complete.

Although there is a greater movement in recent decades for corporations to have a social purpose for good, the primary purpose of a corporation remains to make a profit, as will be discussed later in more detail. This isn't a condemnation of the corporate purpose; it is simply what it was designed to do. Without profit, there would be no investors. Without investors, there would be no corporations. Without corporations, there would be far fewer jobs.

One can look at the capitalist system as half-full or half-empty. If half-full, it creates jobs, produces needed goods, and contributes to the overall economic growth and prosperity. If half-empty, it creates unfair differences in wealth and excludes the uneducated, unable, and unwilling from its rewards. Most unfair, we often see examples of educated, able, and willing people who cannot find reasonable employment.

Capitalism creates inequities and all do not participate equally or even fairly in its prosperity. It is imperfect, as are most systems that are man made. The question is, Is there a better system?

There will be a better one in heaven, but here on Earth, we have not seen it. The only widely experimented alternative has been socialism, and each and every such experiment has created a greater economic divide and left vast numbers of people poor, unemployed, without freedom of choice, and subject to far greater corruption.

Capitalism does not create poverty. In fact, it creates wealth. Every country that has embraced capitalism in the last one hundred years has become wealthier. Some, however, say that many people are left behind, but capitalism has never caused people to *fall* behind. A few simply do not move forward with the rest, for a variety of reasons. It seems wrong to condemn a system that raises the standards and quality of life for the vast majority, but leaves some where they were before. Would we take a medication off the shelf that only cures 90 percent of the people? I think not.

As such, clergy should embrace capitalism and work from within to improve it, to support it, and to help congregants successfully participate in it, rather than stay on the periphery or decry it.

Workers who are casualties of corporate life

If corporations are unjust, then shouldn't it be a mission of the church to minister to those who are victimized? Yes, on both counts—corporations create an imperfect and at times unfair system, and the church should minister to those left out or hurt. Those who prosper in the corporate world should also support this ministry. Just as it may be unfair that an educated, ambitious person cannot find a good job or get started in a successful career, isn't it unfair that you, also an educated and ambitious person, prosper so much?

Give God the thanks for your prosperity and show compassion for the frustrated who have not found it.

I often see the church ministering primarily to the casualties of corporate life. The church's ministry to these individuals is important, but it is not sufficient. In the medical profession, historically the role was only to treat the sick, but it has come to understand that treating the healthy is just as important. "Eat the right foods, maintain a healthy body weight, exercise regularly, and have regular check-ups" are messages that are now central to the medical profession. Preventative medicine may, in fact, be a larger medical focus than treating the infirm, which makes sense since more people are healthy than are sick. How much then, should the church concentrate on ministering to healthy business people, rather than just the wounded? More.

For those out of work, churches often have support groups to help members to network and find jobs.

Those who are work-stressed can get counseling from clergy members.

The church sponsors businessmen's retreats. Today this may seem sexist, but their earlier intent was for Christian men in business to connect. The agenda, however, at such retreats is more on personal testimonies and discussion about honoring family. There is sometimes an emphasis on the unjust claims business has on our lives rather than tackling specific business challenges we face as Christians. It is certainly not to help Christians to be more successful in their careers. *Retreat* is an apt word.

Finally, there are programs for redemptive works. These are short charitable missions that a business person can go on to provide more meaning for his or her life, especially if his/her work life has no connection with a sense of spirituality. A person might spend two thousand dollars on travel and accommodations for this mission to do some tasks that two hundred dollars in local labor would do. The mission may be more for the redemption of the lost businessperson rather than the benefit of the needy. These missions are great, but I'd also like to see more effort developing Christians who are leaders, stewards, and shepherds of corporations.

All of these ministries are good, right, and important, but not sufficient. Where is the clergy devoting energy into preventative medicine? Help us to connect our work lives better with God. Help us to struggle through real world decisions about motivating employees, dealing with unproductive workers, interacting with dishonest vendors or clients, satisfying unethical owners, and competing righteously but successfully.

Laura Nash and Scotty McLennan put it most disturbingly:

> If Church professionals fail to detect and address deeply ingrained assumptions that are hostile to business or hopelessly devoid of practical implementation, they will engage in one of the largest acts of self-marginalization since their support of national prohibition.[22]

Unfortunately, the church may not help you to see God's calling into a corporate vocation because they cannot see it themselves. We, however, need to find ways to help the church to open its eyes and mind to becoming involved and supportive, not a spectator about what we do most of our waking day.

Consider this statement by a theologian about capitalism. It prevails elsewhere in the clergy.

> The main task of Christianity in the West is to assert the command of God in the face of capitalism, and to keep the 'left' in opposition to its champions, i.e., to confess that it is fundamentally on the side of the victims of the disorder and to espouse their cause.[23]
>
> —Karl Barth,
> twentieth-century Swiss theologian

Where Are the Christians?

> A little later someone else saw him and said, "You also are one of them." "Man, I am not!" Peter replied.
> —Luke 22:58

Over the span of my career, I had twenty-one different bosses that I reported to. To my knowledge, not one of these people was a born-again Christian. Some were very good people and others were not, yet none of them were guided at work by their faith, as far as I could discern. I can recall meeting only five people at work who expressed their faith to me. That's one every seven years! Where are the Christians in corporate management?

Perhaps there were quite a few, but they were keeping their faith hidden while at work. I confess that for much of my career, I was reluctant to share my belief in Christ with others at work. Most of those who knew me were probably unaware of my relationship with the Lord. I certainly did not encourage others to share their faith with me.

If your faith and work are not integrated and if your behavior at work does not reflect God's work in you, then you will feel embarrassed to confess your belief. That was the case with me for many years. It is probably true of a lot of people.

The corporate world can also be a dangerous place to witness, particularly if you are in a leadership position. I recall a senior executive who interviewed a candidate for another executive position. Toward the end of the interview, the candidate asked him what his outside interests were. The senior executive happily shared with him his involvement in the church and his belief in Christ. The candidate responded by stating that he did not believe in God.

Another candidate, one who was clearly more qualified, was offered the position. A few weeks later, a letter arrived from the first candidate's lawyer. He claimed religious discrimination as the basis for not getting the job and threatened to sue. Based on advice from the company's attorney, they settled with this candidate for a significant amount of money.

The seeming lack of Christians in corporate leadership may be in part because some are embarrassed to share their faith, while others are afraid of legal risks. Company policy may also discourage it. Yet, I think that there truly are very few believers among the corporate leadership ranks. Perhaps it is because many Christians choose not to "swim with the sharks."

You may have been given the talents and have the skills to become a leader, but your motivation to be a servant leader is not as strong as those motivated by ambition, greed, or a lust for power. God tells us to be content with what He has given us, but I do not think He calls us to relegate positions of influence to non-believers.

Perhaps you feel that your career competition is fraught with people who do anything to get ahead and it seems impossible to succeed unless you join in on the lying, politics, back-stabbing, self-promotion, disregard for family, and other practices not in harmony with our faith. You can still succeed against them. Scripture is filled with examples of godly persons who triumphed over the unrighteous.

Whatever the reasons, my prayer is that if God gave you the required talent and if He is calling you to be a leader of faith in the corporate world, you will consider it. There are dangers in swimming with the sharks. I have discussed many of these in a later chapter called Executive Dangers. But take heart— you can swim with the sharks without being eaten by them. God can help you become a strong leader. The scriptural leaders that He chose became courageous, decisive, innovative, visionary, and had presence.

Why would God not motivate you with a passion into this vocation? Missionaries, when called, are motivated with tremendous dedication to endure hard living situations and even difficulties for their families. They are motivated to be a witness and to bring people to the Lord. As a corporate leader, you can be highly motivated to be a godly steward and a servant leader. The number of people that you can impact as an ethical and caring leader is great.

Where are the Christian leaders? I became one. Once I dedicated my work to the Lord, it became far more fulfilling and my decisions became clearer. It was a wonderful blessing. I hope you will consider doing the same. We need you.

> If you do not choose to lead, you will forever be led by others...but you can make a difference, if you choose to.[24]
> —J. MICHAEL STRACZYNSKI,
> TELEVISION PRODUCER AND DIRECTOR

— Chapter 2 —

ANSWERING the CALL

D ID GOD DESIGN you with gifts and skills to lead in the business world? Are you willing to ask God to help you to develop these skills and to magnify them for His glory? Do you want to serve righteously so that others will experience God's grace in their business environment and be drawn to Him? Are you willing to make the commitment? It takes a lot.

Leadership 101

Do you see a man skilled in his work? He will serve before kings; he will not serve before obscure men.
—PROVERBS 22:29

In 2001, the dean of a leading seminary preached a Sunday sermon entitled "Christian Leadership 101." Here is the dean's advice:

> The qualities of "good leadership" are more gracious gifts of God to be gratefully received rather than skills, techniques, or knowledge to be savvily developed. When the chips are down, all biblical leaders have for credentials is faith in the promise, "Go, I will be with you."[1]

Is this what the church should teach us about leadership; that we really don't need skills, techniques or knowledge, so long as we have faith that God will be with us?

Why then do pastors go to divinity schools where they not only study

Scripture, but also develop public speaking skills and are instructed in many other practical areas pertinent to building and leading a church? Why did the apostle Paul provide so much practical advice to early church leaders?

I recently read a book on the history of Christian missions entitled *From Jerusalem to Irian Jaya,* by Ruth A. Tucker. The efforts and sacrifices of the missionaries who spread the gospel are amazing, but I also found it remarkable and tragic that so many were ill prepared and equipped. For each early missionary (in the eighteenth and nineteenth centuries) that had a lasting impact in China, Africa, and South America, there seem to have been many missionaries that died or returned home in failure. In addition, it seems nearly all these missionaries sacrificed their wives and many of their children. Most received little preparation and training for where they were going. Those that died are martyrs, but many of them were also incompetent to fulfill their calling, though their faith in God was strong. Faith is sufficient for eternal salvation, but not for your vocation, whether it is the ministry, carpentry, or management. Gifts, knowledge, skills, and techniques are also needed.

Is corporate leadership a vocation that God treats in a separate category? Does it not require skills and knowledge in the same way as a trade such as carpentry or plumbing? Imagine telling plumbers not to worry about skills and techniques as long as they have faith that God is with them. I daresay these plumbers would build very leaky homes.

Read Matthew 4. Jesus was sent out into the desert for forty days to be tempted and tested. This was God's preparation; this was His test and strengthening. He needed this before His ministry and His journey to the cross.

In Exodus, God sends Moses out of Egypt to Midian. He lived there with the family of Jethro, a priest, for forty years (Acts 7:30). During this time God prepared him, and I am certain that Jethro was used for this purpose.

Gifts and skills are very different from each other. A gift is a special talent or aptitude endowed by God. *Skill* is defined as a learned power to do something competently. The former is given; the latter is learned.

In the same sense, God gives us gifts, talents, and abilities. We develop those further through experience if we are in harmony with the gifts God gave us. They become skills, techniques, and knowledge.

God forges us. God does not miraculously turn a farm worker into a corporate executive. More likely, a farm worker goes to college; studies diligently; gains experience in entry-level jobs; and works hard developing the skills, techniques, and knowledge necessary to become a successful corporate executive.

Vince Lombardi once said, "Leaders are made, they are not born. They are made by hard effort, which is the price which all of us must pay to achieve any goal that is worthwhile."[2]

Thus, if God gives us the gift of leadership and we feel called to be a corporate executive, we need to understand what qualities, skills, and knowledge must be developed to fully utilize this gift. God gives us the ingredients, the capabilities. Faith in God is necessary to best use them properly, but it takes work to develop them.

> If the ax is dull and its edge unsharpened, more strength is needed but skill will bring success.
> —ECCLESIASTES 10:10

Business Ethics 101

> Do your best to present yourself to God as one approved, a workman who does not need to be ashamed and who correctly handles the word of truth.
> —2 TIMOTHY 2:15

If you are an executive, you are probably exposed to numerous business-people who seem to have weak ethics. If you are considering a corporate vocation and aspire to a leadership position, you can expect to run into many such people. I have. I'm not sure if executives in the last two decades have become less ethical or if I've simply been exposed to more of them as I rose in corporate leadership roles. Whatever the reason, the observation has bothered me.

In doing research for this book, I read the *Harvard Business Review on Corporate Ethics*. Although I was aware that the Harvard faculty, in general, is extremely liberal, I was still sure that those writers and researchers concentrating on the subject of ethics would have some clarity and wisdom. I was wrong. After completing the book, I remarked to my wife that I understood more clearly why many college graduates have little moral clarity. Here are several quotes from this book:

> Instead of acting like moral bookkeepers, quiet leaders bend the rules and own up to their deeper responsibilities.[3]

> Before they take stands or tackle tough problems, quiet leaders calculate how much political capital they are putting at risk and what they can expect in return.[4]

> Like some Triassic reptile, the theoretical view of ethics lumbers along in the far past of Sunday School and Philosophy 1, while the reality of practical business concerns is constantly measuring a wide range of competing claims on time and resources against the unrelenting and objective marketplace.[5]

> Executives who ignore ethics run the risk of personal and corporate liability in an increasingly tough legal environment.[6]

> Many business practices are neither black nor white but exist in a gray zone, a moral free space through which managers must navigate.[7]

> [Defining moments] force us to find a balance between our hearts in all their idealism and our jobs in all their messy reality.[8]

Deeper responsibilities, political capital, competing claims on time and resources, personal and corporate liabilities, messy reality; these are keys to ethical clarity?

Charles Colson, who was involved in the Watergate scandal before becoming a Christian and founding Prison Fellowship, addressed a class on ethics at Harvard University. This is what he had to say:

> You can't teach ethics here because you don't believe there are moral laws. But there are moral laws just as certain as there are physical laws. We are simply unwilling to admit it because it interferes with our desire to do whatever we please, and doing what we please has become the supreme virtue of our society.[9]

My own experience in the business world has exposed me to many CEOs, owners, directors, investment bankers, lawyers, and executives in lending institutions. Each seemed to have their own ethical standards, and I think there is an implicit hierarchy. Based on many meetings with such executives, here is my picture of the hierarchy on difficult ethical subjects.

Of these six levels, I would say that corporate board discussions are mostly focused on the bottom three levels, which deal with the legality of a given action. For many, ethics is mostly a matter of law; however, Jon Huntsman points out that this should not be the first consideration.

> We are not always required by law to do what is right and proper. Decency and generosity, for instance, carry no legal mandate. Pure ethics are optional.[10]

At Young America, I inherited a large issue that fell at Level 3. After a lot of consideration and discussion with our chairman, we moved up to Level 4, prompting us to stop the practice. Some companies operate consistently at levels four and five. The problem, however, is that when each company or CEO defines their own moral values, it is not a standard but rather an opinion that changes with different views. While value statements and codes of conduct are very important to communicate corporate ethics, the only consistent and solid source for these are what God provided for us in the Bible.

Dennis Prager, a popular radio talk show host, TV guest, lecturer, and author on many subjects relating to morality, wrote:

> …the key element to Judeo-Christian morality remains simply this: There is good and there is evil independent of personal or societal opinion; and in order to determine what it is, one must ask, "How would my God and my God-based text judge this action?" rather than, "How do I—or my society—feel about it?"[11]

As a business executive, you will surely deal with executives of lower moral character. In fact, as a Christian, you may deal with few having the same standards. Scripture has a multitude of advice on ethics.

> The LORD abhors dishonest scales, but accurate weights are his delight.
>
> —PROVERBS 11:1

> Do not pervert justice or show partiality. Do not accept a bribe, for a bribe blinds the eyes of the wise and twists the words of the righteous.
>
> —DEUTERONOMY 16:19

> If anyone competes as an athlete, he does not receive the victor's crown unless he competes according to the rules.
>
> —2 TIMOTHY 2:5

> I will judge you according to your conduct.
>
> —EZEKIEL 7:3

> Whatever happens, conduct yourself in a manner worthy of the gospel of Christ.
>
> —PHILIPPIANS 1:27

> A good name is more desirable than great riches; to be esteemed is better than silver or gold.
>
> —PROVERBS 22:1

My advice on Ethics 101 is this: avoid conversations on the ethical hierarchy that are at Levels 1 and 2. Stick to Levels 3 to 6, where legality, reputation and character, values, and the Lord are the criteria used in decision making.

If an issue is stuck at Level 3, a gray area, seek as much advice as possible on its legality and also concentrate on the Level 4, 5, and 6 questions to settle the discussion. On one situation of great complexity, our company actually went to the attorney general for the Minnesota district and posed the question. We received a response indicating they felt certain it was legal.

Hank Paulsen, CEO of Goldman Sachs said, "Whenever there is a close call, you need to seek a second set of eyes and ears."[12] A second set of eyes and ears is good advice. There are times, however, when that second set of ears ought to be God. On particularly unclear ethical issues, ask Him for advice.

God is your business partner. He wants your hard work to be successful and He works by your side to help in that. Honor your Partner by doing business as He would. In hard times or when dealing with unethical competitors, clients, vendors, or owners He will support you. In good times He will celebrate with you.

> And let us with caution indulge the supposition that morality can be maintained without religion. Whatever may be conceded to the influence of refined education on the minds of peculiar structure, reason and experience both forbid us to expect that national morality can prevail in exclusion of religious principle.[13]
>
> —GEORGE WASHINGTON,
> FIRST PRESIDENT OF THE UNITED STATES

It Takes a Lot

I worked harder than all of them—yet not I, but the grace of God that was with me.
—1 CORINTHIANS 15:10

When I started my career as a financial analyst at PepsiCo in 1976, I regularly put in fifty hours or more per week. A very tough guy named Paul Johnson was my first manager, and he made it clear that, in addition to abilities, we needed to demonstrate a diligent work ethic. He often reminded us to never go home before the CFO, since he would walk down the halls on his way out and take notes on who was burning the midnight oil. I used to watch Taylor going home at six o'clock and think how great it would be if I became an executive and could go home early. I got part of my wish—becoming an executive—but the going home early part never happened.

When we had deadlines to hit, during annual planning time, or before financial reviews with senior management, we worked whatever hours were needed. I remember many occasions when I worked until two or three in the morning, even a few where I worked all night to make a morning deadline.

Corporations place a premium on employees who are dedicated and hard working. There are numerous smart and talented managers, but those who demonstrate a willingness to put in whatever hours are needed at times of crises are noticed more often when promotional opportunities arise. It takes a lot of hard work to rise into the top executive ranks. Once there, however, it takes even more. Leo Hindery, a former CEO of AT&T Broadband, Global Center, and The Yes Network commented, "You've simply got to put in the hours—there's no other way to get the job done and inspire others to also give their utmost."[14]

Michelangelo once said, "If people only knew how hard I work to gain mastery, it wouldn't seem so wonderful at all."[15]

Earlier in my career, I could measure the time I worked solely by the hours I spent at the office. I would get my job done, make my recommendations, and leave the weighty decisions on the shoulders of the CFOs or CEOs. During commutes, I would be lost in the music blaring on the radio. At home, work was out of mind, and despite long office hours, I was refreshed by conversation with my wife and friends.

But, as Young America's CEO, whether I was at the office for forty hours or sixty, work was never far from my mind during the rest of my waking time. I would be wrestling with service issues in my mind during dinner, solving client problems as I lay down to sleep, and on my way to work the next morning I might be planning how we would tackle a sales opportunity.

The stereotype of soft CEOs putting in banker's hours, enjoying sumptuous business dinners, conducting business on the golf course, and going on boondoggles for business meetings is a distortion of the reality. In truth, when the CEO is at a business dinner, he or she is probably wishing to be at home with family; and when at home probably feels guilty at times for only listening to the kids with half an ear, as the day's issues are occupying much of his or her thoughts.

Responsibility for shareholder investments and for a great part of employees' lives can be a burden for much of the waking day. That's why John C. Maxwell includes commitment in his listing of the twenty-one most important qualities of a leader. He quotes Stephen Gregg, chairman and CEO of Ethix Corporation:

> People do not follow uncommitted leaders. Commitment may
> be displayed in a full range of matters including the work hours
> you choose to maintain, how you work to improve your abilities,
> or what you do for your fellow workers at personal sacrifice.[16]

Being an executive will take a lot, and you may often feel weary and burdened. Job, the Old Testament figure who endured tremendous trial, said:

> Does not man have hard service on earth? Are not his days
> like those of a hired man? Like a slave longing for the evening
> shadows.
> —JOB 7:1–2

Yet, God promises rest for the weary if we study His Word and call on Him.

The Sovereign LORD has given me an instructed tongue, to know the word that sustains the weary.

—ISAIAH 50:4

Come to me, all you who are weary and burdened, and I will give you rest.

—MATTHEW 11:28

Toward the end of Elijah's ministry, the prophet lay down and asked the Lord to take his life. "I have had enough," Elijah said (1 Kings 19:4). He fell asleep, and an angel of the Lord came and put bread and water by his side. The angel then touched Elijah and said, "Get up and eat, for the journey is too much for you" (v. 7). After eating and drinking what the angel had provided, Elijah got up and traveled forty days and forty nights to Horeb (Mount Sinai). What a tremendous story of how, at our weakest times, God can provide us with strength, give us rest, and nourish us, even giving us tremendous energy and endurance.

To be an executive, and especially a CEO, is a great responsibility and requires a large commitment. If this is your calling, you will find it to be exciting and rewarding, but also very tiring at times. To handle this, I recommend eight practices. Making time for all eight was usually impossible, but I've found that the more of these I did, the stronger I felt to tackle the day.

- Do your best, but when you have done so, take any work burdens to God in prayer and ask Him for strength and guidance to handle them; or when there is nothing else to be done, simply ask God for His will to be done—and unload the burden.

- Frequently share your work concerns with your family and thank them for their support. Their loving response can be a source of strength and peace.

- Take more time to become interested in your family's lives and show them your love. It will reduce your preoccupation with the job.

- Find recreational activities on the weekend that will take your mind off of work. Golf, fishing, or bird hunting with friends worked for me.

- Find a hobby or interest that you can do for a while in the evening to block out work. I usually read a good novel at night until I fall asleep. If I don't, I might roll around for hours thinking about work.

- Have an exercise schedule. Physical exercise creates more energy than it consumes.

- In addition to daily devotional time, open the Scripture when weary to seek comfort and assurance. God's love can help shed a lot of burdens.

- Observe the Sabbath and go to church. So often I have found peace and rest sitting in a pew or singing a hymn on Sunday.

> I [Jesus] am the vine; you are the branches. If a man remains in me and I in him, he will bear much fruit; apart from me you can do nothing."
>
> —John 15:5

The Vine nourishes the branches. Without the water from the Vine, the branch withers in the long, harsh sun. The work of an executive can be mentally and emotionally tiring. It takes a lot. But a Christian executive has an advantage in that God can renew and restore him.

> Luck is a dividend of sweat. The more you sweat, the luckier you get.[17]
>
> —Ray Kroc,
> founder of the McDonald's Corporation

— Chapter 3 —

UNDERSTANDING ᴛʜᴇ RESPONSIBILITIES

Cᴀɴ ʏᴏᴜ sᴜᴘᴘᴏʀᴛ the corporate mission, or is your mission fundamentally different? Are you excited to be a steward for a large number of people? Is it OK to earn wealth when it is used righteously? Does it motivate you to be able to give significantly to the church and the needy? What *are* some of your responsibilities as a Christian and as a business leader?

The Corporate Mission

> The man who had received the five talents went at once and put
> his money to work and gained five more.... His master replied,
> "Well done, good and faithful servant! You have been faithful
> with a few things; I will put you in charge of many things."
> —Mᴀᴛᴛʜᴇᴡ 25:16, 21

There are, of course, numerous books and articles written by academic scholars on mission, core purpose, value, and vision statements. I've read a fair amount of the literature on each and have decided there isn't real clarity on any of these. Most meetings to discuss writing a mission statement get bogged down endlessly in debate over the difference between a mission, a vision, a value, and the core purpose. I figure that leaves room for my own opinion.

When I joined Young America Corporation, the company had just finished a two-year period where profitability had plummeted. Shortly after starting with the company, we had a senior staff meeting to discuss what our corporate mission should be. The vice president of human resources was first to speak up and proudly proposed that our mission should consist of three goals:

- client satisfaction,
- employee happiness, and
- community involvement.

Most of the executive group thought this was pretty good since they felt it included our main constituencies: clients, employees, and our community. I suggested, however, that our mission statement should include the notion of profit growth. This created some obvious discomfort; people looked around the table to read each others' reactions.

The human resources VP broke the tension with an enthusiastic suggestion that we didn't need to say anything about profit because if we simply made our employees and clients happy, we would naturally be profitable. There were several nods and sighs of relief around the room.

I sat there quite amazed at how earnestly the group wanted to avoid using the *p*-word in our mission statement. I then quietly suggested that while we had considered employees, clients, and the community, we left out our most important constituency—the owners. The heavy air of silence and discomfort descended again upon the meeting.

Most people want the office to be a good place, one where we provide honest service to our clients, deal fairly with our vendors, treat employees with respect and kindness, and act responsibly within our community. Those are great values and rightfully belong in a corporate value statement, but is that the corporate mission?

I have seen several examples of companies stubbornly avoiding the notion of profit in their Mission Statement because the *p*-word has become politically incorrect to many today. "Our mission ought to have higher aspirations than just profit," many would say. But ask any owner who has risked his own capital what the mission is, and I doubt you would hear him say, "With this money I want management to delight our clients, make our employees happy, and give generously to the community." If he did say this, I suggest he is confusing an investment with charitable giving.

Imagine that you had invested a substantial amount of your life savings in a company and at the annual shareholder meeting the president made this speech:

> Our company has had another great year. Client satisfac-
> tion is at an all-time high, employee satisfaction ratings have

improved for five years in a row, and we've been voted Best Corporate Citizen for community involvement. It's true that profits have declined for the third year in a row, and we might not even be able to pay our debt next year, but we are proud to remain committed to our client, employee, and community mission despite this.

As an investor, I believe you are likely to demand the president's resignation and instruct the board to hire someone who will manage your investment better. You probably support the client, employee, and community aspirations, but these are not the primary reasons you risked your life savings. Do you suppose your primary investment criterion was, where can I make the most employees happy? Or was it, where can I get the best return on my investment?

Also, consider this: if the company continues to decline in profits, what is the outcome? Without capital to reinvest, service begins to deteriorate, clients become dissatisfied, and the business declines as clients exit. As the business declines, the company is forced to freeze wages and/or lay off employees. Employee happiness diminishes rapidly. And, with no profits, the company can no longer afford to be generous in the community. Eventually, the company may go out of business. There are no clients left, all employees are out of work, and the community has lost its tax base. No happy clients, no happy employees, and not a happy community.

A few years after I became CEO of Young America, our chairman of the board remarked that at the time I took the post we were probably six months from going bankrupt. When I was hired, he and I both saw the urgency to restore profitability. For the owners, it was totally because of concern for their investment. For me, it was more complex—a responsibility for their investment, a fear for my career, and a concern for the three thousand families that our company employed. The week I accepted the position, I met with my pastor and prayed that I could restore the company's health as a steward for the livelihood of so many families. Profitability was the key to being able to do this.

Most mission statements acknowledge the importance of profit and the responsibility to shareholders. Here are some excerpts as examples:

> Our success will ensure: customers will build their business, employees build their futures, and *shareholders build their wealth.*[1]
>
> —PEPSICO, EMPHASIS ADDED

> Our final responsibility is to our stockholders. *Business must make a sound profit.*[2]
> —JOHNSON & JOHNSON, EMPHASIS ADDED

> ...consumers will reward us with leadership sales, *profit*, and *value creation*, allowing our people, our shareholders and the communities in which we live and work to prosper.[3]
> —PROCTOR & GAMBLE, EMPHASIS ADDED

> Achieve enduring *profitable growth*.[4] [This is the last of the three strategic foci in their mission statement.]
> —MCDONALD'S RESTAURANT CORPORATION, EMPHASIS ADDED

> Delight our customers, employees, *and shareholders* by...[5]
> —INTEL, EMPHASIS ADDED

I find it interesting, however, that nearly all mission statements list profit or shareholders last. I'm not sure this is as much honesty as it is an attempt to be pleasing to employees or customers who read it. When Caleb Bradham invented Pepsi-Cola in 1893, I'm just guessing that his primary thought was that the idea could make him some money.

Some companies ignore mention of profit in their mission statement altogether. Academics often seem to love this approach because it is more inspiring than a mission to make profits. Such mission statements may be catchy and marketable, but they're not necessarily true. Walt Disney simply says their mission is *to make people happy*.[6] I suppose someone might have argued that shareholders are people, so growing profits is at least implicitly part of the mission.

Certainly, mission statements should have other components, such as a clear definition of the business and inspirational elements that are harmonious with the core purpose, values, and vision. There is much interesting and insightful literature on this. However, for the purposes of this chapter, I simply want to emphasize that the original mission of the company's founder primarily included profit, and families who invest their savings in stock are expecting the value to grow. This is the core part of the mission.

As Christians, there is nothing wrong with this. It doesn't need to be hidden or buried behind a list of other elements of the mission. It is what the CEO and other executives are paid to deliver. Profits allow companies to employ people and support their families. Profits also permit companies to purchase services or goods from other companies, creating further jobs. Consumers perceive value in the goods produced and thus are satisfied with the purchase. Profits, therefore, enable employee satisfaction, client satisfaction, and giving back to the community at the same time as they provide shareholder satisfaction.

In the parable of the talents, the manager who put the owner's money to work was rewarded. The manager said, "You have been faithful with a few things; I will put you in charge of many things. Come and share your master's happiness" (Matt. 25:21). But the third "investor" hid the money and did nothing to make a profit. The master replied, "You should have put my money on deposit with the bankers, so that I would have received it back with interest. Take the talent from him and give it to the one who has ten talents" (vv. 27–28). The unprofitable manager is punished.

The Old Testament provides a description of an early businessperson. Interestingly, the account is told in Proverbs 31, describing a wife of noble character.

> She selects wool and flax and works with eager hands. She is like the merchant ships, bringing her food from afar.... She considers a field and buys it; out of her earnings she plants a vineyard.... She sees that her trading is profitable, and her lamp does not go out at night.... She makes linen garments and sells them, and supplies the merchants with sashes.
> —PROVERBS 31:13–14, 16, 18, 24

Proverbs 31 ends, "Give her the reward she has earned, and let her works bring her praise at the city gate" (v. 31). God blesses industrious people who earn a profit honestly. A Christian need not be conflicted about a corporate mission to make profit.

> An idealist is one who helps the *other* fellow to make a profit.[7]
> —HENRY FORD

The Christian Executive's Mission

> No one can serve two masters. Either he will hate the one and love the other, or he will be devoted to the one and despise the other. You cannot serve both God and Money.
> —MATTHEW 6:24

The corporate mission may include many ideas to define its business, values, and core strategic direction; but it always, implicitly or explicitly, is on a mission to make money. However, the gospel of Matthew says that you cannot serve both God and money. As an executive, then, how can you serve the company mission and God? What is the mission of the Christian executive? I believe that this is a question that troubles some Christians.

I have heard Christians say to me, "When I go to work, I go to serve the Lord" or, "My primary purpose at work is to be a witness." While this sounds beautiful, I am sometimes confused by it. Although I also am a Christian, I am not primarily looking for Christians who will be a witness in the workplace. I am hiring him or her to help us to be successful in our corporate mission. When Nehemiah led the Israelites to rebuild Jerusalem's walls, he looked for managers who were skilled, who would do the job well, but were also godly. The primary emphasis was on getting the wall built.

Certainly, we should honor God in all that we do. As a corporate manager or executive, and as a Christian, what is your primary mission at work? To begin to answer this question, first decide if you agree that the primary purpose of a corporation is to make profit and that this endeavor, if done according to righteous principles, can be blessed by God. If you do not agree with this, then you possibly should not work for a corporation, because you will always be frustrated with its purpose. I believe there is a great mission for Christian executives to provide a godly example of leadership while pursuing the corporate mission, and to serve hundreds or thousands of people: investors, employees, clients, vendors, and even the community. If you agree, then there is no barrier to becoming a leader in a company with such a mission. There even may be a calling.

Next, consider your contract when you accept employment. I'm not talking about your severance agreement or golden parachute. I am talking about your commitment when you shake hands and accept the responsibility given to you. When the employment offer is made, the contract is essentially this:

> The company will bestow on you great responsibility and quite generous financial reward. In return we expect you to deliver results that will increase shareholder wealth.

Your acceptance of this contract should mean:

> I accept this offer and will endeavor to the best of my abilities to deliver the expected results, provided it is accomplished by honest and ethical means and with integrity and respect for all involved.

If this understanding is accepted, you have a moral contract that is acceptable to God. You also have a mission. Thus, there is no inherent conflict between serving God and serving the company's mission. In fact, the way you pursue the mission will also serve God.

The Christian who accepts responsibility in a corporation but does not energetically focus and commit to contributing to the corporate mission breaks his moral contract and disobeys God's will. Consider what Scripture says about this (although this is in reference to church leaders, it could also be applicable to corporate leaders):

> Obey your leaders and submit to their authority. They keep watch over you as men who must give an account. Obey them so that their work will be a joy, not a burden, for that would be of no advantage to you.
> —HEBREWS 13:17

As Christians, we are commanded to not only obey our leaders but also to make their work a joy by giving our utmost. Our contract with shareholders is also a matter of conscience.

> Therefore, it is necessary to submit to the authorities, not only because of possible punishment but also because of conscience.
> —ROMANS 13:5

If, however, the employer or owner expects behaviors clearly contrary to godly leadership, then we are free to decline the position or to go elsewhere. But, if this is not a problem, we can pursue the corporate mission and endeavor to accomplish it within our Christian principles. The Christian executive mission is the same as the corporate mission. The Christian executive, however, will accomplish it in ways that honor God.

> There is one and only one social responsibility of business—to use its resources and engage in activities designed to increase its profits, so long as it stays within the rules.[8]
> —MILTON FRIEDMAN,
> FREE MARKET ECONOMIST

The Good Steward

Where is the flock that was entrusted to you?
—JEREMIAH 13:20

Clearly being a Christian executive is not an easy calling. The vocation, however, also has great rewards:

- Stewardship for your company
- Providing well for your family
- Generous giving to the church and community

All of these are lasting joys—to see your employees and investors benefit from your labor; to watch your children grow up well-housed, clothed, fed, and prepared for adulthood; and to give back generously what the Lord has given so that others can better serve the needy and spread God's Word. Other professions may provide financial reward and the means to give generously; however, there are few professions that provide such a tremendous opportunity for stewardship.

The word *stewardship* is defined as "the careful and responsible management of something entrusted to one's care."[9] In biblical times, a steward was a servant who was responsible for managing the owner's estate. CEOs and other executives are stewards of the owner's (or shareholder's) estate. The estate includes physical assets, but it also includes the talent pool of employees, the good will of customers, and the relationships with vendors.

Consider the stewardship responsibilities of Jeffrey R. Immelt, CEO of General Electric. According to the 2006 Fortune 500 reports, Mr. Immelt runs a company of $157 billion in revenues with $673 billion in assets. He is also steward for 316,000 employees and, considering an average family size of three to four, directly impacts the life of a million or more people. The company has total market capitalization (the value of outstanding stock) of nearly $400 billion. If the average shareholder has five thousand dollars invested in GE, then the success of the company also impacts the savings and welfare of eighty thousand shareholders, which, including the families, is a quarter million people. Therefore, it is reasonable to say that Mr. Immelt may have some direct responsibility for at least 1.3 million people. If one considers also the strong impact GE has on its vendors, this number may double to nearly three million. That would be nearly 1 percent of the population. Mr. Immelt has some serious stewardship responsibilities.

Even with a much smaller company, your stewardship can be quite vast if you consider all the lives your company impacts, some in major ways and others in smaller ways. Although Young America "only" had about $100 million of revenue, the company impacted a vast number of people during my period as CEO:

- Young America (YA) provided work for up to four thousand people. For an average family of four, this directly impacted about sixteen thousand people.

- YA investors were primarily MidOcean Capital and Ontario Teachers Pension Plan. MidOcean, a private equity firm, has numerous institutional investors in their funds. These institutions are stewards for individuals who have invested with them and through them with MidOcean and Young America. Ontario Teachers Pension Plan is a managed fund with the pension savings of 263,000 current and retired teachers in Ontario. Each of these people had a small part of their retirement portfolio invested with us.

- We handled over sixty million consumer submissions for rebates each year. Our database included more than one hundred million different people who have sent in for a rebate the last ten years; probably representing more than half the total number of family units in America.

- We provided promotion services for at least fifty Fortune 500 companies. How we handled that could also effect the reputation and success of their companies, impacting their employees and investors.

Stewardship is measured more than in just revenue and profit dollars. It is measured in the number of people you impact through your efforts as an executive and as a Christian. When God calls you to be a leader, he calls you to be a shepherd to the people under your care. Being a good shepherd requires character and skill.

> He chose David his servant and took him from the sheep pens; from tending the sheep he brought him to be the shepherd of his people Jacob, of Israel his inheritance. And David shepherded them with integrity of heart; with skillful hands he led them.
>
> —Psalm 78:70–72

Shareholders entrust executives with their investments; employees, with their livelihood; clients or customers, with their purchases; and vendors, with their services. With skill and integrity, we can be good stewards for what they entrust to us. This is the essence of servanthood.

> The true measure of a man is not the number of servants that
> he has, but the number of people that he serves.[10]
> —ARNOLD GLASGOW,
> PSYCHOLOGIST

The Problem of Wealth

> A feast is made for laughter, and wine makes life merry, but
> money is the answer for everything.
> —ECCLESIASTES 10:19

There may be no other topic that is so difficult to tackle as the problem of wealth. The Bible offers numerous passages that praise the fruit of labor and even wealth, as well as many other verses that seem to condemn wealth. Therefore, I begin this section with a most confusing quote from the Old Testament: "But money is the answer for everything" (Eccl. 10:19). A footnote in the New International Version (NIV) translation of the Bible says, "Can be read at various levels—as a wry comment on human values, as sober advice to earn a good living rather than have a good time or as stating the greatest versatility of money." In my opinion, even the footnote doesn't do a good job of clarifying the confusion. A look at other scripture also seems to offer confusing guidance.

Discouraging	Encouraging
Proverbs 23:4–5 "Do not wear yourself out to get rich; have the wisdom to show restraint. Cast but a glance at riches, and they are gone."	Proverbs 29:2 "When the righteous thrive, the people rejoice."
Ecclesiastes 6:7 'All man's efforts are for his mouth, yet his appetite is never satisfied."	1 Kings 10:23 "King Solomon was greater in riches and wisdom than all the other kings of the earth."
Ecclesiastes 5:10 "Whoever loves money never has money enough; whoever loves wealth is never satisfied with his income."	Ecclesiastes 5:13–14 "I have seen a grievous evil under the sun...wealth lost through some misfortune, so that when he has a son there is nothing left for him."

Discouraging	Encouraging
Proverbs 28:20 "One eager to get rich will not go unpunished."	Proverbs 28:20 "A faithful man will be richly blessed."
Ecclesiastes 6:1–2 "I have seen another evil under the sun, and it weighs heavily on men: God gives a man wealth, possessions and honor, so that he lacks nothing his heart desires, but God does not enable him to enjoy them, and a stranger enjoys them instead. This is meaningless, a grievous evil."	Ecclesiastes 5:18–19 "Then I realized it is good and proper for a man to eat and drink, and to find satisfaction in his toilsome labor under the sun during the few days that God has given him—for this is his lot. Moreover, when God gives any man wealth and possessions, and enables him to enjoy them, to accept his lot and be happy in his work—this is a gift of God."
Proverbs 21:5 "Haste leads to poverty."	Proverbs 21:5 "The plans of the diligent lead to profit."
Matthew 19:23 "Then Jesus said to his disciples, 'I tell you the truth, it is hard for a rich man to enter the kingdom of heaven.'"	Proverbs 13:21 "Prosperity is the reward of the righteous."

A close review of these verses leads me to conclude that *earning* wealth is blessed by God, but *yearning* for wealth is wrong and leads to corruption.

Earning wealth

The Bible suggests that it is good for the righteous to thrive and it is even God's blessing.

> When the righteous thrive, the people rejoice.
> —Proverbs 29:2

> A faithful man will be richly blessed.
> —Proverbs 28:20

> Prosperity is the reward of the righteous.
> —Proverbs 13:21

Scripture also affirms that God blesses hard work with wealth.

> The plans of the diligent lead to profit.
> —Proverbs 21:5

> Lazy hands make a man poor, but diligent hands bring wealth.
> —Proverbs 10:4

Finally, Scripture even says that it is a shame if a father is not able to save some wealth for his heirs.

> I have seen a grievous evil under the sun...wealth lost through some misfortune, so that when he has a son there is nothing left for him.
> —ECCLESIASTES 5:13–14

> A good man leaves an inheritance for his children's children.
> —PROVERBS 13:22

Yearning for wealth

Jesus, however, warned us to rely on God to provide our needs and not to have false comfort in our riches.

> Do not store up for yourselves treasures on earth... But store up for yourselves treasures in heaven.
> —MATTHEW 6:19–20

Scripture is clear that we should not love money or be anxious for it. Yearning for wealth reflects a lack of trust in God to determine and provide what you need.

> Whoever loves money never has money enough.
> —ECCLESIASTES 5:10

> Haste [a desire to get rich quickly] leads to poverty.
> —PROVERBS 21:5

> Do not wear yourself out to get rich.
> —PROVERBS 23:4

> One eager to get rich will not go unpunished.
> —PROVERBS 28:20

> A stingy man is eager to get rich and is unaware that poverty awaits him.
> —PROVERBS 28:22

How much is too much?

I'd like to address the concept of too much income and too much wealth separately. I think problems with the former are more quickly dispelled. God gave all of us gifts and He expects us to fully utilize those gifts.

If our gifts call us to into a secular job in the corporate world, our use of these gifts may lead us to be promoted over time into executive positions, which are highly compensated.

It is undoubtedly true, however, that the corporate marketplace needs to come to grips with what is fair and reasonable compensation for executives and CEOs, particularly the latter. In Japan, a CEO typically earns over sixteen times the average worker's salary. In America, it can be more than one hundred times greater. This raises the whole question of merit and how much the performance of a CEO or executive is really worth. To me, the key is to heavily weigh compensation on long-term performance, with salary and annual bonus components being relatively small. The marketplace, however, decides these questions. In the meantime, I do not see how it is wrong for a Christian to accept a job that has a competitive compensation package.

Large earning potential can obviously lead to the accumulation of wealth. A great deal has been written about wealth being OK *up to a point*. Within the church there is often the feeling that a "good Christian" should not be too wealthy, or if he is, that he should hide it.

Sherman and Hendricks suggest that we should live a limited lifestyle.[11] When we purchase an item, the authors say, we should buy the least expensive thing that will get the job done. An example is given of the salesman who needs a car for work that will be suitable for driving clients. He decides that he does not need a Cadillac or a BMW for the purpose of the job and that a high-end Oldsmobile will suffice.

This thinking suggests to me that if you do not entertain clients and only commute to work, that all such Christians should drive a Geo or Hugo. I find this sort of measuring stick to be nonsense. I will give you three examples.

In 1 Kings 3, Scripture tells us that Solomon went to Gibeon to offer sacrifices and that he gave one thousand burnt offerings. God was pleased and promised to grant Solomon anything he would wish for. As we know, Solomon asked for wisdom. God said he was pleased with this choice and especially pleased that he did not yearn for wealth. Therefore, God not only gave Solomon wisdom, but he gave him wealth.

> Moreover, I will give you what you have not asked for—both riches and honor—so that in your lifetime you will have no equal among kings.
>
> —1 KINGS 3:13

First Kings 3 through 10 continue to describe two things: (1) God continued to shower wealth upon Solomon and (2) Solomon continued to praise and thank God. Much of the wealth God granted the king was used to build the temple and for continued sacrifices to praise God. However, he also lived more ostentatiously than all other rulers, including those that did not worship God. Read 1 Kings 4:20–27 for a description of Solomon's "daily provisions."

But, Solomon soon developed an overzealous love for women. First Kings 11:1 says, "King Solomon, however, loved many foreign women," and verse 4 says, "his wives turned his heart after other gods." It is only at this point that God withdraws his blessing and begins to take away his kingdom and all its riches. Sinful and excessive use of God's blessing (he accrued one thousand wives and concubines) led him to turn from God. This is when God withdrew his blessing on Solomon's wealth.

A member of the church that I attended during my high school years was the founder of a large evangelistic outreach organization. When their family moved several miles away to a fairly exclusive township, I recall some comments made that it was unseemly for someone in the ministry to have a nice house in a well-to-do neighborhood.

I think this attitude was wrong. I just finished reading a book on the biographical history of missions and found this family's story featured there. The father struggled financially for many years to start the organization and make his vision a reality. As well, his family grew up overseas in third world countries. Their sacrifices were quite significant. It was only later in life after the organization was large and well established that others were able to take more responsibility, allowing the family to come home so that their children could attend high school in the U.S. The entire family had been dedicated to the ministry that their father struggled to make a reality. Only when it finally succeeded and prospered did they enjoy some luxuries, most of which had been denied to the children in much of their youth. Instead of self-righteously criticizing them for having a nice house later in life, we ought to have thanked them for their years of sacrifice and praised God that they were able to enjoy comforts when their work was largely done.

The final story is about Robert O. Naegele Jr. Bob, a born-again Christian, bought Rollerblade at a time when it was very small and unprofitable, and he endured several years when it was nearly bankrupt. I joined Rollerblade in 1992 as CFO, part of a new team that helped to make it very profitable over the next four years. In 1996 Bob sold his stake in the company and made a sizable fortune. He now is an owner of the Minnesota Wild, having led an investor group to return the NHL to Minnesota. Did Bob become too wealthy to be a Christian? Is he living too ostentatiously? Nonsense.

When Bob sold Rollerblade, he gave back generously to all Rollerblade employees. He participates with and gives generously to various ministries, travels to functions to share his testimony, and, I am certain, runs a high-integrity sports franchise. His wealth opens doors for him to influence and witness to powerful people in business and in government. Despite wealth, however, Bob has always remained a quiet and humble person, totally lacking in arrogance. We should rejoice, as it says in Proverbs 29:2: "When the righteous thrive, the people rejoice."

Conclusions

The scripture and examples we have reviewed can be summarized in the following points:

- It is a blessing from God when He gives us wealth.

- God expects us to be diligent (hard-working) and says this will lead to profit.

- We must not, however, yearn for wealth, or more wealth, but trust in God to provide for our needs in His wisdom.

- We must, therefore, be content with what God has given us.

- God blesses wealth when we remain righteous and give back generously.

- Wealth also affords us to have greater temptations (see Solomon's wives and concubines) so we must ask God to keep our hearts righteous.

- Finally, if God blesses a Christian with wealth, he should not be arrogant with it, nor should he need to hide it.

We should not have ambition to lead because we yearn for wealth. We lead, rather, because God has made us capable. If we *earn* wealth, God has blessed us and made us stewards for these blessings.

> When God gives any man wealth and possessions, and enables him to enjoy them, to accept his lot and be happy in his work—this is a gift of God.
> —ECCLESIASTES 5:19

Giving Back Generously

Command those who are rich in this present world…to be
rich in good deeds, and to be generous and willing to share.
—1 TIMOTHY 6:17–18

When God gives any man or woman wealth, He also gives the person and his or her family a responsibility to be generous and willing to share. In fact, Paul says that giving is more than a responsibility; it is a gift. In Romans 12, he provides seven examples of spiritual gifts, including that of giving. Verse 8 says, "If it is contributing to the needs of others, let him give generously."

As an executive, you probably earn far more than the average person. The gift of wealth and the gift of giving are two sides of the same coin. Having already tackled the question of wealth, we should consider how much giving is enough.

Ancient Israel

Some of the earliest commands in the Bible relate to tithing. Genesis 14:20 says Abraham "gave [God] a tenth of everything," and Deuteronomy 14:22 says, "Be sure to set aside a tenth of all that your fields produce each year." In fact, the word *tithe* comes from the Old English word *teogothian*, meaning "to give or pay a tenth."

Manuel L. Jose wrote in *Accounting Historians Journal* that tithe and tax were the same thing in the early biblical era.

> In the theocracy of ancient Israel, tithing in a religious context was the same as taxation in a governmental context. It is impossible to separate religious and governmental taxation since religion and government were one and the same in ancient Israel.[12]

Manuel Jose further explains why ten percent was adequate:

> The tithe supported the tabernacle worship and priests and was not expended for social welfare purposes, as the poor were left to glean for themselves.[13]

The original concept of 10 percent was only to support the temple, or church. It was treated the same as a tax, but the funds were not used for charity to provide for the needy. Tithes, taxes, and charity: one has to look at all three together.

The kingdom of Israel

The tithe/tax remained a tenth until Israel asked for a king. As instructed by the Lord, Samuel warned the people to be careful what they wished for because of the heavy tax burden that kings would require. Samuel said, "You will cry out for relief from the king you have chosen" (1 Sam. 8:18). Still, the people asked for a king, and what Samuel said came to pass. Solomon increased taxes greatly to build the temple and to provide lavishly for himself and his royal court (1 Kings 4:22–27). When Solomon's son, Rehoboam, took the throne, he said, "My father laid on you a heavy yoke; I will make it even heavier" (2 Chron. 10:11). And so government growth began!

The tithe and tax were still the same thing, except that the tithe/tax had grown so that it would not only support the temple, but also the extravagances of the government. The only charitable use of the tithe/tax in Solomon's era was a fellowship offering, collected three times a year when all of Israel could come to feast on the burnt offerings. It would seem that the tax was not used to help the needy, except perhaps to provide three feasts a year.

This is why the Old Testament talks about giving to the needy as a separate act (in addition to the tithe/tax) to show the love of God and receive His blessing.

> He who gives to the poor will lack nothing, but he who closes his eyes to them receives many curses.
> —PROVERBS 28:27

> A generous man will himself be blessed, for he shares his food with the poor.
> —PROVERBS 22:9

> Blessed is he who is kind to the needy.
> —PROVERBS 14:21

Early Christian/Roman Era

By Roman times, tithing and taxes had taken a different turn. The early Christian church was not supported by taxes, as was the temple in early Israel, a theocracy, so Paul had to reaffirm the church tithe separately: "Don't you know that those who work in the temple get their food from the temple, and those who serve at the altar share in what is offered on the altar? In the same way, the Lord has commanded that those who preach the gospel should receive their living from the gospel" (1 Cor. 9:13–14).

Paul also affirmed that we should still pay taxes: "Give everyone what you owe him: If you owe taxes, pay taxes" (Rom. 13:7). John also reaffirmed the separate calling to give to the needy when he said, "If anyone has material possessions and sees his brother in need but has no pity on him, how can the love of God be in him?" (1 John 3:17–18).

Tithe, tax, and charity is much the same as *church, government, and social welfare.* In New Testament times the church and government became separate and government and social welfare continued to be separate. Today, however, government and social welfare are greatly intertwined.

Modern Era

I have frequently heard Christian Conservatives proudly cite statistics that Americans are far more generous in giving to charities than Europeans. Europeans argue in defense that they pay far more tax, which has two consequences:

- They have less to give.
- The government takes a far greater responsibility for the needy.

I think both views are correct. Americans give more in part because of a far wider Christian ethic than Europe today. However, Europeans are also right because the government has taken more of their money in order to provide far greater social welfare. I am not a fan of the European social model, but I can see that if the state took 20 percent more of my earnings to provide cradle to grave support for people, I might also give less to the needy. Presumably, if the government provided vast social welfare support, there may not even be any needy left within the country (though there is still vast poverty in poorer countries).

Federal, state, and local taxes in the U.S. for a high-income worker can add up to more than 45 percent of his or her income. But in France, state, local, value added (VAT), and other taxes can take up to 65 percent of your wages. As a high-income earner in France, over half of the taxes one pays go to welfare programs. That's a lot of giving to those needier than you.

In the United States, about half of the federal budget goes to social welfare programs (the amount is higher than that in many state budgets) and overseas programs for poor nations. If you pay 45 percent of your earnings in taxes, charitable giving could represent more than 20 percent of your income—even before you give to non-government charities.

I do not make these arguments to convince you that you already give generously, only to point out that in the twentieth century, governments have progressively assumed more responsibility for the needy. At the same time, however, growth in wealth in America has dramatically changed the definition of *giving generously*. It was probably a hardship three thousand years ago to pay the 10 percent tithe/tax. For today's executive, even giving a combined 50 to 60 percent of income to the church, government, and other charities is not sacrificial, and it may not even be generous.

Tithe, tax, and charity: the Bible affirms our responsibility to provide all of these if we are able. Just as we all argue whether taxes are too high or not high enough, I don't think there is any consensus about how much is generous giving. Jesus said to the rich young man, "If you want to be perfect, go, sell your possessions and give to the poor" (Matt. 19:21). The story of the poor widow who gave a small copper coin (Mark 12:42–43) was also used to illustrate the idea that we should give sacrificially.

I don't know how much is sacrificial, generous, or even *enough*. I have not always given as I should, but I have come to believe in four guiding concepts:

Each year, decide what you will give.

Proverbs 3:9 says, "Honor the LORD with your wealth, with the firstfruits of all your crops." I like to give most of my tithing and donations early in the year, trusting God will provide through the year. Whenever I received bonuses in February, I would allocate a large percentage of it to tithing and charities.

Giving is a personal decision and you should seek God's leading.

It should be done because of your gratefulness to God, not because of a desire for earthly praise. Christ said, "But when you give to the needy, do not let your left hand know what your right hand is doing, so that your giving may be in secret" (Matt. 6:3–4).

Enjoy giving.

Don't view it as an obligation, but as a gift. Whenever I have written a large check to the church or a charity, I have had a great sense of joy. After selling Rollerblade, when Bob and Ellis Naegele were writing out very substantial appreciation checks to each of the Rollerblade employees, they described feeling "waves of joy." They gave away millions of dollars.

Imagine the help being done when you pay taxes.

You might be paying four times or twenty times more taxes than the average American and probably don't agree with how all of it is being spent, but imagine how many needy people you are assisting with unemployment, Medicare, Medicaid, Social Security, etc. I'm sure it's a stretch to suggest that you should feel joy when filing your tax return; nevertheless, when you are privileged to earn a hefty income, you also support many people in need through your taxes. Many of us might say we'd rather not trust our government to make these decisions for us, but we also know most people would simply keep it for themselves if the government didn't.

Being able to give generously is a gift and you will also receive a blessing. Proverbs 11:25 says, "A generous man will prosper; he who refreshes others will himself be refreshed." When we are truly thankful to God for what He has given us, giving His wealth away is an act of real joy.

> Nothing is so hard for those who abound in riches as to conceive how others could be in want.[14]
> —JONATHAN SWIFT,
> EIGHTEENTH-CENTURY AUTHOR OF GULLIVER'S TRAVELS

PART II

CHRISTIAN LEADERS IN THE CORPORATE WORLD

— Chapter 4 —
CORPORATE LEADERSHIP QUALIFICATIONS

W HAT ARE THE qualifications for corporate leadership from the perspective of the secular corporation? First Timothy 3:1 says, "If anyone sets his heart on being an overseer, he desires a noble task." The chapter goes on to describe leaders as being "the husband of one wife, temperate, self-controlled, respectable, hospitable, able to teach, not given to drunkenness, not violent but gentle, not quarrelsome, not a lover of money" (vv. 2–3). Does this sound like the job description of most corporate leaders that you know? Probably not.

The secular corporate world has quite different emphases for selecting leaders. But are these qualities in conflict with our spiritual values or not?

The Right Stuff—Executive Qualities

> If the ax is dull and its edge unsharpened, more strength is needed but skill will bring success.
> —ECCLESIASTES 10:10

Do you have the right stuff to be successful as an executive? Numerous books have been written on this topic, and each author has his own list of the key leadership qualities. Some authors list five core qualities, while others describe as many as twenty-one, and the rest list a range in between. I've consolidated many of these into a list of seventeen qualities (in alphabetical order), along with definitions. (A more detailed description and explanation of these qualities will appear in a following chapter.)

Accountability—the willingness to accept responsibility (for both favorable and unfavorable results)

Character and integrity—moral excellence and firmness (character) and firm adherence to a code of moral values (integrity)

Charisma and presence—a personal magic of leadership (charisma) and a quality of poise and effectiveness (presence) that enables a performer to achieve a close relationship with his audience

Commitment and dedication—the state of being emotionally impelled (commitment), a devoting for a particular purpose (dedication). In this context, a commitment and dedication for the purpose of the company

Communication skills—the ability to transmit information, thoughts, or direction so that it is satisfactorily received or understood

Competence—having requisite or adequate abilities and technical knowledge

Courage and risk-taking—Mental or moral strength to venture, persevere, and withstand difficulty (courage) and one who is willing to chance loss for the prospect of a greater win (risk-taker).

Decisiveness, determination, and security—having the quality of deciding conclusively (decisiveness), the habit of deciding definitely and firmly (determination), and the quality of having no doubt (security)

Focus—ability to concentrate attention or effort

Generosity and servanthood—the quality of being liberal in giving (generosity) and the practice of answering needs of others (servanthood)

Initiative and innovation—energy displayed in starting the beginning of an action (initiative) and the talent to introduce something new (innovation)

Listening skills and teachability—the proclivity to hear with thoughtful attention (listening skills) and receptiveness to continual learning (teachability)

Passion—intense, driving, and overmastering feeling or conviction, in this context for the mission of the company

Positive attitude—having a confident, affirmative, and optimistic state of mind, in this context regarding the prospects for success in the company

Problem solving skills—the ability to process information and determine solutions to unsettled questions

Relationship skills—the ability to build affinity with others

Vision—unusual foresight or discernment; the ability to grasp what is obscure

Which qualities are most sought in corporate executives? I surveyed twenty-five corporate executives and asked them which of these qualities were most important in hiring decisions. At least half of the participants were Christians. Each participant was asked to select the five most important criteria and the five least important criteria. The "most important" responses were scored with three points, the "least important" with one point, and the other seven in the middle received two points. Scores for all participants were added up and averaged. The charts on the following pages show the result.

According to the survey respondents, the five most important qualities for selection as a corporate leader were (1) communication skills, (2) competence, (3) vision, (4) charisma and presence, and (5) problem solving skills.

I also asked the executive panel a slightly different question: which are the most important characteristics and traits to *your own* job performance? The answers to this question were somewhat different from the other.

Here is a comparison of the five most important criteria for job selection, as opposed to job success:

Selection Criteria	Job Success
1. Communication skills	1. Character and integrity
2. Competence	2. Vision
3. Vision	3. Competence
4. Charisma and presence	4. Accountability
5. Problem solving skills	5. Communication skills

Competence, vision, and communication skills were common to both criteria. However, two qualities had striking differences.

Survey participants felt that character and integrity, combined into one quality, was the top criterion needed for success, but they thought it was not a highly sought quality for selecting candidates in an executive position. It ranked eleventh for selection criteria! It's remarkable, with corporate corruption being so publicized, that most executives did not feel this was a top requirement in the recruitment and selection of candidates. Executives seemed to feel that integrity is the premier quality for themselves but not necessarily for other potential executives.

The other large perception gap on the survey related to charisma and presence. It was voted the fourth most important *selection* criteria but ranked only sixteenth as important to *job success*. Perhaps they were saying that image will get you hired but substance will make you successful.

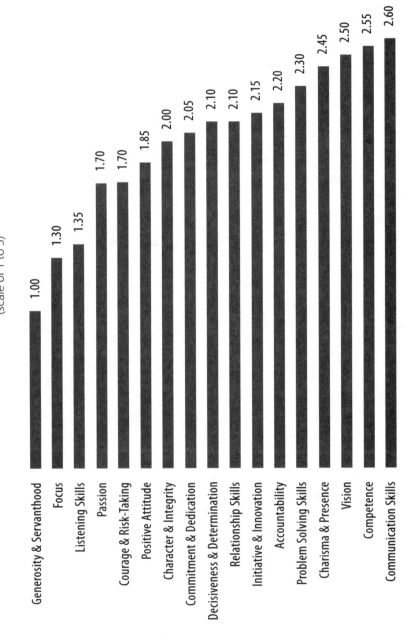

Importance of Selection Criteria for Executive Positions
(scale of 1 to 3)

Generosity & Servanthood	1.00
Focus	1.30
Listening Skills	1.35
Passion	1.70
Courage & Risk-Taking	1.70
Positive Attitude	1.85
Character & Integrity	2.00
Commitment & Dedication	2.05
Decisiveness & Determination	2.10
Relationship Skills	2.10
Initiative & Innovation	2.15
Accountability	2.20
Problem Solving Skills	2.30
Charisma & Presence	2.45
Vision	2.50
Competence	2.55
Communication Skills	2.60

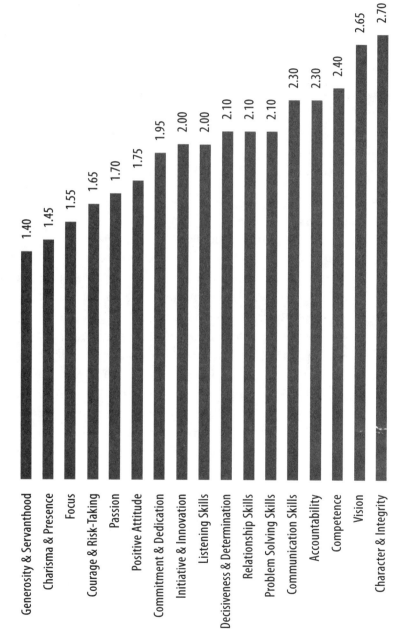

Executive Qualities Most Important in Job Success
(scale of 1 to 3)

The Right Stuff—Characteristics of Christians

Survey respondents were also asked which of these seventeen qualities they thought *others* would perceive to be most and least evident in Christians. Below are the five qualities evident most often and the five qualities least often evident, according to the survey:

Most Frequently Evident	Least Frequently Evident
1. Generosity and servanthood	17. Courage and risk-taking
2. Character and integrity	16. Charisma and presence
3. Positive attitude	15. Initiative and innovation
4. Commitment and dedication	14. Vision
5. Listening skills	13. Decisiveness and determination

The panel was also asked which of these qualities *they* thought to be most and least often evident in Christians' behavior. Surprisingly, there were few differences between their perceptions and what they believed to be the perception of others.

I found these findings interesting since a significant percentage of the respondents are Christians. In other words, their perceptions about themselves seem largely similar to the perception of non-Christians. Yet, I think our own perceptions are influenced by the bias of the secular world.

Christians, according to the survey panel, are generally thought to be generous, high in integrity, having a positive attitude, a sense of commitment, and good listening skills. They're usually not known, however, for taking risks, having charisma and vision, being innovative, and being determined.

The findings also demonstrated a dramatic contrast between what respondents felt were key selection criteria for executives and how Christians are perceived. In fact, *none* of the top five criteria for being selected as an executive were perceived to be Christian strengths.

Top Selection Criteria	Ranking of Perceived Christian Strengths (out of 17)
1. Communication Skills	9th
2. Competence	11th
3. Vision	14th
4. Charisma and Presence	16th
5. Problem Solving Skills	12th

Hide not your talents. They for use were made. What's a
sundial in the shade?[1]
—ATTRIBUTED TO BENJAMIN FRANKLIN

The Christian Leadership Survey Overview

Be strong and courageous.
—DEUTERONOMY 31:6

Having spent my entire career in the corporate world, I often observed significant tensions between the requirements of corporate leadership and the teachings of our faith. It took me over thirty years to sort through these perceptions. This is why I decided to explore these disconnects with a survey that measured how the most sought corporate leadership skills compare to the most evident Christian qualities.

The rankings of the most significant leadership qualities are revealing. The ranking of Christian traits, however, are less so. Because qualities like integrity and servanthood are immediately identifiable as tenants of the Christian moral code and were thus put at the top of the list of Christian behavioral attributes, other traits fell lower on the survey ranking by default. This is not to say that Christians are all poor at any of the lower-ranked traits, but rather that other qualities quickly filled the higher rankings. When I spoke with several respondents, they confirmed this phenomenon: many didn't feel that Christians were weak in the qualities ranked lower; they simply felt these traits were not as distinctive as others. Some of those surveyed, however, did feel that the average Christian could be more deficient in decision making skills, charisma, innovation, or even problem-solving skills. I wished to explore these further to determine what might be secular bias and what might be legitimate criticisms.

What does seem clear is that Christians are best known for the qualities that are least sought in corporate leaders. The graph below clearly describes these findings. None of the top six qualities sought in a corporate executive are seen as Christian strengths. Only two of the seven perceived Christian strengths are listed in even the top half of the qualities sought. The greatest Christian strength (generosity and servanthood) is the quality least sought in a corporate executive!

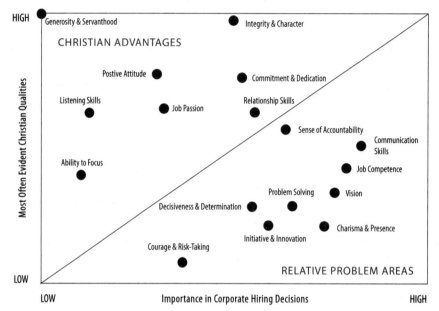

While the lower right quadrant, labeled "Relative Problem Areas," may not really be problems for most Christians in leadership positions or those who feel a call to seek leadership opportunities, for some, however, it might highlight areas where they should concentrate their focus.

Are there real gaps between the profile that Christians project and what business owners or board members are looking for? Or, are there some unjustified biases in our culture that make it difficult for a Christian to be selected? A bit of both, I think. In the next two chapters, we'll look at the qualities that give Christians a leadership advantage, then we'll also examine those qualities that may cause them to be perceived as at a disadvantage.

It seems clearly evident, however, that God designed humans, for good reason, to be responsive to leaders who are decisive and courageous, have bold vision, and possess charisma. These are important leadership qualities, and I believe some Christians have a misunderstanding regarding them. In an attempt to be prayerful, more than some Christian managers act indecisively; in being conservative, they show a lack of boldness; while portraying humility, they loose their charisma. If this behavior truly comes from the teaching of our faith, than we are doomed to have few effective leaders representing Christ.

With few strong Christian leaders, we are doomed to be persecuted by the secular world, as is happening today.

Christian leaders, whether in the clergy, government, or business, need to come together and clarify Christ's message. The Beatitude, "Blessed are the meek" (Matt. 5:5), is an example of a verse often misunderstood by Christians. According to Webster's dictionary, *meek* means "enduring injury with patience and without resentment," but it also means "deficient in spirit and courage."[2] Should Christians who lead be "deficient in spirit and courage"? The NIV footnote on Matthew 5:5 says, "This beatitude is taken from Psalm 37:11 and refers not so much to an attitude toward people as to a disposition before God, namely, *humility*." A footnote to Psalm 37:11 adds, "And betray no *arrogance* towards others." These verses suggest we should be humble before God and not arrogant toward others. It tells us to love, care for, and respect those who struggle and are poor or suffering, as Christ does. It does *not* urge all of us to be downtrodden and deficient in spirit. Leaders are not deficient in spirit or courage. You should be a strong leader. Keep this in mind as you continue to read about Christian leadership qualities in this book.

> Be strong and courageous, because you will lead these people.
> —JOSHUA 1:6

Chapter 5

The CHRISTIAN ADVANTAGE

But the fruit of the Spirit is love, joy, peace, patience, kind-
ness, goodness, faithfulness, gentleness and self-control.
[GALATIANS 5:22–23]

Psychologist and author, Michael Macoby, author of *The Gamesman,* concluded that successful corporate managers develop "traits of the head"—initiative, coop-erativeness, flexibility, and coolness under pressure. "Traits of the heart," however, remain underdeveloped—friendliness, compassion, generosity, idealism, and the capacity to love.[1]

Christians tend to be perceived, however, as strong in the "traits of the heart." Using terms from the list of seventeen executive qualities, the nine characteristics that are perceived to be most evident in Christians are: gener-osity and servanthood, character and integrity, commitment and dedication, positive attitude, listening skills, relationship skills, passion, accountability, and focus.

Many of the Christian's strengths seem to be parallel, as one might expect, to the fruit of the Spirit.

- Generosity and servanthood may be outgrowths of *love* and *kindness.*

- Character and integrity come from *goodness.*

- Commitment and dedication might be evident from *faithfulness* and *patience.*

- Positive attitude comes from *joy and patience.*

- Relationship skills may come from *faithfulness, gentleness,* and *kindness.*
- Listening skills could be a derivative of *patience, kindness,* and *self-control.*

As mentioned in the previous chapter, however, none of these qualities ranked among the top five criteria for selecting executives.

Of the top nine executive characteristics attributed to Christians, only accountability was even in the top half of the most important hiring criteria. The greatest perceived strengths of Christians—primarily relational or "heart-based"—are among the qualities least sought after in an executive. Yet, Christ tells us that we should worship Him not only with all of our heart, but also with our entire mind!

> Love the Lord your God with all your heart and with all your soul and with all your mind and with all your strength.
> —MARK 12:30

In this section, we will consider why both traits of the heart and head are important and how you can make the most of them in your job.

Generosity and Servanthood

The quality of being liberal in giving (generosity) and the practice of answering needs of others (servanthood)		
Survey Findings		
• 17th	Importance relative to hiring criteria	
• 17th	Importance relative to perceived job success	
• 1st	Ranking as a perceived strength of Christians	

Generosity and servanthood were not viewed by the survey participants to be among the critical qualities for selection or for success as leaders. Despite the many books and articles written in recent years on servanthood and value-driven leadership, these qualities still ranked dead last in our survey for importance in the hiring decision and for successful job performance. Christians, however, were seen to greatly exhibit this trait. Are Christians perceived to be more generous and have a greater spirit of servanthood than others? Yes. Does this mean they are more likely to exhibit this in leadership positions? Yes.

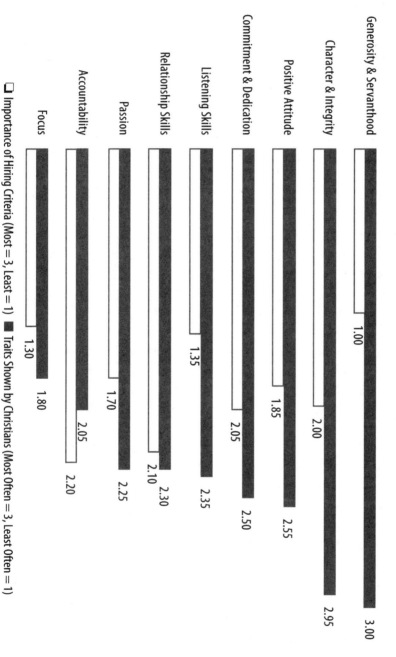

Perceived Christian Strengths Compared to Executive Selection Importance

Generosity & Servanthood — 1.00 ... 3.00

Character & Integrity — 2.00 ... 2.95

Positive Attitude — 1.85 ... 2.55

Commitment & Dedication — 2.05 ... 2.50

Listening Skills — 1.35 ... 2.35

Relationship Skills — 2.30 / 2.10

Passion — 1.70 ... 2.25

Accountability — 2.05 ... 2.20

Focus — 1.30 ... 1.80

☐ Importance of Hiring Criteria (Most = 3, Least = 1)   ■ Traits Shown by Christians (Most Often = 3, Least Often = 1)

People do not yet feel these qualities are as critical as others for an executive, but I believe they are among the greatest reasons why God would call you to be a business leader!

While generosity includes your attitudes to tithing and charitable giving, John Maxwell also lists one of the characteristics of generosity as "putting others first."[2] In this sense it is similar to servanthood, the practice of "answering needs of others."

A spirit of servanthood makes people want to follow you. Employees who feel the leader doesn't have their interests at heart follow only because they have to in order to be safe in their job. Better that they follow willingly out of loyalty and mutual respect.

Christian executives realize that generosity and servanthood are important qualities for leaders. In *God is My CEO,* Larry Julian discusses servant leadership and also provides examples of Christians who were very generous with their money. John D. Beckett, in *Loving Monday,* talks a great deal about having a spirit of servanthood toward his employees and gratefully giving back the wealth God has given him. John M. Huntsman also writes about what he calls "the obligation to give back" in *Winners Never Cheat.*

I recall an example from my early days with PepsiCo. At the time, I was manager of marketing analysis and a friend of mine was manager of financial planning. He and I often worked closely together and were frequently in the same meetings. He was regarded by all as very bright and articulate. We both were known for providing a lot of coaching to our people and working closely with them to ensure a good work product.

There was one difference between us, however. Whenever one of my staff members finished a project, I would spend significant time preparing him or her for the presentation to senior management. He or she would do the entire presentation, and I would sit in the meeting, ready to jump in on hard questions or to provide support, if needed. My friend, on the other hand, would usually be the presenter for his department and his analysts would sit in on the meeting in case he needed to turn to them on a question of detail.

Although I probably had a large role in helping the analyst ensure a good finished project, I wanted to give him or her credit, exposure, and experience presenting under pressure. My coworker, however, more often wanted to glean the exposure and much of the credit for himself.

What was the result in our different styles? We both had successful careers at PepsiCo for many years, and he later went on to take a position as senior executive with another large corporation. I think the difference is that he accomplished this primarily through his own talent and abilities, whereas I believe my style of leadership attracted the best people to my organization.

John C. Maxwell poses these questions:

> Where is your heart when it comes to serving others? Do you
> desire to become a leader for the perks and benefits? Or are
> you motivated by a desire to help others?[3]

Some years ago, a recruiter asked me what my top accomplishments were at Pepsi. I replied, "Bill, Holly, Peter, Jim, Thomas, Boon Tuan, Hector, and Horatio." The recruiter didn't know what to make of my answer, so I explained further: "These were all people that worked for me. I trained them as best as I could, and I marketed their talents internally. They all succeeded in their careers after they left me. While they worked for me, they also did a great job and helped me in my career." I am proud of them and I thank them for their contribution to my own career success.

Finally, having a spirit of generosity and servanthood is emotionally healthy. The Dalai Lama wrote:

> We also find that when we act out of concern for others, the
> peace this creates in our own hearts brings peace to everyone
> we associate with.[4]

This agrees with what Scripture tells us in Proverbs 11:25, "He who refreshes others will himself be refreshed."

If you have an attitude of putting others first, you will also not become prideful, greedy, or arrogant. The apostle Peter tied together the ideas of generosity and servanthood and described them as being incompatible with greed and arrogance.

> Be shepherds of God's flock that is under your care, serving as
> overseers—not because you must but because you are willing,
> as God wants you to be; not greedy for money, but eager to
> serve, not lording it over those entrusted to you, but being
> examples to the flock. And when the Chief Shepherd appears,
> you will receive the crown of glory that will never fade away.
> —1 PETER 5:2–3

You may agree that generosity and servanthood are important qualities of a leader, and they might be real strengths for you. In the selection process for executives, however, they may not be highly sought traits. How then do you "sell" this quality?

While recruiters or decision makers in the hiring process may not see servanthood as a sought-after quality, they are certainly interested in how you motivate people to drive results. Some corporations believe in an organizational culture where motivation is partly based on fear and intimidation, but most do not; you probably would not want to work in such a culture anyway. If you believe in servanthood, you can describe how creating an energizing environment, developing people's abilities, and ensuring respect for individuals results in an organization that wants to work for you and give you their best.

Leading with a spirit of servanthood makes people want to follow with their best energies and skills. For the Christian leader, it is an advantage.

> If anyone wants to be first, he must be the very last, and the servant of all.
>
> —MARK 9:35

> The reason why rivers and seas receive the homage of a hundred mountain streams is that they keep below them. Thus, they are able to reign over all the mountain streams. So the sage, wishing to be above men, putteth himself below them; wishing to be before them, he putteth himself behind them. Thus, though his place is above men, they do not feel his weight; though his place be before them, they do not count it an injury.[5]
>
> —LAO-TSE,
> CHINESE PHILOSOPHER FROM THE SIXTH CENTURY B.C.

Character and Integrity

Moral excellence and firmness (character) and firm adherence to a code of moral values (integrity)	
Survey Findings	
• 11th	Importance relative to hiring criteria
• 1st	Importance relative to perceived job success
• 2nd	Ranking as a perceived strength of Christians

Christians were also perceived as having very high character and integrity. I would have been surprised and disappointed if it were not so. Survey respondents agreed this was also the top quality for success as a leader. Surprisingly, however, it was more than halfway down the list of qualifications sought in executives!

Adrian Gostick and Dana Telford, authors of *The Integrity Advantage*, agree with the survey respondents that character and integrity are essential for success:

> ...it's darn near impossible for a person to have enduring success in business without a reputation of trustworthiness and integrity.[6]

Scripture is certainly clear that we are called to have integrity and good character. For instance, in Paul's second letter to Timothy, he stresses these qualities:

> Do your best to present yourself to God as one approved, a workman who does not need to be ashamed and who correctly handles the word of truth.
> —2 TIMOTHY 2:15

All Christians are expected to have high integrity and strong character, but it is especially clear that *leaders* are to be men or women of strong character. Exodus 18:21 says:

> But select capable men from all the people—men who fear God, trustworthy men who hate dishonest gain—and appoint them as officials over thousands, hundreds, fifties and tens.

Leaders should fear God, be trustworthy, and hate dishonest gain. Note that Moses said leaders must also be capable.

Survey respondents, however, felt that character and integrity were oftentimes not the qualities first looked for in an executive. Instead, charisma and presence, vision, competence, and several other qualities were selected as more important attributes. In a time when there are so many corporate scandals, when the media paints corporations as immoral, and the government feels the need to be more invasive in controls and oversight, survey respondents reported that corporate directors still might not view character and integrity as the number one requirement. Why the disconnect?

I think many corporations and their boards still operate on Levels 1 and 2 of the integrity pyramid, as described earlier:

- Level 1: If it is illegal, will I be caught?
- Level 2: If legality is gray, am I likely to win?

Using these rationales, value statements and codes of conduct become little more than good practices that can be helpful in mitigating legal penalties for a company. The pursuit of winning is paramount, and integrity is defined primarily in legal terms, that is, in a rational risk-versus-reward sense.

Of course, defining integrity in legal terms is grossly inadequate. Ethics *are* often optional. Unfortunately, many corporate leaders opt not to practice strong ethics when it doesn't seem to provide the easiest route to their profit goals. Wayne Sales, the CEO of Canadian Tire, remarked about the prevalence of poor integrity in business:

> You have to think that the average stakeholder can accept the truth. What they cannot accept is dishonesty, breach of integrity, violation of trust. But we see it time and time again.[7]

I had my own experience with this during my tenure as a CFO at a company that was 50 percent owned by an Italian conglomerate. The other 50 percent was owned by a local investor. The board members from the Italian conglomerate decided that the company I worked for should produce several models in one of their manufacturing facilities in Italy. This would enable them to fill capacity at the plant. Management was happy for that manufacturer to participate in the competitive bidding process, but as it turns out, their quotes were considerably higher than our other vendors. Producing at their facility would lower the local investor's half of the company profit, while presumably transferring it to the manufacturer, 100 percent owned by the Italian conglomerate.

Further complicating the matter, the local investor and the conglomerate each owned 50 percent of the voting shares, but the latter had an option to purchase the investor's shares at any time, based on an independent valuation. The company was growing rapidly, so it was in the local owner's best interest for the conglomerate not to exercise the purchase option. This, of course, gave them leverage greater than their 50 percent voting rights. They used this leverage to get the investor's agreement that the company would produce some models in Italy at their quoted prices. Management opposed the decision, but we had to follow the board's direction.

United States law, however, requires that prices between related parties be "arms-length" for tax purposes. In other words, the price paid by our company to the manufacturer in Italy should be no more than the price our company could obtain from unrelated parties for the same product or service. The IRS closely monitors this area when one of the related parties is not a U.S. tax-paying entity. If the transfer price is not considered arms-length, then U.S. taxes must be based on a restatement of earnings using a competitive price.

Therefore, at the end of the first year of production, our auditors asked for proof to demonstrate that the pricing we received was based on competitive quotes. I informed the board of the issue and said that I could not provide evidence that the prices were arms-length. The Italian board members told me that I should convince the auditors that the premium price reflected higher quality not offered by other vendors. But the Italian manufacturer and our other vendors met the exact same quality specifications, so I couldn't make this argument.

I received a letter shortly afterward from one of the Italian conglomerate's board representatives. In essence, it said, "We plan to buy the local investor's shares in the future, and we will reward those executives who have supported us." I responded to the effect that they could do whatever they wanted to do, but I would not fabricate something to satisfy the audit. Very shortly thereafter, the company exercised their purchase option, largely, I think, because of this issue. With the investor out of the picture, and in order to clear the path for resolving the audit, I was terminated. I have no idea to this day how the audit issue was resolved, but I am glad that I did not compromise integrity to preserve my job.

> The ultimate measure of a person is not where they stand in moments of convenience, but where they stand in times of challenge and controversy.[8]
> —Martin Luther King Jr.

Maintaining your integrity under pressure is difficult, but it usually isn't a disadvantage in your career. When I looked for a new opportunity, I was candid in interviews about why I had left. In most cases, I believe this impressed the interviewer. If it didn't, it probably was a red flag for me regarding the job I was interviewing for. Of the five companies I've worked for, I left three at least in part over integrity or character differences. As a leader, you must seek firms where your character and that of the owners or your superiors are in harmony.

Christians clearly should have the integrity advantage. This, more than any other leadership quality, is commanded in Scripture. We are instructed to have integrity not just when it is convenient, but when it is the hardest. Job was utterly tested by Satan; his family, wealth, and health were taken away. Yet Job held on to his integrity and would not turn from God.

I will not deny my integrity. I will maintain my righteousness and never let go of it; my conscience will not reproach me as long as I live.

—JOB 27:5–6

Leadership is a combination of strategy and character. If you must be without one, be without the strategy.[9]

—GENERAL NORMAN SCHWARZKOPF

Commitment and Dedication

The state of being emotionally impelled (commitment), and a devoting for a particular purpose (dedication)	
Survey Findings	
• 10th	Importance relative to hiring criteria
• 11th	Importance relative to perceived job success
• 4th	Ranking as a perceived strength of Christians

Are Christians perceived as having greater commitment and dedication to the purposes of the company? Despite the strong ranking from survey respondents, I don't think so. Are they, in fact, more committed or dedicated? In some cases.

This is one of the qualities that survey respondents were quite split on. Most qualities showed responses that were fairly consistent regarding Christians; those characteristics that scored as strengths had consistently medium to strong scores individually, and those that scored as weaknesses had responses that were consistently medium to weak. Regarding commitment and dedication, however, the scores were all over the board, although more respondents saw this quality as a strength. I spoke with several survey participants to get a better understanding.

The scores seem to reflect three different perceptions. In the some instances, survey participants were thinking in terms of a Christian's commitment and dedication to their faith and did not respond to the question in the context of a commitment and dedication to the purpose of the company. When we discussed this distinction, some said they would not have ranked it as strong.

Other respondents, however, did view Christians as more likely to honor a sense of obligation and commitment to employers. The Christian, in this view, connects his or her faith with biblical commands to be dedicated and committed to the company's mission, such as Hebrews 13:17, which says,

"Obey them so that their work will be a joy, not a burden, for that would be of no advantage to you." Viewed this way, the Christian's work ethic is seen as a strength because it has purpose.

Some, however, viewed Christians as less likely to be committed to the purpose of the company for the very reason that they are fully committed to their faith instead. I've known such Christians; they do exist. These individuals see religion and worship as the only real areas of eternal value and view work as a necessary evil while we are on this earth. As such, they are unable to dedicate themselves to a position they do not view as connected with their faith. Sherman and Hendricks describe these Christians:

> ...many people believe that the only part of life that "really counts" to God is the part that is committed to religious activities like Bible reading, prayer, church activity, and the like. Day-to-day work has no intrinsic value.[10]

Christians who do not believe that their faith and work are integrated can be leaders, but they cannot be Christian leaders. They will always struggle with whether or not their efforts and dedication somehow have any purpose. Why expend so much energy and dedication if it has no eternal value? If they see the goal of work to be only money or prestige, then they will never recognize successful corporate leadership to be in harmony with their faith.

For a Christian to be a leader in a secular corporation, he or she needs to believe that work has a God-blessed purpose and that God desires us to utilize our talents and skills to the utmost in whatever vocation He calls us. Being called to lead is a tremendous way to serve. If this is your view, you are likely to have a strong sense of commitment and dedication.

In Philippians 3:14, Paul expressed how dedicated and committed he was to his mission to lead the early church. So also, Christian leaders in secular corporations should be dedicated to lead well. In Colossians 3:23, Paul commands this:

> Whatever you do, work at it with all your heart, as working for the Lord, not for men.

Although not viewed to be as important to job success as some other qualities, commitment and dedication are still essential. John Maxwell says, "The world has never seen a great leader who lacked commitment."[11]

All strong leaders exhibit these qualities. They inspire a determination to succeed. Merlin Olsen, a member of the Professional Football Hall of Fame, said, "The winning team has a dedication. It will have a core of veteran players who set the standards. They will not accept defeat."[12]

Dedication, however, is not the same thing as obsession. Webster's dictionary defines *obsession* as "a persistent disturbing preoccupation with an unreasonable idea." As leaders, we are dedicated to attainable but ambitious goals, not obsessed with achieving unrealistic plans. An organization needs to believe that the goals are possible, for they will not follow leaders who run into brick walls.

Christian leaders can have a strong commitment and dedication to the job only if work and faith are well integrated. If you believe God called you to be a Christian leader, then you can believe that He wants you to be highly committed and dedicated. It should be an advantage.

> But one thing I do: Forgetting what is behind and straining toward what is ahead, I press on toward the goal to win the prize for which God has called me heavenward in Christ Jesus.
> —PHILIPPIANS 3:13–14

> I know the price of success: dedication, hard work, and an unremitting devotion to the things you want to see happen.[13]
> —FRANK LLOYD WRIGHT

Positive Attitude

Having a confident, affirmative, and optimistic state of mind
Survey Findings
• 12th   Importance relative to hiring criteria
• 12th   Importance relative to perceived job success
• 3rd   Ranking as a perceived strength of Christians

Survey respondents said Christians often have a strong positive attitude. It wasn't one of the more vital qualities, however, for hiring criteria and job success.

When the challenges are great, people look to a leader to reinforce their confidence in success. Military leaders understand this well. Napoleon Bonaparte, for instance, said, "A leader is a dealer in hope."[14] Consider the leadership of Winston Churchill during the bleakest days of World War II. He often gave hope to his countrymen with words such as this, spoken during a radio speech in February 1941:

> We shall not fail or falter; we shall not weaken or tire. Neither
> the sudden shock of battle nor the long-drawn trials of vigi-
> lance and exertion will wear us down. Give us the tools and
> we will finish the job.[15]
>
> —WINSTON CHURCHILL

A corporation will not follow a leader who lacks a positive attitude. Organi-zations look first to their leaders for confidence and encouragement. Without a positive attitude, followers will lose their enthusiasm. Joab rebuked King David when the king withdrew in sorrow and grief over the loss of his disloyal son, even though his army had just won a great battle.

> Now go out and encourage your men. I swear by the LORD
> that if you don't go out, not a man will be left with you by
> nightfall.
>
> —2 SAMUEL 19:7

The most common time that staff members would sit down in my office to talk was when they learned of some significantly bad development in our business. They just wanted to talk about it, and they wanted to see if I was confident that we would overcome it. They were looking for hope. At times, I would also feel exhausted or even dejected over the issue, but it was important to communicate the positive attitude.

Having a positive attitude is one of the most crucial qualities for ensuring you have strong morale in the organization. Peter Kyne, an early nineteenth-century writer said, "The morale of an organization is not built from the bottom up; it filters from the top down."[16] An organization cannot have strong morale and high energy if the leader does not show a positive attitude.

I believe it is easier for Christians to have a positive attitude than for those that do not have faith. The concordance in the New International Version Bible has 236 references to the words *joy, joyful,* or *joyous;* 54 references to *rejoice* or *rejoices;* and 39 references to *hope* or *hopes.* Perhaps this is why survey respondents said this was the fourth greatest strength of Christians. James said, "Consider it pure joy, my brothers, when you face trials of many kinds, because you know that the testing of your faith develops perseverance" (James 1:2). And the apostle Paul said to the Corinthians, "In all our troubles my joy knows no bounds" (2 Cor. 7:4). In the midst of the disagreements in the early church and persecution from outside, James and Paul still had joy because of their salvation and trust in God's will. They had a positive attitude that encouraged their followers.

Where do secular leaders go to find a positive attitude when the chips are down? Like all of us, they share anxiety and fears with a spouse or close friends to seek encouragement. Perhaps they also dig down inside themselves and find the resolve and the determination that gives them a positive attitude in front of those they lead. How deep this well is depends only on the person.

For Christians, however, the well has no bottom when we turn our fears over to God. What an advantage that God promises, "He leads me beside still waters, he restores my soul" (Ps. 23:2–3). And Jesus said, "Whoever drinks the water I will give him will never thirst" (John 4:14). Perhaps this is why our survey respondents felt that Christians are perceived as having a strong positive attitude. In tough times, I too often felt weary. I didn't go to the well often enough to be restored, but when I did, it was an advantage.

> "For I know the plans I have for you," declares the LORD,
> "plans to prosper you and not to harm you, plans to give you
> hope and a future."
> —JEREMIAH 29:11

Passion

Intense, driving, and overmastering feeling or conviction	
Survey Findings	
• 13th	Importance relative to hiring criteria
• 13th	Importance relative to perceived job success
• 7th	Ranking as a perceived strength of Christians

Passion was another quality that the panel felt Christians exhibited. As with most of the highly ranked Christian qualities, though, it wasn't listed as one of the more important factors for a leader's selection or success. Do Christians, in fact, have greater passion for the mission of the company? Probably not. I'll explain why.

Passion is stronger than commitment and dedication. E. M. Forster, author of *Passage to India*, wrote, "One person with passion is better than forty people merely interested."[17] And John Maxwell feels even more strongly: "Passion makes the impossible possible."[18] Maxwell believes passion is one of the indispensable leadership qualities. It can be a differentiator between strong leaders and truly great achievers.

Steve Jobs and Steve Wozniak had a passion to develop personal computers.

Jobs once said to John Sculley (president of Pepsi at that time), "Do you want to sell sugar water the rest of your life or do you want a chance to change the world?"[19] Jobs certainly had passion about what they were doing and he dangled that passion in front of Sculley to entice him to leave Pepsi.

With this passion, Jobs and Wosniak founded Apple computer in 1976. A year later, the president of mini-computer giant Digital Equipment Computer (DEC) said, "There is no reason for any individual to have a computer in his home." Within a short time, a college student named Michael Dell started Dell Computer, and before long personal computers became a reality for much of the United States. DEC, however, no longer exists (though some product lines are produced under the Hewlett-Packard name).[20] Jobs, Wosniak, and Dell—three people with passion to change the world.

If endowment of all other leadership qualities was relatively equal, I believe that passion often separates very good leaders who achieve little from those leaders who achieve truly great things. More than 50 percent of millionaire entrepreneurs never finished college.[21] They have a vision, but they also have extraordinary passion to go with it. Denis Diderot, an eighteenth-century French philosopher, wrote, "Only passions, great passions, can elevate the soul to great things."[22]

Passion is a powerful quality that can elevate energy and drive. However, I have seen many very effective leaders who were highly committed and dedicated, but not passionate. In fact, I don't think any of them had true passion; strong commitment and dedication, yes, but not passion. I believe being committed, dedicated, and determined is often sufficient to be a strong leader—unless you are out to change the world.

Passion put to wrong uses is a dangerous trait and often leads to abandonment of character values. Many bad leaders have extraordinary passion. Steve Jobs, for instance, has been described as an egomaniac.[23] In the extreme example, Adolph Hitler had an intense conviction that he should expand German living space—he called it *lebensraum*.[24] Many politicians also have a driving feeling that they should be in the seat of power. Remember, passion is defined as an *overmastering* feeling. Strong leaders sustain a fairly balanced life, without overmastering aspects, but I'm not sure passionate leaders do. If passion for the business becomes an overmastering conviction, where is the space for God the Master?

As Christian executives, our "intense, driving, and overmastering conviction" should be faith in Jesus Christ. I conceive, however, that it is possible to righteously have tremendous zeal for example, to introduce the personal computer to the world or to lead other business missions. I am a strong believer in commitment, dedication, hard work, and determination to achieve business success. As the apostle Paul qualified, "It is fine to be zealous, provided the purpose is good" (Gal. 4:18). Christian leaders that integrate faith with their mission at work should have such zeal, whether for creating a product that benefits mankind or establishing a work community that strives for correct values.

Billy Graham, the most famous leader in the Protestant church over the last sixty years, has a passion for God and tremendous zeal for his mission. He began his evangelistic ministry in 1943 while attending Wheaton College. His last appearance was in 2006 at the age of eighty-seven. Only Parkinson's disease, hip replacements, and prostate cancer could force him to end his work. During his life, he preached to more than 210,000,000 people in 185 countries. He once said, "I just want to lobby for God."[25]

Given the positive and negative aspects of passion as well as the reasons why some believe it to be essential and others less so, why, then, were Christians reported in the survey as traditionally being associated with a strong quality of passion? Thirty-three percent of survey participants felt it was perceived as a strong quality for Christians, and the rest felt it was either weak or neutral.

I spoke with several of those who felt it was a strong quality. Their rationale fell into two camps: In the first case, some respondents explained that they answered in terms of a Christian's passion *for his faith*. When we discussed that the term referred to passion *for the corporate mission*, these respondents generally said they would have ranked it lower, had they better understood the term. Others perceived Christians as falling into two groups regarding their attitude towards work. The first group, they explained, deems work to have no relevance to its faith and is generally totally passionless (or not even committed) regarding work. One executive participant, however, explained that Christians in leadership positions tended to be "the other type of Christian, one that is passionate about everything." He saw the Christian leader-type as being passionate about all aspects of life.

The apostle Paul wrote about where his passion came from in Colossians 1:29: "To this end I labor, struggling with all his [God's] energy, which so powerfully works in me." Whether you have zeal or passion as a corporate leader, that feeling should come from a conviction that God has called you to be an example in your vocation.

It is fine to be zealous, provided the purpose is good.
—Galatians 4:18

Many believe—and I believe—that I have been designated for this work by God. In spite of my old age I do not want to give it up; I work out of love for God and put all my hope in Him.[26]
—Michelangelo

Relationship Skills

The ability to build affinity with others	
Survey Findings	
• 9th	Importance relative to hiring criteria
• 6th	Importance relative to perceived job success
• 6th	Ranking as a perceived strength of Christians

Scripture abounds in lessons for relationships with family, friends, neighbors, and even enemies. In *Leadership Lessons of Jesus,* Bob Briner and Ray Pritchard explain the relationship skills that Jesus practiced:

> Jesus, the greatest of all leaders, clearly represents the special relationship that can evolve between leaders and followers. He never exhibited a cool detachment toward His followers; they were not simply pawns to carry out His wishes and implement His plans. His followers were very special to Him and, conversely, He was very special to them.[27]

Two excellent books that have many insights into relationship skills are *The Friendship Factor* by Alan Loy McGinnis and Dale Carnegie's *How to Win Friends and Influence People.* I have chosen six practices from these books that I think are most important to developing strong relations, especially with your direct staff. All of these are also important Christian principles.

- Demonstrate that you care for your staff.
- Show respect for the opinions of others.
- Make staff members feel important.
- Be a good listener.
- Become genuinely interested in your staff.
- Give them sincere appreciation.[28]

Demonstrate that you care for your staff.

A central refrain of our faith reminds us that God cares: "For God so loved the world that he gave his one and only Son" (John 3:16). Since God cares for all of us, we should care for all others. The oft-quoted Golden Rule in Luke 6:31 says, "Do to others as you would have them do to you." Relationships are based on caring for each other. As leaders, we will not establish effective relationships with staff members unless we demonstrate that we care for the people we lead.

> People don't care how much you know until they know how much you care.[29]
>
> —JOHN C. MAXWELL

Show respect for the opinions of others.

The most common problem in early Christian churches was division over opinions regarding Jewish law and rituals. Paul had to devote many of his letters to straightening this out, but on matters of opinion rather than fundamental belief he told the church to respect others' views. Regarding disputable matters, Paul told the Roman Church, "Let us stop passing judgment on one another" (Rom. 14:13).

For a leader to build relations with his or her team, respect for their opinions is important. Communication will break down and the leader will alienate followers if respect for opinions is not shown. Respect for another's opinion does not mean agreement; it is an appreciation for receiving a point of view. A leader makes the best decisions when he or she is able to draw from many diverse points of view.

> When two men always agree, one of them is unnecessary.[30]
>
> —WILLIAM WRIGLEY JR.,
> FOUNDER OF THE WILLIAM WRIGLEY JR. COMPANY

Make staff members feel important.

The apostle Paul apparently spent some time in Crete with Titus establishing the church there. Paul left to continue his ministry and later sent Titus a letter with instructions for the new church in Crete. Paul begins the letter by affirming Titus's importance.

> The reason I left you in Crete was that you might straighten out what was left unfinished.
>
> —TITUS 1:5

Paul didn't say he left Crete because he had more important things to do. He left because he was confident that Titus could handle it himself!

If you make your team feel important they will not want to let you down. Respecting the importance of each member is critical to a healthy relationship.

> Everyone has an invisible sign hanging from their neck saying, "Make me feel important." Never forget this message when working with people.[31]
>
> —MARY KAY ASH,
> FOUNDER OF MARY KAY COSMETICS

Be a good listener.

The following chapter specifically discusses listening skills; however, it is worth mentioning here that these skills are also an important component of relationship skills. Proverbs has several lessons on the wisdom of listening, and the book of James also encourages us to be respectful listeners. James 1:19 says, "Everyone should be quick to listen, slow to speak and slow to become angry."

Dale Carnegie covers this twice in his book *How to Win Friends and Influence People.* He says one of the six ways to make people like you is to be a good listener and encourage others to talk about themselves. He also explains that one of the twelve keys to win people to your way of thinking is to let others do a great deal of the talking. Ardent listening communicates respect and will make your staff feel valued.[32]

> A good listener is not only popular everywhere, but after a while he gets to know something.[33]
>
> —WILLIAM MIZNER

Become genuinely interested in your staff.

I am impressed with how genuinely interested the apostle Paul was in all of the people he came into contact with. After spending time in a city and starting a church, he didn't forget it and just move on somewhere else. He stayed in close contact through letters and reports from others that he met in his travels. He called numerous followers by name and demonstrated detailed knowledge of what problems his early followers were experiencing. For instance, in Ephesians 1:15 Paul writes, "Ever since I heard about your faith in the Lord Jesus and your love for all the saints, I have not stopped giving thanks for you, remembering you in my prayers." To have a relationship with people, leaders need to be genuinely interested in their team members.

For several years when I worked at Young America we had a custom that anyone in the company was welcome to join me Fridays after work for a social hour at a nearby restaurant. Work was discussed some of the time but mostly we discussed each other's families, interests, and weekend plans. I got to know more about people in this forum than I would have in decades of business meetings at the office. I was genuinely interested in people's lives outside of the office, and I believe this made relationships back at the office much stronger.

> We are interested in others when they are interested in us.[34]
> —Publilius Syrus,
> Roman poet

Give them sincere appreciation.

Showing appreciation for something is far more effective than pointing out things not done well. Paul wrote a letter to Philemon, asking that he accept back into his household, without punishment, a slave named Onesimus who had run away from Philemon. Paul begins his letter, "I always thank God as I remember you in my prayers" (Philem. 1:4). Paul communicates appreciation for his relationship with Philemon, and later, in verse 19, he says, "I will pay it back." In other words, "I would appreciate it very much."

Relationships are strengthened when leaders frequently show appreciation for the good accomplishments and hard efforts of their staff. Sam Walton, the founder of Wal-Mart, is quoted as saying:

> Appreciate everything your associates do for the business. Nothing else can quite substitute for a few well-chosen, well-timed, sincere words of praise.[35]

More than a few leaders, however, actually avoid relations with their team. They feel that as "commander" it is not appropriate and weakens their superior authority. I've seen a few of these and can assure you that their team members jump ship as soon as possible.

Having strong relations with each member of your team is important, but the key talent is getting the team to have productive relationships with each other. I believe leaders spend more time getting team members to act like a team than any other endeavor. Many years ago my manager confided in me, "I hire eagles because they soar. The problem is I can't get them to fly in formation." As leaders, we all know the challenge to get five or six or seven people on your staff, most of whom are probably Type-A personalities, to work together effectively. Relationship skills are critical to accomplish this. Hiring people who are team players, however, is also necessary.

Our survey panel agrees that relationship skills are highly important to the success of a leader, and Christians have tremendous biblical advice that should help to guide these skills. For Christian leaders, it ought to be an advantage.

> Clothe yourselves with compassion, kindness, humility, gentleness and patience.
>
> —COLOSSIANS 3:12

> Leadership has a harder job to do than just choose sides. It must bring sides together.[36]
>
> —JESSE JACKSON

Listening Skills and Teachability

The proclivity to hear with thoughtful attention (listening skills) and receptiveness to continual learning (teachability)		
Survey Findings		
•	15th	Importance relative to hiring criteria
•	9th	Importance relative to perceived job success
•	5th	Ranking as a perceived strength of Christians

Listening skills and teachability were viewed as being strong qualities in Christians and of some importance to job success. These assets were not seen, however, as key criteria for being selected as an executive.

As a result, many individuals who are chosen to be executives and leaders lack this skill. I've witnessed some executives and many board directors who believe that they understand all of the issues and have superior solutions without having made a serious effort to listen and learn. They often suffer from acute pride and arrogance and, unfortunately, usually make fools of themselves. Dale Carnegie described this type of executive:

> If you want to know how to make people shun you and laugh at you behind your back and even despise you, here is the recipe: Never listen to anyone for long. Talk incessantly about yourself. If you have an idea while the other person is talking, don't wait for him to finish: bust right in and interrupt in the middle of a sentence. Do you know people like that? I do, unfortunately; and the astonishing thing is that some of them are prominent.

Bores, that is all they are—bores intoxicated with their own
egos, drunk with a sense of their own importance.[37]

Such leaders are not only bores, but they communicate to others that their views are not important. As a result, they lead without having the benefit of advice and multiple perspectives. They are likely to lead arrogantly, without a clear picture or sufficient knowledge. A smart leader, however, ensures that he or she listens carefully to subordinates.

In 1984, Pepsi sent me to Singapore as director of finance for the Far East region. My previous positions had all been in the areas of corporate planning, forecasting, and analysis. This was my first real "line job" where I had profit and loss (abbreviated "P&L") responsibility and reported to a general manager. As such, there were many new responsibilities to learn. However, my wife was expecting our first child, which delayed our arrival in Singapore and cut the transition time with my predecessor to only one day. I was immediately dependent upon my new staff to learn the ropes.

I relied primarily on two young and bright local managers. As decisions needed to be made, I would ask for their advice, but usually received little. Instead, they would wait for me to suggest a decision and then enthusiastically agree with it. I recall being quite unsure if I was making good decisions or not. It wasn't long, however, before I discovered that they implemented some of my decisions, but not others.

Over time I came to understand that in Chinese culture, subordinates can be reticent to offer advice and a boss's decisions were always agreed with. However, if they knew it to be a wrong decision, they would simply do what they felt was right in order to protect their superior. I learned that I needed to actively encourage them to offer advice and to disagree with me when their judgment differed. In time, they became active counselors and were of immense value for me to learn and succeed in the job.

John Maxwell said, "A good leader encourages followers to tell him what he needs to know, not what he wants to hear."[38] Listening is an active skill, not a passive one. A leader must be proactive to ensure that he or she is getting as many points of view as possible, and he or she must encourage debate in order to arrive at the best decisions. My best advisors disagreed with me frequently and energetically.

Proverbs has a wealth of advice on the importance of listening and teachability.

> Let the wise listen and add to their learning, and let the discerning get guidance.
>
> —Proverbs 1:5

> Plans fail for lack of counsel, but with many advisors they succeed.
>
> —Proverbs 15:22

> Listen to advice and accept instruction, and in the end you will be wise.
>
> —Proverbs 19:20

> For lack of guidance a nation falls, but many advisors make a victory sure.
>
> —Proverbs 11:14

> He who answers before listening—that is his folly and his shame.
>
> —Proverbs 18:13

Listening and learning not only improve your decision-making abilities, they also make people want to support and follow you. Dean Rusk, former secretary of state said, "One of the best ways to persuade others is with your ears."[39] It is important, as a leader, that employees and advisors feel you actively listen and respect their views.

In my CFO roles in the nineties I often thought of myself as the *consigliere* for the CEO. Many of you were introduced to this Italian word from the *Godfather* movies. Tom Hagen, the unofficially adopted son of the Corleone family, was the confidential advisor for Don Corleone. His advice was always carefully considered, but only the Don made decisions. He didn't always follow Hagen's advice. When Don Corleone made a decision, however, Hagen supported it. In the same sense, I always felt that if the CEO clearly understood and considered my advice, I easily supported whatever decision was made, even if it was not in line with my recommendation. Fortunately, I didn't need to support some of Don Corleone's decisions.

People are motivated to support you more heartily when you listen to them—more often than if you simply provide instruction. Listening validates your team's worth and encourages continued openness on future questions. Of course, if you consistently find an advisor's advice to be poor, the advisor will eventually realize he or she has no impact. You should probably agree to make a change.

Listening and teachability result from a spirit of humility as well as a desire to continually improve. A lack of these qualities often reflects pride and arrogance. John Maxwell says, "You cannot be prideful and teachable at the same time."[40] Proverbs 12:15 puts it this way: "The way of a fool seems right to him, but a wise man listens to advice." The ability to listen and learn are important skills, and scriptural instruction encourages us to practice them. They will put the Christian leader at an advantage.

> Make plans by seeking advice.
> —Proverbs 20:18

> Personally I am always ready to learn, although I do not always like being taught.[41]
> —Winston Churchill

Accountability

The willingness to accept responsibility (for both favorable and unfavorable results).	
Survey Findings	
• 6th	Importance relative to hiring criteria
• 4th	Importance relative to perceived job success
• 8th	Ranking as a perceived strength of Christians

Accountability, the willingness to accept responsibility, was rated in the survey as an important trait, both for being selected as an executive and for success as a leader. Respondents also indicated that accountability is a fairly evident characteristic among Christians.

Scripture makes it clear that Christians will be held accountable for their actions.

> But I will hold the watchman accountable for his blood.
> —Ezekiel 33:6

> I am against the shepherds and will hold them accountable for my flock.
> —Ezekiel 34:10

> So then, each of us will give an account of himself to God.
> —Romans 14:12

Christians ought to understand the concept of accountability, but it is also an important principle that leaders understand. When Harry Truman famously said, "The buck stops here,"[42] he was declaring that he was accountable for all decisions in his administration. Jon Huntsman said, "Leadership is a privilege. Those who receive the mantle must also know that they can expect an accounting of their stewardships."[43]

Twice in my career I worked for an executive at Pepsi who was intelligent and had significant charisma and a great sense of humor. He always sought the advice of his staff with lively discussion and disagreement, but when it came time to make a decision, he often reminded us that he had the final say by saying, "This is like a Latin American democracy. You all get to vote, but I count the ballots!" He was a participative leader, but he never forgot that he was accountable and he needed to "own" the important decisions.

As a leader, you are also accountable for the decisions that you do *not* make. When you delegate authority, you have the responsibility to ensure that those empowered will make correct judgments and that there are participative procedures that bring tougher decisions to your attention. In short, a failure by your people is a failure by you, the leader. That is the essence of accountability.

Some leaders shirk accountability. I was recruited in 1996 as CFO of a Fortune 500 organization with nearly two billion dollars in revenues. The president who hired me had been brought in from GE several months earlier to shake up a stodgy, good-old-boy type of organizational culture. He set out to make changes, perhaps without enough finesse, and a few weeks after I was hired the good-old-boy vice presidents held a palace revolt and convinced the chairman that they would all resign if he didn't fire the president. In my opinion, the chairman should have fired all of *them*. But instead, two weeks into my new job, the guy who hired me was fired. I was then guilty by association with the president who had selected me. I knew before my first few months were up that my tenure was going to be short-term.

The chairman decided to leave the president job open for a year so the vice presidents of marketing, sales, and any other contenders could compete for it. That was his second poor decision. The team politics during this period were horrific.

The vice president of marketing was a classic "empty suit:" his leadership skills were weak and he incessantly played politics against others to campaign for the president position. He was a person we could never trust. He was the last of our peer group that any of us would wish to follow.

After a long period of internal competition, the chairman decided to select him as president. About that time, I saw a weakening in our outlook and my group prepared a forecast reflecting that. On seeing this, the newly appointed president demanded that I raise the forecast. He could not have a poor quarter his first period in the job! He orchestrated pressure from the corporate CFO and controller, each of whom told me they thought I was too conservative. Though I argued, I agreed to raise the forecast. The next quarter we missed forecast. I was held accountable and was fired to appease Wall Street after we announced earnings.

From what I understand, the company went from disappointment to disappointment in the ensuing months, and each time another team member was blamed. I suppose the president was eventually the last man standing or couldn't pretend to hide behind the mistakes of any others. He got sacked. No one wants to follow a leader who does not accept accountability, but instead looks to distribute blame for his or her own job preservation. Such "leaders" are quickly abandoned.

Strong leaders accept accountability. They "own" the results. If a leader does not deliver acceptable results, he should credibly determine how to change course, step down, or accept a decision for someone with a new vision.

In 1997, Michael Armstrong, a thirty-one-year veteran at IBM and a successful executive at General Motors, was hired by AT&T to steer a new course in a deregulated industry with declining margins. Through an aggressive program of acquisitions, Armstrong tried to reestablish the company as an end-to-end carrier. The strategy tanked and AT&T stock dropped from a high of $64 per share in 1999 to $10 in 2002. Mr. Armstrong resigned. He failed, but he clearly understood the concept of accountability. He made this press statement:

> The ancient Romans had a tradition: whenever one of their
> engineers constructed an arch, as the capstone was hoisted into
> place, the engineer assumed accountability for his work in the
> most profound way possible: he stood under the arch.[44]

Christians understand the concept that as leaders they are accountable for the stewardship of the organization's financial and human resources. We are accountable to God, but also for the stewardship given to us by others. It is a highly regarded trait for both selection criteria and job success. It ought to be an advantage for the Christian leader.

> There was a rich man whose manager was accused of wasting
> his possessions. So he called him in and asked, "What is this

I hear about you? Give an account of your management, because you cannot be manager any longer."

—LUKE 16:1–2

Some favorite expressions of small children: "It's not my fault... They made me do it... I forgot." Some favorite expressions of adults: "It's not my job... No one told me... It couldn't be helped." True freedom begins and ends with personal accountability.[45]

—DAN ZANDRA,
AUTHOR

Focus

Ability to concentrate attention or effort	
Survey Findings	
• 16th	Importance relative to hiring criteria
• 15th	Importance relative to perceived job success
• 10th	Ranking as a perceived strength of Christians

Respondents did not indicate focus to be a strength particularly associated with Christianity; it received an average score (ten out of seventeen). I cannot conceive of any reason why a Christian would be more focused on their job than any other person. Additionally, focus was simply seen to be relatively less important for hiring criteria or job success than other qualities.

Leadership focus is having a narrow and select number of priorities and ensuring that the organization concentrates on those priorities. Priorities and concentration are important, as John Maxwell explains:

> A leader who knows his priorities but lacks concentration knows what has to be done but never gets it done. If he has concentration but no priorities, he has excellence without progress.[46]

Robert Shiller, Yale economics professor and author of *Irrational Exuberance*, states:

> The ability to focus on important things is a defining characteristic of intelligence.[47]

Leaders must be able to focus their attention and direct the actions of their staff. It is important to ensure that the individuals you have empowered to lead also focus their attention on what most fundamentally drives success.

A plan is critical to channeling corporate endeavors. Strategic planning is the process of defining the most important objectives, strategies, and tactics so that the organization can be highly focused on them. A business without a strategic plan has no direction. A leader who does not focus his or her organization on a narrow list of priorities has them running around on all sorts of tangents, few of which are likely to be mission critical. There's a popular saying that goes like this: "Anyone who aims at nothing is sure to hit it." It would be just as true to say, "Anyone who aims at too many things will miss them all." I recall the chairman of PepsiCo, Don Kendall, frequently reminding us during strategic plan reviews, "We can focus on three or four things with excellence. But, when we try to achieve six or seven, we fail at all of them." When this happens, efforts on critical goals are diluted and inadequate.

Focus is an important leadership trait, but that is not to say that a leader shouldn't be involved with details. A leader is also accountable for the details. The leader needs to ensure that appropriate levels in the organization are immersed in the details. This is one reason why leaders mandate quality, efficiency, or excellence certifications for their organizations, like the International Standards Organization (ISO), Malcolm Baldridge National Quality Award, Consumer Operations Performance Center (COPC), or Six Sigma. Auditors for these certifications assure the leader that the organization is looking after the details.

There is good advice in Scripture on planning and being focused in the work that we do. Hebrews 12:1–2 exhorts believers to "fix our eyes on Jesus" as we "run with perseverance the race marked out for us." Likewise, Proverbs 24:27 says, "Finish your outdoor work and make your fields ready; after that build your house." In other words, plan carefully to acquire the means to build your house; then go ahead and build it. Proverbs also warns us that energy without planning—and focus—will lead to missing our goals.

> It is not good to have zeal without knowledge, nor to be hasty
> and miss the way.
> —Proverbs 19:2

Proverbs always provides both spiritual and practical advice. In this case, being focused is practical advice; it just makes sense. Although I don't see it as a particular advantage for a Christian, Scripture suggests it makes good sense. It is an important leadership quality.

> So we fix our eyes not on what is seen, but what is unseen. For what is seen is temporary, but what is unseen is eternal.
> —2 CORINTHIANS 4:18

> Leadership must remain focused, must adhere to the mission statement. If a leader loses focus, all the others involved are sure to follow.[48]
> —BOB BRINER and RAY PRITCHARD

— Chapter 6 —
PERCEIVED CHRISTIAN
WEAKNESSES

T HE CHARACTERISTICS LESS often thought to be evident in Christians, based on the survey results, were charisma and presence, courage and risk-taking, initiative and innovation, decisiveness and determination, vision, problem solving skills, focus, communication skills, and competence. The following chart shows this quite clearly.

Seven of these eight qualities were said to be among the top hiring criteria for executives, including all four of the highest-ranked qualities for leadership selection: charisma, vision, competence, and communication skills.

The results should not be taken to indicate, however, that Christian leaders are generally deficient in these areas; they may just be less stereotypically distinctive than their other qualities. Simply by virtue of the fact that Christians are seen to be extraordinarily strong compared to a secular population in such qualities as servanthood, integrity, relationship skills, and listening skills, the other skills would be lower in the ranking. It doesn't necessarily mean that it is a weakness. The concern remains, though, that if those looking for the next person to promote or hire into an executive position are largely concentrating on such qualities as decisiveness, charisma, innovation, vision, and problem solving skills, Christians may not demonstrate these as strongly as other qualities. Nonetheless, it is unfair—and incorrect—to attribute weakness in these areas to all Christian leaders.

In many cases, such perceptions of Christian weaknesses are largely biases. As with most biases, there is not enough truth in it to justify a global

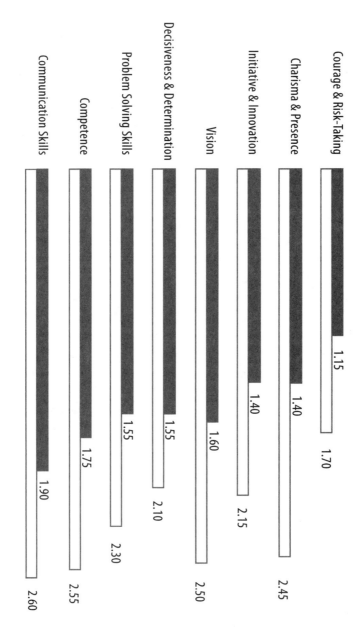

Perceived Christian Weaknessess Compared to Executive Selection Importance

Trait	Importance of Hiring Criteria	Traits Shown by Christians
Courage & Risk-Taking	1.70	1.15
Charisma & Presence	2.45	1.40
Initiative & Innovation	2.15	1.40
Vision	2.50	1.60
Decisiveness & Determination	2.10	1.55
Problem Solving Skills	2.30	1.55
Competence	2.55	1.75
Communication Skills	2.60	1.90

 Importance of Hiring Criteria (Most = 3, Least = 1) ■ Traits Shown by Christians (Most Often = 3, Least Often = 1)

generalization about a population group. In some cases, however, I believe many Christians could be weaker in these areas because of a misunderstanding of Scripture. In the same way that most qualities in the last section were easily seen to be in harmony with the fruit of the Spirit, certain traits may be underdeveloped because the Christian views those qualities as being in conflict with the character of a Christian spirit. For instance, are charisma and presence in conflict with gentleness and humility? How does one reconcile being decisive and determined, but still patient and prayerful? Is taking the initiative and having a sense of urgency wrong when we need to trust in God and wait on His will?

Finally, I want to note that at the beginning of each section in this chapter I have included a quote that is representative of how some people view Christians. Some of these may seem a bit offensive, but it is only meant to illustrate how Christians are often characterized or perceived by secularists.

Charisma and Presence

I cannot follow you Christians; for you try to crawl through life on your knees, while I stride through mine on my feet.[1]

—CHARLES BRADLAUGH,
NINETEENTH-CENTURY ENGLISH ATHEIST
POLITICIAN AND JOURNALIST

A personal magic of leadership that enables a performer to achieve a close relationship with his audience (charisma) and a quality of poise and effectiveness (presence)
Survey Findings

•	4th	Importance relative to hiring criteria
•	16th	Importance relative to perceived job success
•	16th	Ranking as a perceived strength of Christians

Why did charisma and presence come in next-to-last in the ranking of qualities often exhibited by Christians? Are Christians less likely to exhibit charisma and presence? Sadly, I think they often are, though these qualities are ranked fourth among those sought after as the hiring criterion. Respondents did not feel those traits were so important for job success, but they do seem to be premier qualifications to enter "the club."

An executive is supposed to have a certain stature. When he or she walks into a room you can often feel the executive command presence; his or her words have weightiness to them; he or she "fills" the room. The powerful executive also has charisma, a personal magic that makes the audience feel an affinity with him or her.

I think of charisma as the ability to draw people closer to you, whereas presence is the an unspoken air of confidence that immediately commands others' respect and attention. Arnold Palmer had charisma, always smiling and making eye contact with the fans. "Arnie's Army" was drawn to him, cheering and rooting for every good shot. Jack Nicklaus had presence, intimidating opponents with his talent, steely concentration, and determination. People tended to root for Arnie, but were in awe of Jack.

Peter Drucker, however, feels charisma may even be a liability to some:

> Charisma becomes the undoing of leaders. It makes them inflexible, convinced of their own infallibility, unable to change.[2]

Perhaps this is why survey respondents ranked charisma and presence only sixteenth of seventeen qualities for success as an executive; they didn't believe that it was very important. I have worked for leaders who had great charisma but little competence, and I have also seen leaders with tremendous capabilities but no extraordinary quality of charisma or presence. I think we would all prefer to be led by the latter. Charisma and presence make a great impact on initial impressions. Substance, however, is more important for the people who you lead on a daily basis.

I was privileged to be manager of strategic planning during the time when John Sculley was president of Pepsi-Cola USA. John was one of the most highly sought executives at the time, and he later went on to become president of Apple during the eighties and early nineties. Yet, when I knew him he never struck me as having a lot of charisma or even presence. He wasn't a naturally good public speaker, either. He enlisted the help of a former Broadway stage actor to coach and choreograph his speeches—and his audiences thought he was a great speaker!

John, however, had one of the most inquisitive minds I have ever seen. I recall having presented to senior management my group's ideas on regional marketing, and the next day John came down to my office alone, put his feet on my desk, and said, "So let's talk about this some more." Other times, he dropped in to discuss ideas he had seen on new bottle designs or new applications of The Pepsi Challenge. Bear in mind that I was three levels down in the organization, but what I was working on stimulated his curiosity. His mind was a sponge, and his intellect was tremendous. Still, he was not intimidating at all, nor was he particularly magical in his charisma. We simply talked—and argued—and I respected him like few other leaders I have worked with. He had listening and learning skills, vision, competence, positive attitude, and decisiveness in spades.

Moses was another great leader who lacked special charisma or presence. When God chose him to lead the Israelites out of Egypt, he complained:

> O LORD, I have never been eloquent, neither in the past nor since you have spoken to your servant. I am slow of speech and tongue.
>
> —EXODUS 4:10

God allowed Aaron to speak for Moses in front of Pharaoh and the people. However, God still chose Moses to lead, because He recognized Moses' other qualities to be more important! God did this repeatedly: David was a young shepherd, small in stature when he was selected to be king after Saul, and Jesus was raised by a poor carpenter.

In spite of these examples, I have known many Christian leaders and pastors who have tremendous charisma. They are articulate, warm, interesting, and empathetic. We are drawn to them. Some also have presence, confidence, and self-assurance that seem to place them above us. Who would say Billy Graham does not have tremendous presence? In fact, most pastors have more than a fair share of charisma and presence.

Do many of us equate the qualities of charisma and presence in our corporate leaders with pride or arrogance? Do we instinctively try not to emulate this? After all, Scripture tells us, "Make it your ambition to lead a quiet life" (1 Thess. 4:11), and "Be completely humble and gentle" (Eph. 4:2).

There is a significant disconnect between a Christian view of humility and having confidence in God's gifts and the knowledge or skills that we have developed. One of the definitions of *humble* is "ranking low in a hierarchy," yet Numbers 12:3 says, "Now Moses was a very humble man, more humble than anyone else on the face of the earth." How could the most humble man on the face of the earth lead God's chosen people? Moses was humble before the Lord, but he was bold in front of Pharaoh.

We should be humble before God, and we should show humility before others because we respect them as equal in God's creation (and we have the spirit of listening and teachability). However, if we have gifts of leadership, we should also be bold in putting those gifts to use. God would not give us a gift in order to hide it. Charisma and presence are skills to be developed and applied, provided they are not manifested with pride and arrogance but are motivated by a desire to lead effectively.

I don't think I have great charisma, but I try to draw people to me by showing concern, humor, a positive attitude, and candidness. I've been told that I have presence, often in the negative sense: that my problem-solving skills and tendency towards rapid decisiveness can intimidate. So I try to watch out for this by practicing skills in listening, servanthood, and showing respect.

Actually, charisma and presence may describe a package of many other compound skills. Debra Benton, author of *Executive Charisma,* says the foundation of charisma is integrity, confidence, and full disclosure (candidness).[3] She also discusses initiative, listening, giving respect, and a positive attitude as some of the other elements of charisma. You may possess many of these qualities and therefore have more charisma than you think.

There is nothing in the Bible that suggests you should not exhibit charisma and presence. They open up opportunities to lead. However, if these are not your strengths, there are still many opportunities to lead in companies or positions not requiring such skills. Assess your skills and seek the best fit for your leadership. In many leadership positions, charisma and presence have far less import than other qualities. I believe, for instance, that I was better suited to lead privately held organizations that required internal surgery rather than larger, public companies that needed a more gifted external communicator. Charisma and presence are more necessary in roles that require a lot of public exposure.

Charisma and presence are not traits you need to hide out of a sense of humility or a perceived obligation to lead a quiet life. If God calls you to lead, develop your charisma and presence as much as possible so that you might lead better.

> How can you have charisma? Be more concerned about making others feel good about themselves than you are making them feel good about you.[4]
>
> —ANONYMOUS

Courage and Risk-Taking

> Making fun of Christians is like hunting dairy cows with a high-powered rifle and scope.[5]
>
> —P. J. O'ROURKE, JOURNALIST AND SATIRIST

Mental or moral strength to venture, persevere and withstand difficulty (courage) and one who is willing to chance loss for the prospect of a greater win (risk-taker)
Survey Findings
• 13th Importance relative to hiring criteria • 14th Importance relative to perceived job success • 17th Ranking as a perceived strength of Christians

Why did courage and risk-taking come in last as qualities associated with Christians? Fortunately, these traits are not very high in the survey rankings for hiring criteria or executive success either.

People I've talked with, including Christians, tell me that they perceive Christians as generally being conservative and cautious. The word more likely to be used to describe a Christian's attitude toward risk is *prudence*. This word has various meanings, but it is often defined as "caution and circumspection as to danger and risk." Scripture, in fact, teaches us to be prudent:

> The prudent see danger and take refuge, but the simple keep going and suffer for it.
> —PROVERBS 27:12

> A simple man believes anything, but the prudent man gives thought to his steps.
> —PROVERBS 14:15

I own some investments in a mutual fund that is managed by a group of Christians. Would you guess it is highly speculative, or is it quite prudent? If you answered "prudent," you were right, along with 100 percent of the people to whom I have posed this question. This fund usually underperforms the market, but it has almost always had moderate growth.

On the other extreme are the venture capital fund managers. I've known several Wall Street venture capitalists. The nature of their business is to take risks, but most in this industry also "weave and spin" tales in order to make their deals fly. Proverbs 21:5–6 reflects some of them:

> The plans of the diligent lead to profit as surely as haste leads to poverty. A fortune made by a lying tongue is a fleeting vapor and a deadly snare.

Diligence is characterized by steady, energetic, and earnest effort. This is what Proverbs suggests will lead to profit. However, those who are hasty to achieve profit will endeavor to make a fortune by lying and deceiving.

Courage and risk-taking must be ethical, honest, and candid. John Maxwell describes this principle as a key characteristic of courage. He states, "Your dedication to potential must remain stronger than your desire to appease others."[6] If you, as a leader, believe that a risky course is likely to be profitable, the most important thing is to be open and honest about the risks—as open as you are with your belief that it will succeed. When both investors and employees have an honest awareness of the risks and rewards, all can commit to the course without any deception. Nineteenth century preacher and author, James Freeman Clarke wrote, "Conscience is the root of all true courage; if a man would be brave, let him obey his conscience."[7]

The success of capitalism is based on risk-taking. Without leaders willing to take risks and investors willing to risk their savings, nearly all companies would never have started. Most new industries wouldn't survive their early years, and many inventions would never have been commercialized. Commerce and job creation are based on taking risks, so it should be encouraged.

It's interesting that if we take risks and succeed, we are praised for courage. But, if we risk all and fail, we are sometimes mocked for being imprudent. With 20/20 hindsight, historians praise the successful risk-takers for vision and courage but love to mock people who chased wild fantasies.

Howard Hughes had vision and courage. He was a leader in aviation development during the thirties and forties, and Hughes Aircraft Company made him one of the wealthiest people in the world. He is best remembered, however, for his eccentricity and his relentless efforts to create the Spruce Goose. The Spruce Goose was an airplane of 190 tons designed to be built of "non-strategic materials," such as birch instead of aluminum, and to safely fly soldiers and supplies long distances. The design still holds the record for the largest wingspan of any aircraft in history. Hughes worked on the prototype for five years and spent a huge amount of government funds in the process (for which he was called to testify before Congress). It made only one flight, however, and stayed aloft for less than one mile. It only reached an altitude of seventy feet. Although Hughes was a visionary in aircraft design, he is largely remembered for the Spruce Goose fantasy that he chased.

Foolish risk-taking usually ends up being foolish. Proverbs 12:11 warns, "He who chases fantasies lacks judgment." However, when leaders embark on a risk, none believe it is foolish. Most leaders believe they only take prudent risks. Based on our first definition of prudent, this sounds like an oxymoron, but Webster's dictionary also defines *prudent* as simply "skill and judgment in the use of resources." Being prudent doesn't necessarily mean risk-avoidance. It denotes using good judgment in taking risks. Even George S. Patton, known for his aggressive military strategy, said risks should be calculated. He said, "Take calculated risks. That is quite different from being rash."[8]

The two servants in the parable of the talents (Matt. 25:14–30) who took risk and invested their master's money wisely were rewarded. The third servant, the one who feared risking it, buried the money for safekeeping. He was fired.

Courage and risk-taking in business are strong leadership qualities if practiced ethically, openly, and with good judgment. Many corporate leaders should be more ethical and open, perhaps even prudent, but Christian leaders in business should have the courage to be daring.

> Have I not commanded you? Be strong and courageous. Do not be terrified; do not be discouraged, for the LORD your God will be with you wherever you go.
>
> —JOSHUA 1:9

Initiative and Innovation

> One can often recognize herd animals by their tendency to carry Bibles.[9]
>
> —ALLEN WHEELIS,
> CONTEMPORARY AUTHOR AND PSYCHOANALYST

Energy displayed in starting the beginning of an action (initiative) and the talent to introduce something new (innovation)
Survey Findings
• 7th   Importance relative to hiring criteria
• 9th   Importance relative to perceived job success
• 15th   Ranking as a perceived strength of Christians

Initiative and innovation were ranked in the survey as fairly important criteria for being selected and somewhat important for job success in an executive position. It is a trait, however, that was ranked close to last as a perceived quality of Christians. Many individuals in and outside of the corporate arena perceive Christians to be stuck in a rut, adhering to what is tried and true and resisting change. But are they, in fact, likely to be less innovative and have less initiative in the business world? Yes and no.

The very first chapter of the Bible describes God's initiative and innovation. Genesis 1:1 starts, "In the beginning God created." After God completed His creation, He then created man and woman "in his own image" (Gen. 1:27). God's image is Creator and Innovator, and we are one of God's innovations. Nothing that God created is in His image except mankind. Therefore, we are the only species designed to be innovators like Him. It is ironic, therefore, that the people who believe in God the Innovator are perceived as least innovative!

How often have you heard these types of things said, particularly by the media, Hollywood, and others in the so-called cultural elite?

- "Christians don't have an open mind."
- "Christians want to preserve the status quo."
- "Christians are old fashioned."

Where does the perception that Christians are likely to be less innovative and lacking initiative come from? It is a generalization drawn from secularists' realization that Christians have values that never change. Since the second half of the twentieth century, age-old cultural values have undergone dramatic redefinition in the Western world, values about pre-marital sex, sanctity of marriage, the family unit, education, patriotism, and even clarity between good and evil. Hollywood, the mainstream media, and universities all consider part of their mission to be the reeducation of America to conform to this new way of thinking. They deeply resent the fact that Christians hold firm to values and oppose their supposedly enlightened thinking. Rejecting new values or thinking that it is at odds with our faith shouldn't carry over to a perception of our being less innovative or lacking initiative in business, but it does.

Let's begin by looking at initiative. I believe survey respondents were correct to say that people with Christian values have a solid sense of commitment, which leads to a stronger work ethic. The question is, do we simply follow instructions energetically or do we also pursue our own initiatives? Personally, I believe Christians are more likely to show initiative because they have a *greater* sense of accountability and stewardship. Therefore, I think the perception that Christians have less initiative is largely bias.

Innovation, however, involves an element of risk-taking. Michael Eisner, former CEO of the Walt Disney Company, said, "When you're trying to create things that are new, you have to be prepared to be on the edge of risk."[10] As discussed in the previous chapter, Christians may be accurately perceived as more risk-averse, or conservative. There is often a stronger wish not to fail than a desire to wildly succeed.

I have gone searching for recent examples of Christian innovators. Mark Galli's book, *131 Christians Everyone Should Know*, breaks a list of important Christians down into thirteen groups including theologians, musicians, missionaries, rulers, poets, and scientists. With twenty centuries of history to account for, it is certainly tough competition to make the top ten in any of the thirteen categories. It is interesting, however, to note that there was at least one twentieth-century representative in every category, except for those of rulers and scholars and scientists. Twentieth-century hall of fame nominees in each category were:

- Theologians (Karl Barth)
- Pastors (Harry Fosdick)
- Poets (Fanny Crosby and T.S. Eliot)
- Writers (George MacDonald, G. K. Chesterton, Dorothy Sayers and C. S. Lewis)
- Inner Travelers (Oswald Chambers and Andrew Murray)
- Evangelists (Billy Sunday and Billy Graham)
- Denomination Founders (Aimee Semple McPherson)
- Missionaries (Hudson Taylor)
- Martyrs (Dietrich Bonhoeffer)[11]

The last ruler to make the list of *Christians We Should Know* was King Henry VIII, who ruled England during the sixteenth century. He had six wives and numerous mistresses. Two wives were beheaded. He is presumably on the list, however, for having broken England from the Roman Catholic Church.

The last scholar or scientist to make the list of *Christians We Should Know* is Galileo, from the seventeenth century. There are none listed *for the last four hundred years.*

I know, however, that there are many examples of Christian leaders in business who are known for their innovation. Wheaton College, my alma mater, graduates more doctoral students than nearly any other liberal arts school of its size. But, I think it is sad that our hall of fame list of Christians does not include any contemporary examples from the business world, much less any names in the last four hundred years. Wouldn't it be inspirational if someone like Bill Gates or Steve Jobs was an outspoken Christian and on the hall of fame list of Christians we should know?

True to the stereotype, I have probably been less of a risk-taker or innovator than many leaders. That is not to say that I did not initiate radical change. At both Rollerblade and Young America we implemented dramatic changes in our processes, organization, and marketing strategy. Each of these followed well-made plans and resulted in successful turnarounds. I never considered them to be risky, however, because in both cases the companies were on the brink of bankruptcy. Doing nothing was risky. When you are hanging on the edge of a cliff, the struggle to find a foothold isn't risky at all, compared to the consequences of hanging on until you have to let go. As Winston Churchill said, "I never worry about action, but only inaction."[12]

I believe most leaders innovate out of dire need. When business is on a nice upward trend, many leaders avoid new risks and innovations, keeping the course, but true innovators innovate constantly. Bill Gates said, "Microsoft is not about greed, it's about innovation and fairness."[13] Microsoft was founded on innovation and having attained famous success, it is still about innovation.

Continual innovation is needed to be a successful leader in the long-term. Peter Drucker warned, "An established company which, in an age demanding innovation, is not able to innovate, is doomed to decline and extinction."[14] There are highly effective turnaround specialists who, through cost cutting and efficiencies, rescue companies and get them on a stronger footing, but the ability to continually reinvent comes from a different skill set. If innovation is not your key strength, collect some true innovators on your team and listen to their ideas with an open and eager mind.

Winning companies succeed through continual progress and innovation. Strong leaders are never happy with the status quo. They continually look for ways to change. David Ogilvy, founder of Ogilvy Advertising, remarked, "The best leaders are apt to be found among those executives who have a strong component of unorthodoxy in their character. Instead of resisting innovation, they symbolize it."[15]

But innovation or unorthodoxy, and an adherence to conservative values are not mutually exclusive. C. S. Lewis describes paradise in his book about a planet called Perelandra. The hero, whose name is Ransom, is transported to this planet, and during his wanderings in the land he often pauses to taste fruit from a tree or a bush. Having sampled several different fruits, Ransom tastes another and remarks:

> It was none of the fruits he had tasted before. It was better than any of them. Well might the Lady say of her world that the fruit you ate at any moment was, at that moment, the best.[16]

This is Lewis's vision of paradise, where everything is new, different, and the best; each experience an innovation.

Man and woman were gifted with God's ability to innovate. God's gifts are meant to be used—fully! Christian leaders should reflect His nature by being bold and innovative.

> So God created man in his own image, in the image of God he created him; male and female he created them.
> —Genesis 1:27

Decisiveness, Determination, and Security

> Nothing can be more contrary to religion than reason and common sense.[17]
> —Voltaire

Having the quality of deciding conclusively (decisiveness), the habit of deciding definitely and firmly (determination), and the quality of having no doubt (security)
Survey Findings
• 8th   Importance relative to hiring criteria
• 6th   Importance relative to perceived job success
• 13th   Ranking as a perceived strength of Christians

Decisiveness, determination, and security were viewed by respondents as moderately important in both the hiring and job success criteria. It was ranked low, however, among qualities perceived to be evident in Christians.

There is a secular perception that Christians are easily led and therefore must be told what to believe or do. What I most often heard from survey respondents, however, is that this image of a Christian who is slow to make a decision comes from two honored Christian practices. The first I call "seeking answers in prayer" and the second I will call "relinquishing control."

Seeking answers in prayer

I heard the story of a new CEO hired to salvage a failing company that was owned by a fundamentalist Christian. The CEO's charter was to take action and save the company. He needed to move quickly to put a plan in action because the company was near default on loan agreements. He came up with a plan that called for major restructuring, including relocation of a significant part of the operations. He was sure he could find refinancing behind this plan to rebuild the business. However, when the owner was presented with the plan he was distressed about the need to lay off many employees, quite a few of whom he knew. He would not give the CEO permission to go ahead with the plan until he had time to pray about it and seek God's guidance. The CEO waited a few days and checked back, but the owner was still praying.

In the mean time the bank threatened to call the loan, so a week later he checked in with the owner again—still praying. The bank demanded huge penalties as a concession for another week of time. The CEO finally had a face-to-face meeting with the owner and explained that he could not keep the company out of bankruptcy and preserve as many jobs as possible if he were not given the authority to do his job. In a final act of indecision, the owner said he was not sure if this was what God wanted him to do, but would trust the CEO to go ahead. The business did survive, but the CEO always remembered the owner's indecision and seldom again ever asked for agreement or approval.

Relinquishing control

I've also heard a few stories about CEOs who found themselves in the midst of a crisis and, despite their greatest efforts to resolve the course, could not extricate the company from the dilemma. Finally admitting that they were insufficient to find the solutions, they gave the problem to the Lord. I have read some books with testimonies about this and about how, once the CEO turned the problem over to the Lord, things miraculously worked out. In most cases, when I listen to these stories closely I realize that what the CEO did was to get out of the way and stop micromanaging, leaving it to his/her team to work it through.

This really hit me when I read Larry Julian's book *God Is My CEO*. There seemed to be so many miraculous examples of Christians who just gave up control, and things then turned out wonderfully. I read this with mixed interest and bewilderment until I got to the last chapter. It was the story of Rollerblade.

Larry tells how the company was struggling financially. Though Rollerblade had been renting the Metrodome a few times a month for in-line skating enthusiasts, the organization simply didn't have the resources to market its product.

He relates how Bob Naegele, the owner, recalled one particular night when he was growing fearful and anxious about whether the company was going to make it. He cried out, "God help us. Nobody knows about Rollerblade." Two weeks later, the Minnesota Vikings were playing the Chicago Bears on *Monday Night Football,* and Mike Ditka commented on TV, "We are playing the Vikings at that 'Rollerdome' up in Minneapolis." By giving the Metrodome this nickname, Ditka gave Rollerblade some free but very widespread publicity. The sport gained tremendous national recognition, which proved to be a great boost for the company. Larry Julian concludes the story of Rollerblade right there by saying, "The rest, as they say, is history."[18] It was a miracle.

The Ditka story occurred before I joined Rollerblade. After reading Larry Julian's version of it, I called one of the other vice presidents who had joined the company shortly after me. I read Julian's account of the story to him. His response was the following:

> I guess they left out the part about how a few years later the company was nearly bankrupt and the more they sold the more they lost. I guess he forgot the part about how the Board decided they needed to change the entire senior management team. I guess he forgot the part about how we totally changed the product line, the pricing, the terms, the sales force, the financing, the production and the assembly. I guess he forgot the part about making the organization a lot leaner and bringing in a lot of new talent to run it more successfully. But as they say, the rest is history.

I wish Larry had explained that Bob's prayer that night gave him great peace and comfort, and the Ditka story was a great answer to prayer. It was a turning point, but even after that Bob continued to work hard, guiding and directing the business towards its success. "The rest is history" is inspirational, but it is not accurate at all.

It is right to seek answers in prayer, and it is right to relinquish control. Both, however, can be wrongly employed to excuse passivity and a lack of action or decisiveness.

As a leader, many nights I went to bed and said, *Lord, I don't know what I am going to do tomorrow. There is a decision that needs to be made and I ask you to guide my thoughts and heart to make the right one tomorrow.* Decisions are time-sensitive. Leaders have to make them in a timely manner. George Patton said, "I would rather have a good plan today than a perfect plan two weeks from now."[19]

It is also correct to relinquish control. This is not to be confused with giving up responsibility, nor with inaction. No one writes about the Christian who didn't take further action because he "turned the problem over to God"—and then things failed. I am sure there are many examples of this, but we don't really want to hear about them. Relinquishing control is *not* giving up when there is still more that needs to be done; it is putting your faith in God that no matter what happens He will still be your counselor. All CEOs experience crossroads that require a decision with uncertain results. This is when you pray, *I will not fully control how this works out, but I am going to make decisions with the best judgment I can make. I trust that You will be beside me no matter how it turns out.* Relinquishing control is not about the success stories, when things turn out well. It is about doing your best and trusting that God has a plan. As Romans 8:28 says: "And we know that in all things, God works for the good of those who love him, who have been called according to his purpose."

Decisiveness and determination are critical characteristics of business leaders. A survey of CEOs by Deloitte and Touche found that 75 percent of the CEOs polled said determination to succeed was one of the things they attributed to their success.[20] Lee Iacocca had this to add:

> If I had to sum up in a word what makes a good manager,
> I'd say decisiveness. You can use the fanciest computers in the
> world to sum up numbers, but in the end you have to set a
> timetable and act.[21]

Leaders are decisive. Almost one hundred years ago the humorist Will Rogers observed, "Even if you're on the right track, you'll get run over if you just sit there."[22]

Christians, however, are sometimes viewed as being indecisive and lacking determination. It stems mostly from bias, but some of it is true. As a leader, you intently listen to your counselors and then you make a decision, even if you are not sure. That is what leaders do. God is one of your counselors—ask Him for guidance. I have often jokingly said to my team when I was about to make a rather risky decision, "I'm not always right, but I'm always sure." Leaders need to be decisive and sure. If the decision is wrong, change course.

> Is any one of you in trouble? He should pray.
> —JAMES 5:13

Vision

Lighthouses are more helpful than churches.[23]
—BENJAMIN FRANKLIN

Unusual foresight or discernment; the ability to grasp what is obscure	
Survey Findings	
• 3rd	Importance relative to hiring criteria
• 2nd	Importance relative to perceived job success
• 12th	Ranking as a perceived strength of Christians

Over fifty percent of survey respondents said that vision was one of the least-evident skills for Christians. Only one respondent thought it was traditionally one of a Christian's top strengths. Still, vision was voted third in the criteria for hiring leaders and ranked even higher as a component of job success among executives.

I think the perception that Christians lack vision is bundled up in the biases relating to independent thinking and reasoning. Vision is related to forward-thinking, and Christians are perceived as rigidly adhering to tradition. Bertrand Russell, a well-known twentieth century British philosopher and mathematician expressed a view that many secularists believe today: "...the Christian religion, as organized in its churches...is the principle enemy of moral progress in the world."[24] I would certainly argue that the direction morality is going today is not to be considered "progress," but many people associate Christians with resistance to all progress. They are thought to defend the status quo rather than imagine a new future.

It is unfortunate that people confuse adherence to principles of right and wrong with a lack of creativity, imagination, or vision as it relates to commerce. This perspective is confused and largely lacking in basis. One could argue that Christians may tend to be somewhat cautious and conservative and as such could be more near-sighted in vision, but I think many Christians are just as likely as nonbelievers to be strong visionaries.

There are, I think, three kinds of visionaries: the prophet visionary, the history-making visionary, and the successful corporate visionary.

The prophet visionary

The greatest visionary in all of history is God. Numbers 12:6 says, "When a prophet of the LORD is among you, I reveal myself to him in visions."

It is certainly true that some Christian business leaders have responded to a vision from God about what they should do. We have all probably heard or read stories about Christian leaders who felt the leading of God in some important decision. I have also had occasions where I felt God speak to me about a particular path to take. John Maxwell calls this the higher voice.[25]

The Bible gives us a very powerful example. God said to Moses that He would lead the Israelites "into a good and spacious land, a land flowing with milk and honey" (Exodus 3:8). It was a vision that God gave to Moses. Moses shared this vision with the Israelites. In response, six hundred thousand Israelites left Egypt to follow Moses to the Promised Land.

Egypt and Palestine are only about two hundred miles apart; about the same distance as New York City to Boston. Even at a pace of ten miles per day, the distance ought to be covered in less than a month. There was significant trade between nations even in those days, and I am sure there was good knowledge about where the land of Abraham and Isaac was. The directions from Egypt should have been quite clear—"Just keep the Mediterranean on your left shoulder until you get there." It is remarkable, then, that the Israelites followed a leader who wandered for forty years to cover a relatively short distance. Quite understandably, most grumbled all the way and God delayed their arrival in the Promised Land until that unfaithful generation had all died.

A vision is often lofty and the detours uncertain. Only those that share the vision will follow. A vision statement, however, describes the "promised land;" it inspires the committed people to persevere together towards the goal. The promised land is what all corporate vision statements are about.

The history-making visionary

Inventors such as Galileo, Leonardo da Vinci, Copernicus, Einstein, and Edison were visionaries; but they are primarily visionary scientists, not business visionaries. When we think of history-making business visionaries, we may think of these examples:

- Henry Ford had a vision to put a car in every home.
- Steve Jobs had a vision to put a computer in every classroom.
- Sam Walton had a vision of discount stores in every town.

- Bill Gates had a vision that there would be a computer running Microsoft software on every desk.

There are but a handful of these famous business visionaries in each lifetime. Their description of the promised land they sought was succinct, powerful, far-sighted, and clear.

The successful corporate visionary

The accomplishments of the history-making visionaries inspire us, but most leaders can hardly aspire to visions that will change history. Great vision, however, does not need to be at the world-changing level of a Bill Gates or a Henry Ford to be effective. Thousands of strong leaders have excellent vision to make their company a success, though few are historical figures.

The leader's vision can be successful merely by describing the promised land in a powerful way that inspires the organization. The vision describes a journey that will bring the organization to a land "flowing with milk and honey."

When I worked for Rollerblade the mission statement was simply "to teach the world to skate." The sport was actually in-line skating, but the company wasn't simply designing and marketing in-line skates; it was in the business of creating a national craze that would be forever identified with Rollerblade. During this period, every employee, whether in marketing or finance, shared the excitement and promise of achieving this vision.

Many companies, however, are in less exciting businesses, but the vision can still be articulated in a way that will inspire the organization. Young America, for instance, is in the business of processing and fulfilling for its clients the consumer responses to marketing promotions. Such marketing programs include rebate offers, "collect-and-win" premium promotions, and sweepstake contests. It mostly involves data entry and customer service—not particularly inspiring as a business. Young America is also the largest company in a long-established industry, but at the time I became CEO there were three problems:

- pricing for its services were at a premium to our competitors,
- the industry had a reputation for slow and often inaccurate processing of consumer submissions, and
- the company was unprofitable; employees had not earned bonuses in three years.

In response, we developed a vision that said, "We will delight clients with superior value and delight consumers with redefined standards for speed and accuracy." Employees were responsive to this vision, but they didn't become excited until I internally added, "We will achieve a 'three-peat;' maximum bonuses earned in each of the next three years." The whole vision communicated major changes and hard work, but the vision also described a land flowing with milk and honey. Although there was surely skepticism, employees loved the vision because it included them. When profits beat plan for the first quarter, people got excited for the next update. By the time we maxed on bonus the first year, they believed we could do it again. When we did it the second year, everyone was talking optimistically about the three-peat. We also did it the third year.

Early-twentieth-century French novelist Antoine de Saint-Exupéry described the essence of vision:

> If you want to build a ship, don't drum up people together to collect wood and don't assign them tasks and work, but rather teach them to long for the endless immensity of the sea.[26]

When your sights are on the horizon, you also need to aim high to allow for *trajectory*. As Henry David Thoreau said, "In the long run, men only hit what they aim at."[27] But you should aim high!

Christians ought to have a strong inclination and talent to create a vision for three reasons: they are motivated by a higher goal than short-term wealth, they seek vision to inspire and include the whole team, and their vision can be enhanced by "the higher voice."

Visionaries have a long-term view, rather than a desire for quick gains. This perspective is scriptural. Proverbs 21:5 says, "The plans of the diligent lead to profit as surely as haste [such as a desire to get rich fast] leads to poverty." Visionaries also believe in the importance of inspiring their team. Christian leaders don't get results through fear and dominance, as some leaders try to do. A spirit of servanthood leads them to want everyone to join the journey with them. Finally, Christians recognize that only God knows their true capabilities. John Maxwell talks about listening to "the higher voice" and explains that a truly valuable vision must have God in it.[28] Only He encourages you to look beyond yourself, even beyond your own lifetime.

> And I will bring you to the land I swore with uplifted hand to give to Abraham, to Isaac and to Jacob.
> —Exodus 6:8

Problem-Solving Skills

So far as I can remember, there is not one word in the Gospels in praise of intelligence.[29]

—BERTRAND RUSSELL,
BRITISH PHILOSOPHER AND MATHEMATICIAN

The ability to process information and determine solutions to unsettled questions	
Survey Findings	
• 5th	Importance relative to hiring criteria
• 6th	Importance relative to perceived job success
• 14th	Ranking as a perceived strength of Christians

Problem solving skills ranked near the top in importance for both hiring criteria and job success. The survey panel, however, ranked it very low among qualities that Christians are known for. In fact, nearly 50 percent of the respondents rated problem solving as one of the least-prominent Christian skills, and none thought it was the most prominent.

Most of the individuals that I spoke with did not feel that Christians actually have less problem-solving ability than others, but they often felt that other people consider believers in God to be less intelligent. This prejudice seems tied to the view that for one to have faith he or she must give up reason.

Contrary to this perception, the individual said to have the greatest wisdom and problem-solving skills in the world during his lifetime was a devoted believer in God, King Solomon. His wisdom was a gift from God!

One of my favorite stories about Solomon relates how he mediated a dispute between two women who both claimed a baby as their own. (See 1 Kings 3:16–27.) Today, the solution would easily be determined with a DNA test, but in that day it seemed impossible to discern who the true mother was. King Solomon told the two women that he would simply cut the baby in two and give half to each. Of course, the real mother, out of love for her child, cried out and asked Solomon to give the baby to the other woman. In this way, Solomon knew who the mother was and gave it to the correct woman. It is the story of a difficult problem solved with great discernment.

Christians are just as likely to have strong problem-solving skills as anyone else. John Hapgood earned a PhD in 1952 from King's College at Cambridge University in physics, mathematics, physiology, and chemistry. He later became a devout Christian and was appointed Archbishop of York. He authored several books, including *Truths in Tension*. Hapgood wrote:

> Christianity insists that knowledge carries responsibilities, and that we only know the world truly as we use it rightly for God…Science gives us power; Christianity shows us the power of God in action in a rejected man on a cross; it turns upside down our ideas about the abuse of power. These contrasts do not exclude each other. There is no need for science and Christianity to be in fundamental conflict…It is possible to be both an honest Christian and an honest scientist, and to find the two allegiances both illuminating and correcting one another.[30]

God "created" and He also gave us the intellect to discover the DNA of His creation. Intellectual ability and problem solving-skills, however, are gifts given by God to some in greater proportion than to others. Some see an array of seemingly disparate information, find the pattern, and arrive at a solution easily. Such people usually have stronger analytical gifts. Problem-solving skills are clearly a strong asset to the leader, but they are not always critical if you have a team around you with this skill. Some leaders need to work harder at doing this or even ensure they are surrounded with a team possessing stronger problem-solving skills. John Maxwell says, "If you aren't a good problem solver, bring others onto your team who are."[31] Good leaders identify problems quickly, collect complete and accurate information, analyze it, and deduce a solution; but much of this can be done as a team. The leader need not always be the problem-solver.

The common theme for strong leaders, however, is that they do not avoid problems but constantly look for them. Each problem solved is an opportunity to strengthen the organization. Norman Vincent Peale, author of *The Power of Positive Thinking*, suggested the following:

> When a problem comes along, study it until you are completely knowledgeable. Then find that weak spot, break the problem apart, and the rest will be easy.[32]

There can be times when a leader is burdened with many problems, but in general I usually found problems to be invigorating in their challenge. A good problem solved always yields the greatest sense of accomplishment. American psychiatrist and author, Karl A. Menninger, said:

> Unrest of the spirit is a mark of life; one problem after another presents itself and in the solving of them we can find our greatest pleasure.[33]

Christian leaders are no more or less likely to have strong problem-solving skills than any other leaders. It is one of many gifts that God dishes out in no seemingly particular order. My own analytical skills made me a strong problem-solver, but I also worked for leaders less gifted in this skill who were excellent leaders. If God gave you strong problem-solving skills, it is an asset. If He gave you other skills more abundantly, develop and draw from a team that has counselors with great problem solving skills.

> Then the king said, "Bring me a sword." So they brought a sword for the king. He then gave an order: "Cut the living child in two and give half to one and half to the other." The woman whose son was alive was filled with compassion for her son and said to the king, "Please, my lord, give her the living baby! Don't kill him!" But the other said, "Neither I nor you shall have him. Cut him in two!" Then the king gave this ruling: "Give the living baby to the first woman. Do not kill him; she is his mother"
> —1 Kings 3:24–28

Communication Skills

> If you don't think that logic is a good method for determining what to believe, make an attempt to convince me of that without using logic.[34]
> —Brett Lemoine,
> cofounder of Internet Infidels, Inc.

The ability to transmit information, thoughts, or direction so that it is satisfactorily received or understood		
Survey Findings		
• 1st	Importance relative to hiring criteria	
• 4th	Importance relative to perceived job success	
• 9th	Ranking as a perceived strength of Christians	

Communication skills were ranked as the most highly sought quality for executives in candidate selection and also placed near the top in skills required for job success. The survey participants, however, responded that communication skills were not one of the top perceived Christian assets, though Christian history is replete with examples of leaders who were great communicators—Jesus, Martin Luther, Charles Spurgeon, Martin Luther King Jr., and Billy Graham, just to name a few. President Reagan was a Christian, and he was known as The Great Communicator.

I spoke with several survey respondents who gave Christians a low score regarding communication skills. In each case it seems communication skills fell lower in score simply because traits like integrity, servanthood, commitment, positive attitude, relationship skills, listening skills, and a sense of accountability ranked as larger hallmarks of Christian behavior. They didn't feel that Christians are perceived as having lesser communication skills at all, but rather that it was not one of their distinguishing characteristics. It is, however, a hallmark of what people seek in an executive.

Communication skills enable you to project your competence. American writer and broadcaster Lowell Thomas wrote the following about the importance of communication skills:

> The ability to speak is a shortcut to distinction. It puts a person in the limelight, raises one head and shoulders above the crowd. And the person who speaks acceptably is usually given credit for an ability out of all proportion to what he or she really does.[35]

Some survey respondents differentiated between informal communication skills and presentation skills. They felt that Christians' informal skills were likely to be as good as anyone else's, but that they were probably less skilled in formal communication, such as doing presentations. This perception seems connected to feelings that Christians might lack charisma or presence.

Unlike charisma or presence, presentation abilities, however, can be a taught skill. When I was about twenty-eight, Pepsi enrolled me and several of my peers in a course on presence and presentation skills. The instructor was Jack Byrum, a former Broadway actor that Pepsi used extensively to coach middle managers who were thought to have abilities for senior management. Jack worked with all of us on the execution and organization of presentations, but the program also devoted a lot of time to one-on-one coaching on presentation style and presence. I recall Jack telling me that I came across in a very competent and knowledgeable manner but far too serious. I also didn't articulate well. Jack told me, "I'll bet everyone wants you to work for them but no one wants you to be in their country club."

That got my attention. There was something definitely wrong with my presentation abilities. Jack had me repeatedly do presentations in front of a camera with three marbles in my mouth—and I had to laugh at the end of each sentence! He told me to practice smiling until the muscles around my mouth ached. Jack helped me to become a much better public speaker. I have never forgotten the lessons he taught me. With instruction and practice, everyone can improve their presentation skills and most can become good presenters.

Formal presentations are all about speaking, but informal communication is about speaking and listening. Doc Childre and Bruce Cryer, authors of *From Chaos to Coherence,* say that coherent communication is based on four key principles:

1. Achieve understanding first.
2. Listen non-judgmentally.
3. Listen for the essence.
4. Be authentic.[36]

Two of the four principles have to do with listening! John Marshall, fourth chief justice of the United States said, "To listen well is as powerful a means of communication and influence as to talk well."[37] Listening intently and non-judgmentally is a prerequisite to being heard and understood.

I was not only a poor formal communicator before Jack coached me, but I was also a poor informal communicator. Anxious to display the speed of my thoughts, I often spoke before I listened to the views around me. I had to learn to consciously keep my mouth shut in meetings in order to encourage discussion. I now try to keep my mouth shut or just ask questions until the discussion is exhausted and then add my thoughts or communicate a decision. When I practice listening, I find one of three possibilities happens:

- After some discussion, the person or people in the meeting suggest exactly what I would have communicated. "I agree" is never ignored or misunderstood. It is a great communication phrase.
- The discussion results in new information that leads me to a change of mind, to adopt another's idea. "Your proposal is

better than what I had in mind," is a message that is heard and embraced even more than "I agree." It confirms people's value.

- I may not agree with the views of the team, but I communicate a decision only after I have listened and confirmed understanding of everyone's opinion. People hear, understand, and accept communication better when they believe their views have been heard and respected.

Effective informal communication is made up at least 50 percent by listening skills. Survey respondents felt Christians tend to be good listeners, and Scripture encourages leaders to be good listeners. This aspect of communication skills should be an advantage for Christian leaders.

The other aspect of communication is delivery of the message. There are four components to doing this successfully.

1. Keep it simple. This applies to both verbal and written communication. Keeping the communication as simple and concise as possible is important for clarity. Lengthy communications burdened with oration, details, and tangential facts risk confusion of the core message.

2. Explain the benefit or importance. Understand the needs of your audience. Dale Carnegie says one of the most important practices to ensure people understand is to talk in terms of the other person's interests.[38] Explaining why a message is important to the team or why it will contribute to their benefit makes people listen more intently. Christian leaders, believers in servant leadership, ought to be particularly in tune to the needs of their followers.

3. Seek understanding. After communicating and explaining the message, always ask questions like, what does everyone think? or, are we clear about this? Communication needs to stay open until the leader is sure everyone understands.

4. Finally, ask for acceptance and support. If the message is purely informative, this might not be necessary; but if the communication requires follow-up and action by team members, always ask everyone if they feel comfortable to support it. If there is any hesitation on the table, flush it out then and there rather than discover later that someone was not committed.

Christ was obviously a very effective communicator. He spent a great amount of time with people and listened to their needs. He often began communications with questions and spoke in parables so followers could figure out answers for themselves. He very clearly communicated the eternal benefits of following Him (John 6:47). He asks for acceptance (John 13:20). And most of all, he keeps it simple. Read the Beatitudes (Matthew 5:3–11) for an excellent example of communication that is simple.

Christian leaders understand that communication skills are highly important. Communication skills can be developed, especially formal presentation or writing skills. Important aspects of informal communication skills are natural results of a spirit of servanthood: listening, understanding the audience, respect, and acceptance. Christians ought to be better-than-average communicators.

> He who answers before listening—that is his folly and his shame.
> —PROVERBS 18:13

Competence

Organized religion is a sham and a crutch for weak-minded people.[39]

—JESSE VENTURA,
FORMER MINNESOTA GOVERNOR

Having requisite or adequate abilities and technical knowledge
Survey Findings

•	2nd	Importance relative to hiring criteria
•	3rd	Importance relative to perceived job success
•	11th	Ranking as a perceived strength of Christians

Competence is one of the top criteria for hiring and job success, as it should be. John Maxwell describes competence as "…the leader's ability to say it, plan it, and do it in such a way that others know that you know how—and know that they want to follow you."[40] It is distressing, however, that competence ranked in the bottom six of perceived Christian qualities. Once again, Christians, for good reason, are perceived to be strong in so many other qualities that secular leaders don't traditionally possess, such as integrity, servanthood, and others, that Christians' competence ranking generally got pushed lower on the list.

Yet, there does seem to be some bias that Christians rate less-than-average in competence. There is clearly a prejudice in secular circles that Christians must be less rational, thus making them less competent. Liberal elites who assert that President Bush is incompetent as a leader sometimes try to connect their reasons for criticism to his religious faith. I suppose conservatives could similarly argue that Nancy Pelosi or Ted Kennedy are incompetent because they seem to lack religious commitment, but that would be equally absurd.

The truth is, however, that Christian institutions *embrace* learning, including the sciences. My alma mater, Wheaton College, an evangelical Christian liberal arts college, ranks among the top schools in the nation:

- Tenth (just behind Yale and M.I.T.) among all colleges and universities in percentage of National Merit Scholars.[41]

- Number 14 among all National Liberal Arts Colleges for student selectivity.[42]

- Ninth from 1986–1995 among 250 liberal arts colleges for graduates who went on to receive a doctoral degree. In the sciences, Wheaton ranked in the top 8 percent of the nation for doctoral degrees.[43]

Faith and knowledge are complementary to Christians, not exclusory. Scripture praises competence. Proverbs 22:29 says, "Do you see a man skilled in his work? He will serve before kings; he will not serve in obscurity." A physician who believes that God can heal the sick still relies on his or her knowledge and skills to treat the patient. Christian physicians believe that, although God can and does often intercede with miraculous healings, He set up laws of nature and science for us to discover and use for ourselves.

The story of Daniel is a great example of a biblical leader who demonstrated the highest level of competence.

> Then the king ordered Ashpenaz, chief of his court officials, to bring in some of the Israelites.... Among these were some from Judah: Daniel, Hananiah, Mishael and Azariah.... To these young men God gave knowledge and understanding of all kinds of literature and learning.... In every matter of wisdom and understanding about which the king questioned them, he found them ten times better than all the magicians and enchanters in his whole kingdom.
> —DANIEL 1:3, 6, 17, 20

> Then the king placed Daniel in a high position and lavished
> many gifts on him. He made him ruler over the entire prov-
> ince of Babylon and placed him in charge of all its wise men.
> —Daniel 2:48

It is God that gives us our gifts and abilities. Clearly, it would not be His wish that we employ them incompetently; rather, it His joy that we might develop them and put them to good use. In fact, I believe that God wishes to *magnify* your abilities that you may glorify Him.

As a Christian leader, you must have competence for two reasons. First of all, it is absolutely necessary for success as a leader. And secondly, the gift of intelligence is one that God wishes you to develop and use to your maximum ability. With stewardship for an organization comes a responsibility to lead with as much competence as possible.

> Then I will give you shepherds after my own heart, who will
> lead you with knowledge and understanding.
> —Jeremiah 3:15

PART III

MANAGING RIGHTEOUSLY—
THE APOSTLE PAUL'S EXAMPLE

— Chapter 7 —
MOTIVATING the TEAM

IN HIS BOOK *There's No Such Thing as "Business" Ethics*, John C. Maxwell says that employees want six things: to be valued, to be appreciated, to be trusted, to be respected, to be understood, and that no one should take advantage of them.[1] Responding to these needs by providing encouragement, coaching and honest feedback, trust, reward, care, and respect is important in creating a well-motivated organization. I also would add that it is important for a leader to celebrate at appropriate times and to be vulnerable at other times. These actions clearly resemble biblical standards of behavior.

The apostle Paul planted churches in Italy (Rome), Greece (Corinth, Philippi, and Thessalonica), and Turkey (Galatia, Ephesus, and Colossus). We know that he also established churches in Syria, Cyprus, and Crete. In a sense, Paul is an early example of the CEO of a vast, multi-national organization. He was only able to physically visit most of these churches one or two times during his journeys, so he relied a great deal on sending letters. Paul's letters to the early churches reveal a great deal about motivation, clearly needed since the early churches suffered from persecution and internal disputes. We will review how Paul used different practices to motivate.

Care and Respect

We always thank God, the Father of our Lord Jesus Christ, when we pray for you, because we have heard of your faith in Christ Jesus.

—COLOSSIANS 1:3–4

In each of Paul's letters, he begins with words that communicate care and respect. He even does so in those letters in which he is largely scolding the church. In all cases, Paul affirms that he cares. Even when the church is troubled, he shows respect. (See Ephesians 1:16; Philippians 4:1; 2 Thessalonians 1:3; and 2 Timothy 1:3.) In much of Corinthians, for example, he criticizes the church for its numerous problems, yet he opens the letter by saying, "I always thank God for you because of his grace given in you in Christ Jesus" (1 Cor. 1:4).

Not only does Paul communicate care and respect to each church as a body, he also commands the churches to demonstrate the same to each other. The apostle Peter also wrote, "Show proper respect to everyone" (1 Pet. 2:17). As leaders, we should not only be an example with our own staff, we must demand this of each of our subordinates and their teams.

Paul develops this idea in 1 Corinthians 12. He says the church is a unit with many parts. All of the parts are important and none are weaker. I encourage you to read the entire chapter, but verses 12 and 22 capture the essence of it:

> The body is a unit, though it is made up of many parts...they form one body.... Those parts of the body that seem to be weaker are indispensable.

These principles are also true of secular organizations. The seemingly weaker parts are still indispensable. Some in the early church seemed to feel they were more important than others, and Paul needed to remind them that all were important to the work of the church. In Romans 12, he reminds them of the many important roles people play: prophesying, serving, encouraging, contributing, and last, leadership. It is interesting that Paul mentions leadership last. In verse 5 he says, "Each member belongs to all the others." Leaders are not first; all members are equal and deserve equal respect.

Everyone should remind themselves of the original meaning of the word *corporate*. Before it became a term to describe a legal business entity it meant "relating to a unified body of individuals,"[2] exactly what Paul describes in Corinthians. A corporation is a unified body of individuals all working to achieve the same business goals. Each individual is important to the mission and deserves respect from all in the corporation.

Robert Schuman was an intensely religious man who served briefly as prime minister of France after World War II. He used another analogy to make the same point as Paul did:

> If we were all determined to play the first violin we should
> never have an ensemble. Therefore, respect every musician in
> his proper place.[3]

As in an orchestra, each player in the organization is important to the mission. Each person is also important to God. Together, this suggests that all should be considered with care and respect.

At Young America, the vice presidents of client services, customer care, finance, human resources, information services, marketing, operations, and sales reported to me. I continually heard arguments about why one VP or the other was more important. It is true that if the VP of sales brings in a 20 percent increase from new business, the company will have a great year; but if the VP of human resources mishandles an organizational grievance, that plant could become a disaster and the company could suffer greatly. Each section of the orchestra—and the organization—is critical to a well-played symphony. Each function in an organization is important and critical. That is why it is called a function; without it, the business does not function.

If I had given, as many leaders do, a great deal more respect and attention to the VP of sales or marketing than I gave to the other vice presidents, would I have created a hierarchy in my team which caused some to speak up less and others to dominate their views? Would I have encouraged the VP of sales to be less of a team player? I think so. An aggressive marketing strategy, not tempered by the advice of the CFO as to the risks of such a plan, might result in a tragic decision. Each perspective is critical.

It is not only right to regard all functions and all employees as important, but it is also a strong motivator for them. John Maxwell says, "Most people greatly desire the respect of the people they work for. And when employers give it freely, it creates a very positive working environment."[4] Seventeenth-century author James Howell wrote very simply, "Respect a man, he will do the more."[5] There is a profitable return in giving care and respect; respecting and caring for your employee generates in him or her a greater desire to perform well. However, as a Christian, caring and respect are primary feelings generated by love for our fellow brothers and sisters.

The spirit of servanthood means that we care for the people we lead. Two of the most important occasions in my tenure as CEO of Young America were opportunities in which I was given the chance to demonstrate this. In the first instance, we had two young employees, both three levels down in the organization, that were dating. Everyone knew they were dating, but since it was kept pretty discreet at the office I always pretended I didn't know. When they decided to get married, they surprised my wife and me with an invitation to their reception. Perhaps they were surprised that the president accepted the invitation, but, in fact, it was I who was honored to be included in their celebration.

The second story, unfortunately, deals not with celebration but with loss. An account manager who had been a good and loyal employee for many years tragically lost a teenage daughter in an accident several months after I left the company. I went to the funeral to show my respect; and so did nearly all the vice presidents in the organization, for which I was proud. I sat by myself and prayed for the mother and her family in their grief. I went not to be seen, but because I cared.

Perhaps it is easy to show care and respect for employees you have known directly and who are loyal and hard working, but care and respect should be extended also to the employee who is not succeeding. (A later chapter will discuss showing care and respect to an employee that may need to be terminated.) Remember that Christ cared for all people: the physically handicapped (Mark 2:5), the demon-possessed (Matt. 9:32), the sick (Mark 1:40), an adulterous woman (John 8:7–11), and even tax collectors (Mark 2:14). If a person is unable (or even unwilling) to perform well, that person is in some pain and we should care for that problem, even as we do what is right for the corporate body.

Caring, compassion, empathy, and sharing—all of these should be more common among Christians, even Christian business leaders, than their nonbelieving peers. Laura Nash writes:

> Employee relations were just about the distinctive area of spiritual relevance for the (Christian) CEOs—second only to their...personal relationship with the living God.[6]

Care and respect for your employees is an important leadership practice. It has a practical return by encouraging a more positive work environment, but it should largely be a natural outflow of our Christian concern for others.

> Let every man be respected as an individual and no man idolized.[7]
>
> —ALBERT EINSTEIN

Encouragement

> You then, my son, be strong in the grace that is in Christ Jesus.
> —2 Timothy 2:1

A primary objective of Paul's letters to the early Christian churches and to other missionary leaders was to provide encouragement. In most letters, following a greeting that expresses care and respect, Paul writes of his empathy for their trials and offers words of encouragement. The early church was persecuted, and many of the believers were mocked. As a leader, Paul knew how important it was to continually encourage them. Here are some examples of Paul's encouraging words:

> He will keep you strong to the end, so that you may be blameless on the day of our Lord Jesus Christ.
> —1 Corinthians 1:8

> We sent Timothy, who is our brother and God's fellow worker in spreading the gospel of Christ, to strengthen and encourage you in your faith, so that no one would be unsettled by these trials.
> —1 Thessalonians 3:2–3

> I long to see you so that I may impart to you some spiritual gift to make you strong—that is, that you and I may be mutually encouraged by each other's faith.
> —Romans 1:11–12

> I am sending him to you for the express purpose that you may know about our circumstances and that he may encourage your hearts.
> —Colossians 4:8

Efforts are energized by words of encouragement. As leaders, part of our job is to set stretch objectives, aim high, and set expectations for extraordinary achievement. This creates tensions and pressures in our organizations. Most of the team will want to make the extra effort to achieve the goals, but they may have doubts about whether the sacrifice is worth it. Our encouragement gives them the extra faith to put out the effort.

I remember a TV scene in which a child's dog was being swept downstream by the current or away from shore by the tide. The child ran down to the bank and yelled out, "You can do it! C'mon, you can make it!" Amazingly, the dog found some reserve of strength and paddled harder. Slowly, agonizingly, the dog inched toward shore and, exhausted, finally made it. Robert Collier captured the essence of this scene and circumstances that feel like it when he said, "Most of us, swimming against the tides of trouble the world know nothing about, need only a bit of praise or encouragement—and we will make the goal."[8] Similarly, John Maxwell says, "Encouragement is oxygen for the soul."[9]

Well-timed words of encouragement enable people to forget their doubts and continue the effort. In 1986, I led a functional team in Asia to restructure the operations of an important independent Pepsi franchise operation in Thailand. I was confident that the plan would be successful, but the franchisee needed capital. We decided to do an initial public offering (IPO) of stock in the company, but with the franchise's poor track record there was some doubt that the IPO would be successful. I decided it needed PepsiCo's financial backing.

I pulled a presentation together and flew to Purchase, New York, for a meeting with our division president. He was known for being gruff, and when I met with him, he certainly was. "What do you want?" he asked impatiently. I replied, "I'm here to explain a plan for rescuing our Thailand franchise. It involves backing their IPO by purchasing 30 percent of the issued stock." He glared at me and replied, "There's no way I am going to sink another penny in there," before ushering me out of the office.

That evening, depressed, I called my boss in Singapore and told him I would be back on a plane the next day. He encouraged me to stay another day and try again since I had worked hard on the plan and he felt it was sound. So I stayed.

The next morning, I was sitting outside the division president's office when he arrived. "What are you doing here?" he asked. "I thought you'd be in the air back to Singapore by now." I told him I didn't plan to leave until he gave me thirty minutes to explain the plan in some detail. For a moment I thought he would literally kick me down the hall, and then he sighed, "OK, thirty minutes...and then you leave." I made the most of it. He agreed to back the plan. When we later announced Pepsi's intent to purchase a significant percentage of the IPO, the market confidence resulted in a fully subscribed offering. The turnaround plan worked, and Pepsi's investment value grew tenfold within a few years.

Without those words of encouragement from my boss, I never would have completed the project, and our business may have failed. Encouragement at the right time provides confidence to make further effort.

Having trust and giving encouragement can also enable followers to grow and develop. Benjamin Disraeli, nineteenth-century prime minister of the United Kingdom said:

> The greatest good you can do for another is not just share
> your riches, but reveal to them their own.[10]

At Young America, I gave one of my vice presidents a goal to decrease operating cost in his function by 50 percent and to significantly raise service levels. After studying this a bit with his team, he came to my office and said, "I can do one or the other, but I can't do both. You need to decide which you want." I said, "You can do both, I know you can."

He studied it a bit longer, then came back and said, "I can reduce cost by cutting people, but service will go down." I said, "Don't focus on cutting people; focus on improving processes and you'll get both. I know you can do it." I can't recall how many times I had to encourage him, but he plugged away at it—and he eventually hit the goal! Afterward, he said with pride that my encouragement had shown him how much greater his abilities were then he imagined. Encouragement helps people to grow and develop.

Encouragement is a strong motivator. Paul provided encouragement to his followers in the church at all times. As Christian leaders, we may receive encouragement from family, friends, peers, or our own team at times. Even more important than these sources, Paul reminds us of "the God who gives endurance and encouragement" (Rom. 15:5).

> The final test of a leader is that he leaves behind in others the
> conviction and will to carry on.[11]
>
> —WALTER LIPPMAN,
> WRITER, JOURNALIST, AND POLITICAL COMMENTATOR

Coaching and Honest Feedback

> I gave you milk, not solid food, for you were not yet ready for
> it. Indeed, you are still not ready. You are still worldly.
> —1 CORINTHIANS 3:2–3

The apostle Paul was certainly a preacher that spread the gospel, but much of what he did in his letters to the Romans, Corinthians, Galatians, Ephesians, Colossians, and Thessalonians was provide honest feedback and coaching. The early church had many troubles, misunderstandings, and divisions. His letters were blunt, even brutal, in giving these churches honest feedback:

> You, therefore, have no excuse, you who pass judgment on
> someone else.
> —ROMANS 2:1

> My brothers, some from Chloe's household have informed
> me that there are quarrels among you.
> —1 CORINTHIANS 1:11

> You foolish Galatians! Who has bewitched you?
> —GALATIANS 3:1

> We hear that some among you are idle.
> —2 THESSALONIANS 3:11

What is the difference between criticism and honest feedback? The former is meant to tear down. The latter is intended to build up. In office politics, people criticize others to make themselves appear better and to gain an advantage. A Christian leader, however, provides honest feedback in the sincere hope that the person will respond and become better.

Honest feedback is not always negative. Encouraging feedback is just as important. Paul also provides examples of this:

> I always pray with joy because of your partnership in the
> gospel from the first day until now…
> —PHILIPPIANS 1:4–5

> We continually remember before our God and Father your
> work produced by faith, your labor prompted by love, and
> your endurance inspired by hope in our Lord Jesus Christ.
> —1 THESSALONIANS 1:3

Business leaders must make it a practice to provide continual feedback and coaching to improve both individual and corporate performance. Annual performance reviews are an important formal feedback process, but a strong leader also provides frequent informal feedback and coaching throughout the year. Nothing in a formal performance review should ever be a surprise to your staff. If it is, you have not done an adequate job in providing feedback throughout the year. A formal performance review should be anti-climatic, simply documenting the feedback you gave during the year.

Feedback and coaching should be motivational. But why do people often emerge from their formal review dejected and feeling demotivated? First of all, that individual probably encountered surprises in the review. Second, the leader probably did not communicate well the purpose of the feedback: the sincere wish that the person become more successful.

At Young America we had an account executive that had been with the company for twenty years. Through much of this time he had been the company's star salesperson. In the most recent three years, however, he had won little new business. Rather than being constantly out on the road, he was usually shut in his office. He had no recent successes, and he'd lost energy. He was failing, and the vice president of sales and marketing was ready to pull the plug on him. I was reluctant to watch this person fail.

The three of us arranged a dinner, and I am sure the account executive expected a verbal beating from me. He did get honest feedback. I communicated a wake-up call—"we can't hang on to legacies," I said. I confronted him with facts about his recent record and his noticeable lack of effort, but I also gave him facts about his great earlier successes. I communicated a strong desire to see him succeed and expressed confidence that he could be a star again. That night he committed to us that he would rekindle the old fire. He went on to be one of our top performers the next two years. I rejoiced in his success more than I would celebrate over the solid performer who never fell down.

Author W. A. Nance said:

> No person can be a great leader unless he takes genuine joy
> in the success of those under him.[12]

Honest feedback is often uncomfortable to give, and many leaders avoid it until too late. Unfortunately, many leaders do not provide feedback until it is time to document performance as legal protection for firing someone. Nothing is as disappointing as a manager who wants to terminate an individual whose files reveal neutral or even good reviews. That manager has failed. The individual has never had a chance to receive honest feedback and improve, but by that time, it is often too late to correct such mismanagement.

Strong leaders don't provide honest feedback and coaching just to improve corporate performance. After all, it is sometimes easier to replace a person than to work with him or her on the areas where improvement is needed. However, such leaders do it because they genuinely wish people to succeed. This is the essence of a servant leader. It is the essence of a *Christian* leader.

The boss drives people; the leader coaches them.[13]
—Harry Gordon Selfridge
retail chain owner who coined the
slogan "The customer is always right"

Trust

I myself am convinced, my brothers, that you yourselves are full of goodness, complete in knowledge and competent to instruct each other.
—Romans 15:14

Many of Paul's letters also show that he expressed trust in his followers. Oftentimes, a lengthy criticism of the young church is quickly followed by a reassertion of his trust in them.

I have great confidence in you; I take great pride in you.
—2 Corinthians 7:4

I am glad I can have complete confidence in you.
—2 Corinthians 7:16

We have confidence in the Lord that you are doing and will continue to do the things we command.
—2 Thessalonians 3:4

I think the best example of communicating trust is found in Paul's letter to Titus. In Titus 1:5 the Apostle says, "The reason I left you in Crete was that you might straighten out what was left unfinished." Paul and Titus had begun the work of starting a church in Crete, but Paul left to go elsewhere before they had organized the church leadership. Paul wanted Titus to know that the reason he was able to leave was because he trusted Titus to complete the mission. When Titus read Paul's letter, his response was surely to feel even more committed and determined to successfully finish the work in Crete. Because Paul trusted him, Titus had a new motivation to his task and a desire not to let Paul down.

Bob Briner and Ray Pritchard also explain:

Leadership is lacking when it is not invested in followers in a way that empowers them to independently advance the cause.[14]

Strong leaders select a trustworthy team and empower them with trust. Here's another story about our gruff division president at Pepsi International. My boss in Singapore sent me down to Sydney in 1986 to negotiate a new deal with our franchisee, Cadbury Schweppes, Australia. We felt they had been under-investing on the Pepsi line, and our goal was to offer them increased marketing support if they would match it. I had a long afternoon of negotiations with the Cadbury Schweppes president, and we seemed to get nowhere. He welcomed our additional support but would not agree to match it. We went round and round for a few hours. Late in the afternoon, I said, "I have a plane to catch in three hours. I'm going to head to the airport and relax in the business lounge. If I do not hear that you are willing to meet us at least partway by the time I get on that plane, I will have to return next week to discuss canceling your Pepsi franchise rights." I got up and left.

I sat in that airport wondering if I had done the right thing. Meanwhile, Frank was infuriated that I had walked out. He was important enough to have immediate access to our president, so he called the division president in New York, catching him early in the morning. He demanded an apology for my hardball position. The division president replied, as only he could, "I'm not sure of all the details, but I strongly suggest you head to the airport."

Thirty minutes later, one of Frank's people walked into the lounge and asked that I extend my stay. We worked out a deal the next day and our investment spending made a positive impact on shares the next few years. The division president's trust in my decision did a great deal for my personal development.

Christian modern-mythology author, George MacDonald once said, "To be trusted is a greater compliment than to be loved."[15]

You cannot, however, trust an incompetent manager with a lot of responsibility. Giving trust requires having competent staff members with strong character. You cannot trust a person with weak character or one that is disloyal and unsupportive. Ancient Greek philosopher Democritus advised us, "Do not trust all men, but trust men of worth; the former course is silly, the latter a mark of prudence."[16]

Strong leaders first select a team that is trustworthy and then empower them with trust. The prophet Nehemiah indicates that a key quality in selecting those to be given responsibility is trustworthiness.

> I put Shelemiah the priest, Zadok the scribe, and a Levite named Pedaiah in charge of the storerooms and made Hanan son of Zaccur, son of Mattaniah, their assistant, because these men were considered trustworthy.
>
> —NEHEMIAH 13:13

You cannot lead effectively unless you have a team that you can invest trust in. Some leaders, including myself, have attempted to lead team members in whom they have little trust by supervising more closely. The times I did this I came to regret it. It may be expeditious in the short term, but the team member will resent scrutiny, become even more secretive, and damage team morale. It is best to replace such a person as soon as possible.

Strong leaders demand trustworthy followers and then empower them by giving trust. Trust increases their sense of ownership and the desire to exceed expectations. Giving trust makes people determined to not let you down.

> Trust men and they will be true to you; treat them greatly and they will show themselves great.[17]
> —RALPH WALDO EMERSON

Vulnerability and Humility

> I have labored and toiled and have often gone without sleep; I have known hunger and thirst and I have often gone without food; I have been cold and naked. Besides everything else, I face the daily pressure of my concern for all the churches. Who is weak, and I do not feel weak?
> —2 CORINTHIANS 11:27–29

Paul always showed a positive attitude and confidence despite the hardships and persecution he suffered. However, he also displayed vulnerability. In 1 Corinthians 2:3 Paul says, "I came to you in weakness and fear, and with much trembling." When Paul says in 2 Corinthians 11:28, "Besides everything else, I face daily the pressure of my concern for the churches," we might better grasp his meaning by rewording it to say, "Besides everything else, I face the daily concern of my company or team."

A strong leader is not afraid to show vulnerability and humility to his followers. It is a means to empathize and connect with your people. It validates their fears and concerns by communicating to them that you have also felt the same. It can also be the lead-in to restoring their strength and confidence. The strong leader can say, "Like you, I have felt fears, but I am confident that we will prevail—and you can be confident, too."

Paul does this effectively time and time again. He begins by relating to the concerns and hardships of the church and then follows by stating that he found strength and confidence, as in 2 Corinthians 12:10:

That is why, for Christ's sake, I delight in weaknesses, in
insults, in hardships, in persecutions, in difficulties. For when
I am weak, then I am strong.

A scene in *The Sands of Iwo Jima* also depicts this principle. A private on the brink of a battle turns to his sergeant, played by John Wayne, and says, "Sarge, I'm scared!" John Wayne turns to him and calmly says, "So am I, son...I'm always scared."[18] When the sergeant charges onto the beach and into the fray, the young private follows with new courage, surely thinking, "If he can do it, so can I!" If John Wayne had told the private that he was never afraid, I doubt the private would have overcome his fear.

All leaders have fears and doubts at times. The leader who acts invulnerable and fearless all the time is probably hiding insecurities behind a spirit of arrogance. These leaders discourage counselors from opening up about their own concerns, fearing to be seen as weak, or even simply weaker than their peers. This "invulnerable" leader hands out direction without complete counsel, and as a result poor decisions are made and organization fears grow as the staff loses confidence in the leader.

Jeroen van der Veer, the former CEO of Royal Dutch/Shell Group made this observation:

> The one common value that most leaders lack today, whether
> in business, politics, or religion, is humility.[19]

Jesus said, "Whoever humbles himself will be exalted" (Matt. 23:12), and the fourth-century theologian St. Augustine also believed humility is the foundation of strong leadership:

> Do you wish to rise? Begin by descending. You plan a tower that
> will pierce the clouds? Lay first the foundation of humility.[20]

Strong leaders are always conscious of their vulnerability and have a spirit of humility. Showing vulnerability is helpful to validate your staff members' own fears so that they can deal with them. It also releases them to share concerns more openly, providing the leader with more candid counsel from the team. Showing vulnerability, however, needs to be accompanied with expressions of encouragement, confidence, and a positive attitude.

If you as a leader are more deeply in doubt and searching for confidence, you are better to share your concerns only with an inner circle at the company or perhaps with friends and family outside your organization who are closest to you until you are strengthened. It is even more important to share your fears with God during such times. The story of Jesus in the Garden of Gethsemane is a great example of how Jesus sought the Father during His time of worry.

> They went to a place called Gethsemane, and Jesus said to his disciples, "Sit here while I pray." He took Peter, James and John along with him, and he began to be deeply distressed and troubled. "My soul is overwhelmed with sorrow to the point of death," he said to them. "Stay here and keep watch." Going a little farther, he fell to the ground and prayed that if possible the hour might pass from him. "Abba, Father," he said, "everything is possible for you. Take this cup from me. Yet not what I will, but what you will." Then he returned to his disciples and found them sleeping.
> —MARK 14:32–37

Jesus knew that He was approaching a painful death, and He was troubled with apprehension and sorrow. So what did He do?

- First, He told most of His disciples to stay behind. He did not confide in them. He only took His closest disciples with Him: Peter, James, and John (v. 33).

- Second, He confided partially with His inner circle, sharing with them that He was "overwhelmed with sorrow to the point of death" (v. 34).

- He then told even His inner circle to wait while He walked off by Himself. Alone, He fully opened up His anguish in prayer, pleading to somehow be relieved of the burden. "Take this cup from me," Christ says in verse 36.

- When Jesus returned to Peter, James, and John, He found them sleeping. Not yet ready, however, He went away two more times by Himself to pray, and each time He found them asleep when He returned (vv. 37–41). After the third time, He told His inner circle get up; He was ready to face the challenge and to lead again.

Strong leaders are not afraid to show vulnerability and humility. By sharing some of their doubts or fears, they validate similar feelings on the team and make a stronger connection with their staff by doing so. When combined with the leader's positive attitude, the team deals with doubts and strengthens its resolve. However, when leaders are searching for their own confidence, they should seek their inner circle for support, not all members of the staff. In the toughest times, Christian leaders derive their inner strength and confidence from God in prayer. It is an advantage.

> I claim to be a simple individual, liable to err like any other fellow mortal. I own, however, that I have humility enough to confess my errors and to retrace my steps.[21]
> —MOHANDAS GANDHI

Rejoice and Celebrate

Rejoice in the Lord always. I will say it again: Rejoice!
—PHILIPPIANS 4:4

Celebration at appropriate times is another important part of motivating the team. There are several verses in which the apostle Paul instructs the churches to rejoice, and in each case it is a reminder to be glad in our salvation by Christ. Nearly all of these verses offered encouragement to the churches during seasons of suffering and trials, as in the example in Philippians 2:17–18:

> But even if I am being poured out like a drink offering on the sacrifice and service coming from your faith, I am glad and rejoice with all of you. So you too should be glad and rejoice with me.

As a leader, Paul clearly demonstrated a positive attitude to his followers by encouraging them in the face of terrible difficulties.

Rejoice, however, has a different meaning than *celebrate*. *Rejoice* means "to feel joy or great delight."[22] It seems more an inward action than *to celebrate*, which means "to observe a notable occasion with festivities."[23] Celebration is more active, outward, and inclusive of a group of people. I wish there were some Scripture verses noting that Paul and/or his followers *celebrated* completion of an arduous task, perhaps safe arrival on one of his journeys or his release from prison. I feel certain that he celebrated joyfully with some of his followers when he was released from prison, but there is no mention of it. In fact, when Paul finally returned to his friends in Jerusalem after years of dangerous journeys, persecution, and hardships to spread the gospel, he wrote in Acts 21:17, "When we arrived in Jerusalem, the brothers received us warmly." Received *warmly*! Paul had accomplished something akin in his travels to the first walk on the moon. Can you imagine the first astronaut on the moon returning and simply saying, "I was received warmly"?

There are a number of possible reasons that we do not find examples of Paul celebrating. During the time of Paul's ministry there was great hardship and persecution against Christians. It was a difficult time for Christians, and there may not have been much to celebrate. Hence, Paul importantly concentrates on encouraging followers to rejoice in Christ, even during trials and hardships. Perhaps he doesn't talk of celebrations because he felt that it would be unseemly to talk about a celebration he had with some followers when other Christians were so persecuted. Also, a celebration usually marks the end or the beginning of something, as in a marriage or harvest feast; Paul was singly focused on his mission to spread the gospel, which he said had no end for him except in death and salvation.

My own theory, however, is that there were times when Paul celebrated with his followers for some joyous event—whether it was the conversion of a soul, a marriage, safe arrival from a dangerous trip, or completion of a missionary visit—but he felt it was not so appropriate to share with churches who were dealing with problems of persecution and internal strife.

In fact, I've found no secular or religious authors on leadership who discuss the topic of celebration, but I feel it is an important and distinct practice for three reasons.

First, leadership is about getting the most out of your organization. Such messages to the organization that we must work hard, aim higher, and achieve excellence need to be positively reinforced and balanced with reward. Merit increases, bonuses, and promotions are individual forms of reward. Recognition may also be an individual reward. Celebration, however, is a group reward.

Second, when people work their hardest, they are worn down by the exertion and pressure. A good merit increase or bonus pleases them, but a celebration does more to renew them.

Third, too many Christians are seen as dour or restrained, even though we may have a positive attitude. We should rejoice, as Paul instructs, but as leaders we should also celebrate the great efforts and accomplishments of the people in our organization. The Old Testament describes many festivals, such as the Feast of Booths, the Feast of Dedication, the Feast of Harvest, the Feast of Passover, the Feast of Pentecost, and the Feast of Trumpets. All were celebrations to mark an event and to praise God's goodness. They were also occasions for the Israelites to have fun and to celebrate together. The Feast of Ingathering was observed after the hard toil to harvest crops, and Moses commanded, "Celebrate the Feast of Ingathering at the end of the year, when you gather in the crops from the field" (Ex. 23:16). In the same sense, I think it is appropriate and important to celebrate the completion of challenging business objectives.

I initiated a custom for celebration at Young America each time we won a major new client. I had a cowbell hung outside the door of the vice president of sales' office. Whenever an account executive closed a sale with a large new customer, he or she would walk down to the VP's office to ring the bell. When I heard the sound of the bell, I would grab a bottle of chilled champagne and some glasses. The account executive would bring to my office all members of the team that contributed to the successful sales process. This often included an account manager, a systems programmer, and persons from operations or customer service. We'd sit down in my office and the account executive would have the honor of pouring a glass for each team member. He or she and I would make the toast, and we'd enjoy thirty minutes to savor the win, discussing the contributions of each member. What was also special was that people from all over the office, when hearing the bell, would wander over to see who was participating in the ritual and to learn what new account we had won. (We would send an E-mail out to all employees later.) There were often up to fifty employees that did this. Each would offer his or her congratulations and go back to their work area to share the good news with others.

We also had celebration meals at each of our facilities for Thanksgiving and at year-end. I tried to visit as many of these as possible to celebrate with them and thank them. Bob Briner and Ray Pritchard describe social gatherings around a meal as a critical part of building a team.

> Leaders do not neglect the power that food and mealtimes
> have to set the stage for building lasting, productive relation-
> ships and imparting important lessons.[24]

Ecclesiastes 3 begins, "There is a time for everything, and a season for every activity under heaven" (v. 1) Verses 4 and 5 say there is "a time to weep and a time to laugh, a time to mourn and a time to dance."

My favorite example of celebration in Scripture is the story of Jesus at the wedding feast at Cana. It was Christ's first miracle. To run out of wine at a wedding celebration was a social embarrassment, so I presume the family had taken appropriate measures to prepare. Nonetheless, the celebration must have been great, for the wine ran out during the feast. Jesus' mother turned to her son and said, "They have no more wine" (John 2:3). Jesus might have replied, "It's just as well. They've had enough to drink and they ought to go home." Instead, He performed a miracle and turned six stone jars of water, each holding twenty to thirty gallons, into wine. That's between 120 and 180 gallons of wine. (Remember that a wedding feast in those days could last for three days to a week.) When the master of the banquet tasted the wine, he said to the bridegroom, "Everyone brings out the choice wine first and then the cheaper wine after the guests have had too much to drink; but you have saved the best till now" (John 2:10).

While I was a college student, a Wheaton professor remarked in a chapel address that *choice wine* was translated from the original Greek word meaning "strong wine," which was higher in alcoholic content. You can understand why the master of the banquet was surprised that a stronger wine was being served after the guests had already consumed so much.

Of course, in the spiritual sense, this story is meant to tell us that the new wine that Christ will give us, eternal life, will never run out. I do not mention this story as an argument that Christians should all feel free to drink at such occasions. There are enough other verses warning us not to drink too much, and you may feel it is better not to drink at all. Nevertheless, there is no denying that Christ chose to be at this wedding and certainly seemed to encourage the celebration to continue.

There are occasions when the most important thing we do as a leader is to celebrate with our people. It is a powerful recognition of their efforts and achievements, and it is an occasion to be renewed and energized for the next race.

Celebrate what you want to see more of.[25]

—THOMAS J. PETERS,
AUTHOR OF *IN SEARCH OF EXCELLENCE*

— Chapter 8 —
SETTING EXPECTATIONS

As an executive, you have a responsibility to provide a motivating environment. Your employees also have responsibilities: to work hard, deliver results, to be team players, and to have total integrity. Failure to meet these expectations should have consequences. These are expectations not often discussed by Christians, many of whom feel patience, forgiveness, compassion, and understanding are always commanded instead.

Scripture tells us not to be judgmental. Matthew 7:1 says, "Do not judge, or you too will be judged." As a result, Christian managers and executives can often be too reticent to hold their people accountable. Many Christians are perceived as too soft to be able to handle the tough demands of getting results from the organization. I have to agree that I've often seen evidence to support this.

Paul, however, was never shy in setting expectations or in administering consequences when followers fell short. Scripture supports the setting of expectations and has surprising examples of what the consequences should be for falling short.

Hard Work

For even when we were with you, we gave you this rule: "If a man will not work, he shall not eat."
—2 Thessalonians 3:10

One of the expectations that Paul established for his followers was hard work. Paul also set an example of this through his ministry. In fact, he went so far as to set a rule for himself that he would provide for his own needs, rather than depend on the support of the churches. In addition to leading the church, he worked as a tentmaker, as described in Thessalonians and elsewhere. He worked hard.

> We worked night and day, laboring and toiling so that we would not be a burden to any of you.
> —2 Thessalonians 3:8

> To this end I labor, struggling with all his energy, which so powerfully works for me.
> —Colossians 1:29

Effective leaders work hard but also set expectations for hard work. Paul indicated that his "executives" should work hard.

> Now we ask you, brothers, to respect those who work hard among you, who are over you in the Lord and who admonish you.
> —1 Thessalonians 5:12

And he encouraged all in the church to work hard in their vocations.

> Whatever you do, work at it with all your heart, as working for the Lord, not for men.
> —Colossians 3:23

"Work at it with all your heart," is a clear encouragement by Paul for all Christians to do their best in whatever they set out to do. This instruction applied equally to leaders in the church and members in secular workplaces.

Scripture has many other lessons regarding hard work. In particular, Proverbs includes much practical advice.

> Diligent hands will rule, but laziness ends in slave labor.
> —Proverbs 12:24

> Laziness brings on deep sleep, and the shiftless man goes hungry.
> —Proverbs 19:15

> Lazy hands make a man poor, but diligent hands bring wealth.
> —Proverbs 10:4

> The sluggard craves and gets nothing, but the desires of the
> diligent are fully satisfied.
>
> —PROVERBS 13:4

Scripture clearly encourages hard work as the means to satisfy both needs and desires. At the beginning of the twentieth century, Max Weber popularized the term *Protestant work ethic*. He ascribed the prosperity of Europe and the United States to Reformation thinking, which emphasized giving one's best to work.

I imagine that in the nineteenth and early twentieth centuries, there were numerous sermons delivered in church about God's instruction to work hard and work well. In all of my fifty-plus years, however, I have never heard a minister address a congregation even remotely on this subject. It might make too many people uncomfortable. Rather, the clergy often focuses on the problems of the corporate casualties, and they largely ignore the employed congregants, some of which could be reminded that they should work hard if they do not wish to be a casualty.

We have evolved from a society that believed in *earning* to one that believes in *entitlement*. My father never believed he was entitled to anything, and he probably couldn't spell the word. He emigrated from Norway as a young boy along with his mother, three sisters, and four brothers. His father was an alcoholic who was thrown out of their home shortly after they came to Brooklyn. It was the Depression, and all of the kids went to work as soon as they could to provide support for each other. Dad had to learn English, and he barely got a tenth grade education. He became a machine operator, then a foreman, then a supervisor, and eventually started his own company. His business became prosperous, and he worked hard at it. There were thousands of stories like this during that era.

The definition of working hard, however, has changed a lot over the last two centuries. In 1830, a manufacturing employee worked an average of sixty-nine hours per week. In 1900, it was down to fifty-five, and by 1955 it was about thirty-nine.[1] The 2006 US Census Statistics indicate that the thirty-nine hour work week held steady over the following fifty years.[2] This means that since 1830 average work hours decreased by 43 percent.

Not only have official work hours decreased, but I think attitudes about work have changed. Proverbs 13:4 says, "The sluggard craves and gets nothing," in other words he or she feels entitled. Today, many young people feel that they are entitled to a job, and even to advancement. The people who whined most in my organizations about not getting a good raise or a promotion were almost always the people who worked the least.

I've noted this change in work ethic during my career. In 1975, the parking lot at Pepsi was full at least fifteen minutes before starting time, and few would go home until a half hour or more after quitting time. However, in 2000 when I first became president of Young America, there would be a steady stream of cars in the morning pulling into the parking lot fifteen to thirty minutes after official business hours, and there was nearly a traffic jam leaving the lot ten minutes before close of business. So often I heard about an employee who felt they should have gotten the last promotion, but usually that same employee was one who drove by my office each evening fifteen minutes before quitting time.

Judith M. Bardwick wrote a great book in 1991 titled *Danger in the Comfort Zone*. Bardwick writes:

> Gradually, insidiously, prosperity created the crippling condi-
> tion called Entitlement, where workers have no real incentive to
> achieve and managers have stopped doing the work of requiring
> real work. How did this happen? For most of its history, the
> United States has honored a tradition of self-sufficiency; indi-
> viduals have been expected to take care of themselves and to
> earn their way. But by the 1950s, we had become a nation that
> expected our society to provide for its citizens and we expected
> U.S. companies to take care of their employees.[3]

I feel that a declining work ethic and a spirit of entitlement are real problems. We can look to declining productivity in other countries as an example.

In 2002, we closed down a data keying operation in Minnesota, moving it to Canada where the labor rates and exchange rate offered us a 30 percent advantage. Unfortunately, with the same policies and practices, employee productivity was 30 percent lower in Canada. We saved nothing. We put tremendous effort into finding the best candidates and providing productivity incentives but could not fix it. In our experience, the work ethic was simply inferior. Over the next few years, Canada raised the minimum wage and the exchange rate gap narrowed. As the wage and exchange rate advantage disappeared, lower productivity resulted in higher costs than in America. Once this happened, we decided to close the operation and move the jobs to India. I fear that the United States is on the same course.

Scripture suggests that we should be self-sufficient and *earn* our liveli-hood. As Paul says, "If a man will not work, he shall not eat" (2 Thess. 3:10). However, there are two specific concepts to consider in this verse. First, he said "will not work." He was not referring to people who are *unable* to work.

Second, he addresses this to men; he couldn't contemplate a future where both the men and women were working full-time and also caring for a family.

As wealthy a nation as we are, all Americans should have an opportunity to earn a decent living, and the state ought to support the basic needs of those who cannot. Paul said that a man should not eat if he would not work. The Bible, however, is clear that we should support the needy, those who cannot work whether due to physical or mental infirmity or because of prejudices and disadvantages that prevent people from work opportunities. Christians should provide support for these individuals, and businesses also have a moral responsibility to facilitate opportunities, where possible, for the willing. The biblical, political, and corporate question, however, is how to discern between those who *cannot* and those who simply *will not*.

According to a White House Report, at the turn of the twentieth century only 19 percent of women sixteen or older were in the workforce.[4] In 2004, about 60 percent of women in this group were in the workforce.[5] The days of *Father Knows Best*—where dad comes home to a wife who has the kids all taken care of, his slippers and paper ready, and dinner on the table—are gone. The demands on dual-income families are great. Work expectations must be balanced with an understanding of the real demands on dual-income families. It is important for both employee and employer to understand expectations when entering into employment. If job responsibilities require greater time commitments than are possible for the employee, it will not succeed. On the other hand, employers can sometimes benefit by creatively structuring responsibilities that facilitate a talented and dedicated employee's other commitments.

As leaders, we work hard and we should set expectations for our employees to work hard. An unprofitable corporation of one hundred employees with a lazy work culture might be able to survive and prosper with eighty productive employees who do the same work. Proverbs 18:9 has a very interesting insight:

> One who is slack in his work is brother to one who destroys.

The employee who is slack in his or her work robs all of the other employees in a corporation. The unproductive employee hurts the corporate success. As a result, pay increases are less affordable, bonuses are less (or nonexistent), and lack of growth prevents employing others, or even results in layoffs. All are hurt by the employee who will not work hard.

A successful work ethic needs to balance work, family, and other responsibilities during downtimes. However, when there is a crisis do you wish to be carrying the entire load, or do you expect your team to be there pulling with you? Select a team that is willing to commit as much as you are.

Strong leaders set an example of hard work, and they also set expectations for employees to work hard and well. Hard work plus a desire to give extra when needed are qualities that a leader expects.

> Plans are only good intentions until they degenerate into hard work.[6]
>
> —PETER DRUCKER

Results and Performance

> Remember this: Whoever sows sparingly will also reap sparingly, and whoever sows generously will also reap generously.
>
> —2 CORINTHIANS 9:6

How are Christian leaders to judge the performance of employees? This is a serious question I have seen Christians struggle with when they must evaluate performance of subordinates.

Paul warns Christians not to judge one another. He says in Romans 2:1, "You, therefore, have no excuse, you who pass judgment on someone else, for at whatever point you judge the other, you are condemning yourself, because you who pass judgment do the same things." Christ also said, "Do not judge, or you too will be judged" (Matt. 7:1). In the context of both verses the meaning is clear: we should not judge our peers hypocritically or self-righteously.

Paul, however, makes it very clear that appointed leaders have a responsibility to judge performance. He reminds Titus to "encourage and rebuke with all authority" (Titus 2:15), and he also tells Timothy to "correct, rebuke, and encourage" (2 Tim. 4:2). In many of his letters, Paul provides an evaluation for the early church. He provides honest feedback, he rebukes, and he praises.

Throughout Scripture, people in authority are anointed to judge performance and results. Judges and rulers, anointed by God, were commissioned to judge the actions of their people. The prophet Ezekiel said:

> But if the watchman sees the sword coming and does not blow the trumpet to warn the people and the sword comes and takes the life of one of them…I will hold the watchman accountable for his blood.
>
> —EZEKIEL 33:6

The watchman's job was to be alert and, if he saw an enemy coming, to blow the trumpet in order to wake people so that they could defend themselves. Ezekiel said the watchman should be judged for his performance and the results.

I have known Christian leaders and managers who struggle with evaluating the performance of their subordinates. They tend to find all kinds of excuses and explanations for poor performance or lack of results. They don't want to judge, and even if the performance was clearly poor, they want to forgive, provide a second chance, and a third, and a fourth. This is not what a strong leader always does. It is not what a Christian leader should do.

In the parable of the ten minas (see Luke 19:11–27), a nobleman left ten servants in charge while he traveled. To each he entrusted ten minas (about three months' wages) and told them to "put this money to work" (v. 13). When he returned, the master asked each servant what he had done with the ten minas. The first had earned ten more. The second had earned five more. The third earned nothing. The nobleman judged their performance. He gave to the first servant responsibility over ten cities, the second received responsibility for five cities, and the third lost all his responsibilities. To the third servant, he didn't say, "Maybe I wasn't clear about what I wanted you to do," or "I know you'll do better the next time," or "Perhaps some more training will help." The master said his performance was poor; the results were poor—performance review done. The master took his responsibilities away. He was fired.

The Gospel of Matthew, however, has a slightly different version of the same story in the parable of the talents. (See Matthew 25:14–30.) In this parable the servant actually *hid* the money and didn't even try to invest it. He didn't even make an earnest attempt to do his job. It makes me wonder how the story would have been told if there were a younger, fourth servant who tried diligently to invest the money but wasn't successful in making a profit. Perhaps the master would have felt the servant had potential; at least he showed initiative.

In these parables, however, we see that the person in authority is to discern between poor, good, and best performance and reward people accordingly. The Christian leader whose conscience makes it tough to give a poor performer an honest evaluation actually *robs* from the good performers.

If a budget requires overall merit increases to average 5 percent and the worst performers get 4 percent, the best performers can only get 6 percent. The leader has given the poor performers an unearned gift only by taking away from those that should have earned a greater reward. He or she has robbed from the achievers in order to give to the poor performers. What's worse, the achievers soon realize there is little reason to work hard.

A friend of mine made it a custom to pass out bonus checks at the annual Christmas party. A sales executive who was last in generating business that year came up to him after the party and said, "Jerry, I think you should know I was very disappointed with my bonus check." Jerry simply looked at him and said, "Then we're in agreement. I was very disappointed too!"

According to Mitchell Kaplan, CEO of E-Trade Group, "To succeed as a team is to hold all members accountable for their expertise."[7] If a member of the team fails, the whole team may fail. To overlook or not correct the performance of one team member may unjustly condemn the rest of the team to fail. The poorly performing team member needs to be developed or replaced. A leader needs to discern quickly between development needs and poor abilities or character. As a good shepherd, we wish for the success of our employees, but we need to be realistic about it. It's wonderful for the shepherd to return the lost sheep to the flock. However, if a particular sheep keeps wandering off, it should soon be selected for dinner.

Strong leaders, strong Christian leaders, set expectations and judge results wisely, impartially, and with no self-righteousness. Yet, they must judge. They must set expectations for results, wisely reward those who achieve, and fairly withhold from those who do not. To accept responsibility requires it. God expects it.

> It is no use to say, "We are doing our best." You have got to succeed in doing what is necessary.[8]
>
> —WINSTON CHURCHILL

Team Players

> I urge you, brothers, to watch out for those who cause divisions and put obstacles in your way that are contrary to the teaching you have learned.
>
> —ROMANS 16:17

Paul frequently encountered division in the early churches about matters of theology and ritual. His letters endeavored to make such matters clear, but they also directly addressed those who were being divisive. Paul repeatedly warned against these individuals.

> We hear that some among you are idle. They are not busy;
> they are busybodies. Such people we command...to settle
> down and earn the bread they eat.
> —2 Thessalonians 3:11–12

> They get into the habit of being idle and going about from
> house to house. And not only do they become idlers, but also
> gossips and busybodies, saying things they ought not to.
> —1 Timothy 5:13

> Don't have anything to do with foolish and stupid argu-
> ments, because you know they produce quarrels.
> —2 Timothy 2:23

> Let us not become conceited, provoking and envying each
> other.
> —Galatians 5:26

> May the God who gives endurance and encouragement give
> you a spirit of unity among yourselves as you follow Jesus
> Christ, so that with one heart and mouth you may glorify the
> God and Father of our Lord Jesus Christ.
> —Romans 15:5

Paul set the expectation for everyone to be a team player. He knew that for the church to be unified he couldn't allow divisive people to stir up dissension. Strong leaders expect a team spirit from each of their followers. In fact, a leader may spend more time on getting his or her team to act as team players than on any other activity. Authors Bob Briner and Ray Pritchard had this to say about building a unified team:

> A wise leader does all he or she can to build with those who
> contribute to unity while eliminating the cause of disunity
> from the team.[9]

Teams that cooperate are more powerful than the sum of their parts, and the inverse is also true. When I reflect back on periods in my career in which the business was most successful and those that were least successful, the common denominator was the team. When the team was coherent, business was successful; when business was unsuccessful, there was little teamwork among members of my staff.

In 1992, the owners of Rollerblade decided they needed a new team to grow the business and to make it profitable. During that year, they replaced every single senior executive, from the CEO to the vice president of human resources. The team clicked, and the level of cross-functional collaboration was extraordinary. Over the next four years the business was transformed. It grew rapidly and became very profitable. However, in the fifth year the team became split over some board-level issues. Disunity among the team was destructive. Within two years the entire senior team resigned or was dismissed, and the company began a severe downward slide.

In 2000 I became the CEO of Young America Corporation. I replaced three of the executives that year and built a team that largely worked well together for the next four years. During that period we doubled units processed and increased profit five-fold. In 2004 we acquired a company, and I brought the three owners on board in senior executive roles in order to have continuity with their system's transition and key clients. Company philosophies and cultures, however, were different, and the addition of three newly wealthy executives with sharply different views divided the teams. Our sales message became confused, and inter-functional projects nearly ground to a halt. The tensions drove the team further apart and sapped our energies. It was a mistake to bring the former owners on board or not to usher them out soon afterwards, regardless of the risks. Jon Huntsman has it right:

> If a member of your team no longer believes you can attain
> success, that person—or you—should leave.[10]

No matter how strong an individual performer is, I would urge leaders to replace him or her right away if that individual is not a team player. There is no room on a team for the prima donna or subversive member. Paul made this very clear to his friend Titus:

> Warn a divisive person once, and then warn him a second
> time. After that, have nothing to do with him.
> —TITUS 3:10

The team is more important than any individual. For this reason, I am not a fan of differential senior executive titles like vice president, senior vice president, or executive vice president. The same would be true for a vice president who has directors and senior directors reporting to him or her. Once you do this, you start to create divisions. I made this error once by promoting a vice president to executive vice president, hoping to groom a successor. That person, already weak on team skills, became a true prima donna and drove the rest of the team away from him.

A team is made up of critical parts. There is no sense in saying that the carburetor is more important to an engine than the fan belt. If either breaks, the car does not run. Jesus said, "If a house is divided against itself, that house cannot stand" (Mark 3:25).

Leaders build strong teams rather than simply collecting strong individuals. Good teamwork is like fuel on a fire. Poor teamwork is like throwing water on the fire. Christian leaders understand and honor the value of each team player. Christian leaders must also cull out members who are divisive. Teamwork should be an expectation.

> Gettin' good players is easy. Gettin' 'em to play together is the hard part.[10]
>
> —CASEY STENGEL

Total Integrity

> Finally, brothers, whatever is true, whatever is noble, whatever is right, whatever is pure, whatever is lovely, whatever is admirable—if anything is excellent or praiseworthy—think about such things.
>
> —PHILIPPIANS 4:8

Of course, a central message of both the Old Testament and the New Testament is that we ought to have goodness and integrity at the core of our character. The apostle Paul understood how especially important it is to ensure that those appointed to responsibility and leadership have these traits at their core. First Timothy 3 and Titus 1 go into great detail on the qualities needed in deacons and elders as church leaders. Prominent among these qualities are being upright, holding to the truth, sincerity, and being above reproach. Paul understood that building a successful organization requires a leader to be surrounded with total integrity.

It is not sufficient for you as a leader to have high integrity and character. Leaders must set expectations in their organization for integrity and create a culture where it is required and supported. You should have a clear strategy for establishing integrity as the core of your culture. There are several books available on this, and I would particularly recommend *Absolute Honesty* by Larry Johnson and Bob Phillips.

Although you can do a great deal to create a high-integrity culture, it is difficult to train people in integrity. It is usually just part of the package they bring—or not. Integrity needs to be a requirement of everyone who works for you, especially those in key positions. Selecting and deselecting people on the basis of integrity and character is critical. John M. Huntsman gives this the right emphasis:

> The first and most important decision in one's success is carefully choosing the people who will surround you. Make sure they share your values, make certain their character defaults to higher moral ground in times of stress, ensure they are bright and comprehend results, and be confident of their loyalty.[12]

Adrian Gostick and Dana Telford also believe in the importance of being sure you are surrounded with integrity:

> To have the Integrity Advantage, you hire and surround yourself with straight arrows who have a strong sense of personal integrity. You promote those who demonstrate an ability to be trusted.[13]

The reasons for this are clear. Trust in a person's character and loyalty as well as his or her competence are prerequisites for empowering the employee. Empowering a person who lacks integrity and loyalty is likely to have serious consequences, *for which you will be accountable.* Many corporate scandals are planned at the top, but many are also hatched further down in the organization, unknown to the CEO. The leader, however, is always responsible for having the controls, communication channels, and culture to prevent such problems. Proverbs warns that harm comes to us if we "walk with fools." Proverbs 13:20 says, "He who walks with the wise grows wise, but a companion of fools suffers harm."

When delegating responsibility, the wise leader ensures first and foremost that those entrusted have integrity. Nehemiah, governor of Jerusalem, cites integrity as one of the mandatory qualifications for responsibility.

> I put in charge of Jerusalem my brother Hanani along with Hananiah the commander of the citadel, because he was a man of integrity and feared God more than most men do.
> —NEHEMIAH 7:2

Warren Buffet, CEO of Berkshire Hathaway, also expressed a belief that integrity is the most crucial qualification to ensure responsibility in his organization:

> I look for three things. The first is personal integrity, the
> second is intelligence and the third is a high energy level. But,
> if you don't have the first, the second two don't matter.[14]

If you have worked in the corporate world for long, you have certainly encountered people who quite clearly do not have integrity. They shouldn't be leaders, but sometimes they are. It is most important to make sure they are not on your team. I've had several experiences where I discovered lack of integrity or poor character traits in people on a team that I inherited from a predecessor. Sometimes I did not act on that discovery until a significant act of dishonesty or deceit was proven and some damage was already done. Twice this occurred with sales account executives. In both cases we terminated the person after discovering his behavior; however, in each case, all my instincts had convinced me much earlier that these people were not trustworthy and would eventually do damage to our company. I should have dealt with the problem earlier when the infractions were not as serious.

In another example, I had a vice president on my staff that generally got good results but was deceitful and dishonest in his efforts to gain influence. I kept a close eye on him and several times confronted him, verbally and in writing, regarding such deceitful actions. He resented the scrutiny but did not change his character. He finally gave his notice just a few weeks before I was going to announce that I was leaving the company. I was pleased with his decision and quite happily accepted his resignation.

My successor, however, came in a few weeks later and, even though he had already been briefed on this vice president's behavior, talked him into staying by promising a great deal more autonomy and money. On hearing of this, I called up my replacement and warned him that what he was doing was a large risk. I was right. This vice president did significant damage to the business over the next year before making another exit ahead of the bullet.

Hiring people with integrity and character is critical, but sometimes it is tough to discern these qualities in the interview process. Once on board, it can be difficult to correct a mistake. If your instincts tell you that a person on your team lacks integrity and character, begin right away to keep a close eye on the person and to build up a file on his or her behavior. Provide written feedback and, in a severe situation, seek legal counsel. It's not as simple for us today as it was for the apostle Paul whose simple instructions were, "Expel the wicked man from among you" (1 Cor. 5:13).

Surrounding yourself with integrity is critical for strong and successful leadership. As a leader, you not only set an example, but you communicate the highest expectations for all employees to have solid integrity and character. When hiring your team, investigate the person's background thoroughly, but also use your instincts. If there is any doubt during this stage, walk away from the candidate. For problems already in place within your team, rely also on your instincts. Before damage is done, keep a watchful eye and document instances of poor or unethical behavior carefully and completely. Remember, even though God can change a man's heart, you cannot coach integrity.

> Whoever is careless with the truth in small matters cannot be trusted with important matters.[15]
> —Albert Einstein

You're Fired

> I already gave you warning when I was with you the second time. I will now repeat it while absent: On my return I will not spare those who sinned earlier or any of the others.
> —2 Corinthians 13:2

I wondered for a moment if 2 Corinthians 13:2 is where the term "three strikes and you're out" comes from, but then decided baseball probably did not take its guidance from this verse.

Paul provided the churches with a lot of honest feedback and coaching. However, he didn't hesitate to draw the line when necessary and tell church leaders to expel people who repeatedly fail to repent and who may damage the community. In 2 Corinthians 13:2, he reminds the church that he warned some of the members two times already, and if they have not changed, there will be no further warnings.

I'd like to use the parable of the talents from Matthew 25:14–30 again to illustrate this further. We've already discussed the blessing given for being a good steward by making profit or wise investments with what you are given responsibility for, but the parable also contains a harder lesson of instruction.

The first two servants invested the master's money, and when the master returned they gave back more. To both of them, the master said, "Come and share your master's happiness!" (v. 23). But the third steward hid the money in a hole and did not put it to work. When the master returned, the servant dug up the money and returned the same amount he had been given. The master was not happy. "You wicked, lazy servant," he said, "You should have put my money on deposit with the bankers, so that when I returned I would have received it back with interest" (v. 26–27). The master then instructed his other servants to take the money away from the third steward before adding the command, "Throw that worthless servant outside, into the darkness" (v. 30). In other words, "You're fired!" And in those days there was no severance, unemployment insurance, or welfare.

This sounds overly harsh, and perhaps it is. Christians often have a terrible struggle to make decisions related to firing unproductive employees. Laura Nash notes in her book, *Believers in Business*:

> Of all the situations that have tested the interviewees' sense of what is right according to their faith, the underperforming employee has been the hardest one.[16]

This is hard because we are commanded to show love to others: "Do to others what you would have them do to you" (Luke 6:31). Colossians 3:12 also says, "As God's chosen people, holy and dearly loved, clothe yourselves with compassion, kindness, humility, gentleness and patience." How can we reconcile firing an employee with the command to show compassion, kindness, and patience? Would you have them do that to you?

This is an area where Christians are often indecisive because they struggle with feelings of guilt in their decision. But they shouldn't feel this way. Concern for the individual must be weighed against concern for others on the team. An underperforming individual affects the overall staff performance. Certainly coaching, training, feedback, and other efforts should be made to raise the performance of the individual, but not past the point where it hurts the team.

In the army, recruits are taught to act as a team. The team totally depends on each other, especially for survival in battle. The individual is accountable to the team. Other members of the team may be working hard, supporting the mission, and performing well, but one poorly performing member can hurt the performance of the team, especially in battle.

Several years ago I had a very talented department director working for me. He was a Christian, and he had a great team, except for one individual who was causing the team to miss their goals. The director assisted and coached the weaker contributor, but his performance continued to hold the department back from making their objectives. The employee was a very good and likable person, probably just in the wrong job. While the director agonized over the decision of what to do, the department continued to fall behind and team morale suffered.

Halfway through the year, I sat down with the director and said, "You have a choice. You can keep him on board the rest of the year, in which case you will probably have a few resignations from the able people on your team, and those remaining—including you—will get smaller bonus payments for having missed your goals. Or, we can help him to find a better fit elsewhere. The latter may be better for him and will certainly give your team a chance to make their objectives." From this conversation, he saw that his compassion for the individual was doing harm to all of the other individuals on the team. He was able to take the needed action.

If an individual is not performing or contributing to the mission, he or she is either unable or unwilling. If unable, better coaching or training may resolve it. If unwilling, honest feedback may help. However, it may simply be a bad match that will hurt others on the team and frustrate their efforts. In my own career, I would estimate that I waited too long to make the inevitable decision in 80 percent of the cases in which I felt an individual was a poor fit.

Jesus told a parable with an interesting application to this point:

> A man had a fig tree, planted in his vineyard, and he went to look for fruit on it, but did not find any. So he said to the man who took care of the vineyard, "For three years now I've been coming to look for fruit on this fig tree and haven't found any. Cut it down! Why should I use up the soil?"
>
> "Sir," the man replied, "leave it alone for one more year, and I'll dig around it and fertilize it. If it bears fruit next year, fine! If not, then cut it down."
>
> —LUKE 13:6–8

A field only has room for a certain number of trees, a sports team only has so many positions, and a company can only support so many employees. For a farmer to be a success, he needs to use the soil efficiently; a coach needs to draft the best players; and an executive needs to hire the best talent. If you have an unproductive employee, you might ask, "Why should I use up the office space?"

We are told to be compassionate, but compassion does not mean lowering standards. If an employee does not meet the standards, action needs to be taken. If an employee is clearly a bad fit and coaching fails to resolve the situation, outplace or move him or her to another position immediately. If there is a reasonable chance for performance improvement, set a timetable and determine measurable criteria in advance for efforts to improve the individual's performance through feedback, coaching, and training. Circumstances dictate the timetable: wait long enough to give the individual a reasonable opportunity but never so long that it risks company performance or morale of team members. Be sure the individual understands the process and commits to it.

Whatever the course of action, treat the individual with respect and dignity. All people are created by God, and He has a plan for each person. An unable employee in one area may be a star in another position or career. An unwilling employee may be in a time of struggle with personal or emotional difficulties. Pray that the employee may succeed in the job or that a job transition will lead to a better fit, success, and happiness. I'm surprised how often a person who I had to terminate later told me that it led him or her to a more fulfilling and satisfying job.

If, at the end of the remedial period, the improvement criteria have not been met, take action to outplace or, if possible, move the employee into a position that is a better fit. Compassion leads us to be as generous and creative as possible to make a transition successful for the individual.

Firing an employee is something that will always be hard. We care and pray for the individual's success elsewhere but must decide what is right for the team.

> Compassionate leaders care deeply about the feelings of individuals, and they seek to deliver painful decisions in the most humane and caring manner. However, the greatest good for the group mission must also be considered.[17]
> —Bob Briner and Ray Pritchard

Corporate Layoffs

> Now there was a famine in the land, and Abram went down to Egypt to live there for a while because the famine was severe.
> —Genesis 12:10

Laying off numerous employees because of business conditions rather than individual performance is oftentimes more difficult than terminating an underperforming employee. There are no lessons from Paul on this subject. He was *building* a church during his lifetime.

When corporations grow and create jobs, the organizations are viewed positively. When they suffer downturns and must lay off people, they are viewed as bad organizations. Neither is true. A corporation is neither good nor bad. Corporations operate under a free market system wherein they employ people in proportion to the labor needs for the product. If the proportion is competitive, their products are attractively priced. If not, the business declines.

Businesses prosper and adapt in order to survive. It was much the same in the agrarian economies described in the Old Testament; sometimes agriculture was good, but there was famine at other times. In Genesis 12 we read that Abram went down to Egypt because there was a famine, probably from a lack of rain. The famine in Israel put people out of work. Abram and others went elsewhere to find work.

The story in the book of Ruth is similar.

> In the days when the judges ruled, there was a famine in the land, and a man from Bethlehem in Judah, together with his wife and two sons, went to live for a while in the country of Moab.
>
> —RUTH 1:1

Why did God allow famines that caused so many people to be laid off? I can't answer that, but I do know that people had to make moves to adapt to a changing environment. Similarly, leaders sometimes need to make hard adjustments to adapt to the competitive environment.

It is a difficult problem that Christian leaders face. There are several stories in Scripture about the good shepherd who risks the flock to save one lamb. Christ said, "Suppose one of you has a hundred sheep and loses one of them. Does he not leave the ninety-nine in the open country and go after the lost sheep until he finds it?" (Luke 15:4). Does this mean a Christian leader should risk the whole company to preserve the job of one employee?

Christian leaders face this problem all the time. You can read many testimonies by Christian leaders that describe how they found solutions to profit pressures that enabled them to avoid laying off employees. Larry Julian tells the dilemma of one CEO:

> The company had lost one of its biggest accounts and was faced with the need to downsize by laying off thirty employees.[18]

The CEO prayed about it, consulted the board, and put together a plan to preserve the jobs. The plan was adopted. She said that employees were so grateful that instead of 10 percent improvement, "I got 24 percent!"[19] The business was able to recover.

Bill George, CEO of Medtronics, is also proud that his company found a way to preserve an unprofitable medical device division that they thought would need to be shut down. The device was unique and critical to the health of some people.[20]

I have also read testimonies from CEOs who felt they were in a temporary downturn and preserved jobs through job sharing and reductions in hours until the business recovered. Each of these CEOs is a servant leader who cares about his or her employees in balance with a sense of responsibility to shareholders. They are excellent examples for each of us. If there are options to preserve both the business and jobs through alternatives with a good chance for success, the good leader will choose this path.

Unfortunately, many Christians only hear these wonderful stories about how a CEO put aside profit pressure and did "the right thing" to save jobs. These testimonies alone can be misleading and unbalanced instruction for Christian leaders. Well-meaning Christian leaders who put aside profit pressure to preserve jobs may destroy the long-term viability of their company. The Christian executive's employment is based on his or her agreement to lead in a way that preserves and grows shareholder capital. If a Christian cannot honor that contract, he or she should not lead. Corporate success and survivability are not driven by preserving jobs. However, job preservation *is* dependent on maintaining profitability. When the competitive environment changes and famine threatens, it can be necessary for some people to go elsewhere for employment so that other jobs may be preserved.

The week I became CFO of Rollerblade in 1992, our bankers threatened to foreclose on the company's loans. If that had happened, many could have been out of work. We had a limited time to resurrect the business. One of our first decisions was to close the local assembly of foreign components and to assemble overseas. The savings were compelling, but it would result in the loss of many jobs. However, it would give hope to several hundred other employees that the company could survive. We decided to make this decision, along with some other tough ones, that helped preserve the security of many more jobs than were lost. We also coordinated with neighboring companies that required similar job skills and were able to arrange job offers for each of the employees that were affected. In the end, the company prospered, and within a year or two we were growing and adding jobs with different skills.

More recently, as CEO of Young America, I was faced again with the need to have layoffs. We employed about three to four thousand people, more than 80 percent of which were relatively low-wage data entry or customer service jobs. In 2000 all of the operations were in the United States. Telecommunications and data processing technology, however, rapidly evolved such that geography became a less distinct factor. Our competitors began to do data entry in Mexico and customer service in India. While our service and quality remained superior, it was evident that we could not survive long against a three-fold or four-fold labor rate advantage. Ninety percent of our variable cost was labor.

Imagine how I struggled with the decision to embark on a strategy that would eventually put out of work all but four or five hundred of our US employees. With the way the industry and technology were going, however, it was evident that we could not survive long with a ten-dollar per hour wage rate when competitors were paying two or three dollars per hour. I had to focus on preserving the four or five hundred jobs in the US, along with our shareholder's capital. We went ahead with outsourcing, but we also invested significant effort to help employees with job transitions through lengthy notice periods, severance, and job fairs. Frankly, it was deeply depressing to say good-bye to friends in the company each quarter as we executed the outsourcing strategies. Had I not done it, however, the company would not exist today. There would be no jobs for anyone.

Christian leaders need to be able to make tough employment decisions. The Christian executive has accepted the mission to be a steward for shareholder capital. Both physical and human resources must be used wisely. In many cases, servant leaders cannot put job preservation ahead of profits, because in the long term they will fail in both.

> Always look at what you have left. Never look at what you
> have lost.[21]
>
> —Rev. Robert H. Schuller

PART IV

DANGERS AND BLESSINGS

— Chapter 9 —
EXECUTIVE DANGERS

*They have acted corruptly toward him; to
their shame they are no longer his children,
but a warped and crooked generation.*
[DEUTERONOMY 32:5]

Unfortunately, executive ranks are filled with "casualties" of the position. It is worthwhile to consider some of the most common danger signs among executives so that you can intelligently and prayerfully avoid them.

Douglas LaBier wrote a groundbreaking book in the 1980s called *Modern Madness*. His study focused largely on people who he describes as "fast-track career winners:"

> What I discovered was that within this group were people who were very sick. Some were dominated by unconscious, irrational passions of power-lust, conquest, grandiosity, and destructiveness, or conversely by cravings for humiliation and domination. Yet their pathology did not seep into the arena of their daily working lives and on-the-job behavior. They appeared very well adapted to their work, very competent, and intellectually skilled. From the outside, (they appeared) perfectly "normal."[1]

Power-lust and greed, or pride and arrogance, are among the most common executive issues that I have observed. Getting sucked into the cultural rationalization that everyone cheats is also very common. Pressure and responsibility can cause obsession and burnout and result in serious family casualties. For many executives there is also a large price for success.

As a Christian corporate leader you are surrounded by these dangers and often influenced by them. It's best to be aware and deal effectively with it.

Power and Greed

When the wicked rise to power, people go into hiding.
—PROVERBS 28:28

All man's efforts are for his mouth, yet his appetite is never satisfied.
—ECCLESIASTES 6:7

Richard Nixon's downfall was an unchecked desire for power. He was also exceedingly greedy and selfish. In 1971, Richard Nixon gave only $500 to charity on income in excess of $400,000—barely 0.1 percent of his income![2] The lust for power and greed often go together.

Before you vote in the next election, check the public record on the candidates' charitable giving. Most politicians who are anxious to tax your income give surprisingly little of their own wealth to the poor.

Power-lovers

Perhaps you have met power-lovers in your corporate career. They are excessively self-promoting. They view teammates as competition up the corporate ladder. They primarily see opportunity when a superior loses his or her job. They view subordinates as tools to be exploited for their own success. They hunger for recognition and credit. They are quick to point out weaknesses in peers. As a result, they are unable to trust subordinates or others. They assume others also carry a knife.

Some organizations have a culture in which the behavior of power-lovers is rewarded. They tend to be highly political places where "survivors" are promoted, rather than the most able. Douglas LaBier describes such organizations:

> The organizations in which we find the power lovers support,
> in effect, the development of exploitive, sadistic tendencies,
> and the methods of manipulation, betrayal, or seduction, in
> order to reach the top and get power.[3]

When I joined Pepsi, there was a saying among employees: "The day you are hired, a heat-seeking missile is fired behind you. The moment you stop running, ducking, and weaving, it nails you." Nice image. It was a strongly "up or out" culture, and missiles were flying all over the place. If you were hired straight out of business school, the rule of thumb was to make manager in four years, make director in another four, and vice president in another six. If you missed any of these milestones, the missile was right behind you. It's no wonder many young and aspiring Pepsi execs were political, trying to put the heat on peers so the missile wouldn't track on them. Ambition had become corrupted.

Ambition is good if it is rooted in a desire to do one's best and to seek challenges that can fully utilize your abilities. Ambition for leadership is good if it includes a desire to serve others more effectively. Power-lust, however, is different; it is ambition founded in visions of grandiosity and driven by the defeat of others in the pursuit of one's own glory. It is sinful for several reasons.

- Self-glorification is the opposite of giving God the glory and thanks. When the Pharisees challenged Jesus as to whether He were greater than Abraham, even He said, "If I glorify myself, my glory means nothing" (John 8:54).

- A desire to defeat others, particularly fellow employees, in the effort to rise up the corporate ladder (or stay there), is in sharp contrast with a spirit of servanthood. Christ said, "So in everything, do to others what you would have them do to you" (Matt. 7:12).

- God instructs us to be humble. It is impossible to be a seeker of power or self-glorification and remain humble. "For whoever exalts himself will be humbled, and whoever humbles himself will be exalted" (Matt. 23:12).

- Power-lust almost inevitably corrupts one's morals and ethics. Political historian Lord Acton made the well-known statement, "Power tends to corrupt and absolute power corrupts absolutely."[4]

Many leaders lust for power. Christian leaders should be careful of this danger. The wise use of authority is good and necessary, but it is not to glorify yourself; it is to serve the shareholders and employees.

> It is a mistake, that a lust for power is the mark of a great mind; for even the weakest have been captivated by it; and for minds of the highest order, it has no charms.[5]
> —CHARLES CALEB COLTON,
> NINETEENTH-CENTURY CLERIC AND WRITER

Greed

Power-lovers are self-centered, and because of this they also tend to be greedy. One would think that powerful people who have great wealth also would be relatively generous. Richard Nixon's miserliness, however, showed that this is not necessarily true. Doug LaBier provides another example from his research in *Modern Madness*:

> The effects of money-lust are seen, for example, among the highly successful Silicon Valley careerists who find that success has its price. Studies of their life-styles and problems have found an atmosphere of enormous money-lust, wealth and self-ishness. The rate of giving to charity is one of the lowest in the nation, relative to the income level of careerists.[6]

A lack of generosity in charitable giving is one symptom of greed in many leaders. There are two other types of greed, however, that I find more egregious: greed for unearned gain and greed for the first share.

CEO salaries in the US have gotten out of control. Compensation for CEOs of large corporations grew at an annual rate of nearly 23 percent from 1992 to 2000. The average American CEO in large companies makes approximately seventy-eight times as much (in salary alone) as the average worker. This compares to twenty-one times in Germany and sixteen times in Japan. There is a growing sentiment that boards need to rein this in.

Of even greater concern, however, is the huge severance "earned" by CEOs when they are dismissed for poor results. During the four and one-half years that Carly Fiorina was CEO of Hewlett-Packard, the stock price dropped about 64 percent, a loss of more than $100 billion to shareholders. Yet, when she was terminated, she received a $42 million severance package and benefits.[7] Americans were shocked and offended by this. Shareholders sued.

There are frequent examples of leaders in public corporations who deliver terrible results but walk away with huge payouts. There is no honor in this; only greed. Daniel Yankelovich, author of *Profit With Honor*, explains the view of most Americans:

> Americans harbor little class resentment toward the huge rewards that our society gives to star performers, be they in sports, entertainment, or business. But when these rewards go to people who don't deserve them, especially when they

come at the expense of hardworking employees, Americans feel anger and disappointment.[8]

In addition to avarice for unearned gain, greedy leaders are often too greedy for the first share. A good shepherd feeds his flock before he eats. A father lets his family draw from the well before he drinks. Leaders greedy for the first share have insufficient gratitude for those whom they lead.

At one company where I served as the CFO, we had just finished a spectacular year in sales and profit growth. Despite this performance, the board decided not to give senior management, including the president, any merit increases. Their rationale was that they had never anticipated performance would be so strong that it drove bonuses and the value of stock options this much. Rather than being grateful for their unexpectedly high share value, ownership decided to partially offset our gains with a pay freeze. Senior management, not surprisingly, was furious over this ingratitude.

Our president vowed to fight the decision. Following his return from the next board meeting, he called all of us into a staff meeting. He explained that he had fought very hard for us and that he came close to losing his job, but the board did not change their position. He asked all of us to accept the decision, and when the meeting ended everyone thanked him for his efforts. We promised to continue our hard work. We later found out that he hid from us that the board had given him a *very* hefty increase. That was the day he stopped being a leader. He was greedy for himself, insufficiently grateful, and deceitful with his staff.

Ezekiel issued a warning to leaders and rulers who selfishly used their power:

> This is what the Sovereign LORD says: I am against the shepherds and will hold them accountable for my flock. I will remove them from tending the flock so that the shepherds can no longer feed themselves. I will rescue my flock from their mouths and it will no longer be food for them.
> —EZEKIEL 34:10

Leaders make a lot of money. I will leave it to compensation specialists whether the compensation is justified. However, Christian leaders should not seek great rewards that are not earned. A synonym of *greedy* is the word *covetous*, which means desiring something that belongs to someone else. Christian leaders should not seek generous rewards unless shareholders and employees are awarded their share of the profits as well.

Power-lust and greed are frequent dangers for corporate leaders. Christian leaders accept responsibility and wield authority wisely in order to serve. Servant leaders measure success by bringing the whole team with them rather than greedily claiming their share.

> Greed is a bottomless pit which exhausts the person in an endless effort to satisfy the need without ever reaching satisfaction.[9]
>
> —ERICH FROMM,
> EARLY TWENTIETH-CENTURY PSYCHOLOGIST AND PHILOSOPHER

Pride and Arrogance

> I hate pride and arrogance.
>
> —PROVERBS 8:13

Success potentially breeds pride and arrogance. It is a danger that leaders face. Strong leaders exhibit courage, decisiveness, and a positive attitude. They have confidence to lead but are not arrogant. It's instructive to look at how the definitions of confidence and arrogance differ.

> *Arrogance*: a feeling or an impression of superiority manifested in an overbearing manner or presumptuous claims
>
> *Confidence*: faith or belief that one will act in a right, proper or effective way

The arrogant leader exhibits a manner of superiority over every one else. In contrast, the confident leader believes in his competence but also acknowledges the many competent people on his staff.

An arrogant leader is a poor listener. He or she is less teachable because subordinates are viewed as inferior. Subordinates are seen as useful for gathering facts and information, but arrogant leaders assume their judgment is poorer. Arrogant leaders have poor relationship skills, except among people they wish to mix with at the yacht club.

There are a lot of arrogant leaders in the corporate world. Many are CEOs, but more than a few are board directors. Jon Huntsman wrote the following about this problem among executive board members:

Unfortunately, many of today's boards are little more than social clubs that do a poor job of protecting the long-term interests of stockholders.[10]

In 2004, a major stockholder at Young America added a new person to the board of directors. We had finished a third year of extraordinary results, as profits had grown four-fold in the previous few years and we had just completed the acquisition of a significant competitor.

The new board member arrived for his first director's meeting. This person had never met with me before or toured our facilities, and neither had he engaged my staff or me in any discussion about the history of the business, our industry, or our competition. He had never asked our opinion on business-related matters or inquired to develop knowledge about the business, although he had reviewed a few of our previous board presentations.

I was about fifteen minutes into a review of the 2005 plans when he interrupted to provide a long list of advice on what we needed to do with the company. Without understanding current services and recent innovations, he declared that we needed new services quickly. Without inquiring about the present challenges to integrate systems for the two companies, he said we should dramatically enhance systems. With no knowledge about our sales compensation structure, he lectured that we needed to ensure the sales team was well compensated. He minimized the strategic importance of our service focus and said we needed to concentrate more on marketing efforts instead. Fifteen minutes into his first meeting with our team he felt he had "fixed" everything. He didn't even seem interested in a response; the "Great Oz" had spoken.

He was an empty suit, spouting proud and arrogant statements to seem important. The book of Proverbs has good advice for him.

> Arrogant lips are unsuited to a fool.
>
> —Proverbs 17:7

> Even a fool is thought wise if he keeps silent, and discerning if he holds his tongue.
>
> —Proverbs 17:28

> Do you see a man who speaks in haste? There is more hope for a fool than for him.
>
> —Proverbs 29:20

A look at his resume showed that he had jumped from job to job, staying less than two years, sometimes less than a year, in most positions. Yet, in each case he claimed that he had dramatically turned around the business. After the meeting, my staff had dinner with the board. This new board member spent the whole evening talking about yachting or his country club. My staff members didn't have sailboats or belong to country clubs, so why was this the subject that he most wanted to discuss after work? They all had the same reaction—they felt he was pretentious. Their impressions remind me of Proverbs 28:11:

> A rich man may be wise in his own eyes, but a poor man who
> has discernment sees through him.

He wasn't authentic. Bill George, former CEO of Medtronics, speaks about a leader's need to be authentic. He says good leaders "are genuine people who are true to themselves and what they believe in…they are more concerned about serving others than they are about their own success or recognition."[11] I heard Mr. George speak recently, and I was impressed with how understated but wise he was. He fielded some questions that others might have thought were naïve, but he treated each question as if it were of utmost importance and depth. The apostle Paul would have approved of Bill George's attitude. Paul wrote in 1 Corinthians 8:1–2:

> We know that we all possess knowledge. Knowledge puffs
> up, but love builds up. The man who thinks he knows some-
> thing does not yet know as he ought to know.

A leader is appointed to lead because he or she is perceived as more capable than others in that job, at that time. A wise leader, however, understands two things: First, some team members may become more capable than him or her as they develop. In fact, a strong leader tries to make this happen. The arrogant leader, however, is often mystified by how successful a supposedly inferior subordinate later is in his or her career. Second, most team members are more capable of doing their own job than the leader would be. A good leader will add strong judgment and perception but does not bring as much expertise.

I was a successful CFO during much of my career, but as CEO at Young America I worked with a CFO who brought different talents to the job, talents that I was weaker in. Likewise, I was knowledgeable and had some good instincts in the areas of marketing, sales, human resources, and operations, but my department heads had more expertise. These factors helped us to complement each other. You can never complement the abilities of your team when you believe that you are complete.

Poet Ralph Waldo Emerson wrote, "Every man I meet is my superior in some way. In that, I learn from him."[12] Similarly, French author Antoine de Saint-Exupéry wrote, "I have no right to say or do anything that diminishes a man in his own eyes. What matters is not what I think of him, but what he thinks of himself. Hurting a man in his dignity is a crime."[13]

Arrogance is a danger for successful executives. Only God is omniscient, but I've seen some leaders who act like they are in the same league. The Scriptures offer many warnings against arrogance, including Jeremiah 9:23 and James 4:6. The Christian leader should be confident, not arrogant; wise, and humble enough to seek wisdom, counsel, and expertise from others.

> A man wrapped up in himself makes a very small bundle.[14]
> —BENJAMIN FRANKLIN

> People who look down on other people don't end up being looked up to.[15]
> —ROBERT HALF,
> FOUNDER OF ROBERT HALF RECRUITING FIRM

Everyone Else Cheats

> You are always righteous, O LORD, when I bring a case before you. Yet I would speak with you about your justice: Why does the way of the wicked prosper? Why do all the faithless live at ease?
> —JEREMIAH 12:1

You ask, how can I be successful when everyone else cheats? In order to compete effectively and be successful you might think you need to walk on the edge of ethical boundaries. Perhaps it's just little lies, exaggerations, or simply skirting the truth. Maybe it's a bigger action, not *really* illegal, and because everyone else is doing it, it may seem that you will be at a disadvantage if you don't.

Job 34:8–9 talks about people in business who think this way:

> He keeps company with evildoers; He associates with wicked men. For he says, "It profits a man nothing when he tries to please God."

We are surrounded by people with these thought patterns. In some corporations or industries it may even be normal and accepted behavior. I think one of the most profound examples of this may be found in the Wall Street venture capital and private equity sectors. Most of these professionals are consumed with an eagerness to become wealthy. Many believe that the chances of making a shrewd deal are maximized by as much deception or selectively chosen information as is legally safe. As a result, private equity and venture capital professionals never really believe what they are told in a business transaction, relying totally on their rigorous due diligence to discover where the exaggerations and "half-truths" are. The onus is much more on the buyer to *discover* the truth than the seller's responsibility to *tell* the truth. But noted journalist and satirist H. L. Mencken observed, "It is hard to believe that a man is telling the truth when you know that you would lie if you were in his place."[16]

I encountered this mind-set with some of our board members at one organization. Whether making a presentation to commercial banks for financing or a business review for potential venture capital buyers, they encouraged me to omit issues, put positive spin on risks, and inflate the good news. "They expect this," I was told. "They'll discount the picture you give them, so you have to make it rosier to allow for this." In other words, "The only way to give a balanced picture is to leave out the bad stuff and exaggerate the good stuff. If you tell the whole truth, they will assume the situation is worse than the reality. A little 'shaving on the truth' is OK because everyone else does it; it's expected."

Such people might agree with the advice from the Marquis de Sade in the eighteenth century: "In an age that is utterly corrupt, the best policy is to do as others do."[17]

It's sadly true that in some business sectors this is the way people operate. But I've found that a long-term reputation for honesty works better. As CFO of Rollerblade, we consistently provided our lead banker, Harris Trust and Savings, with a balanced assessment of our outlook, and then usually exceeded it. Years later, when Young America was in need of financing and our historical results were poor, I met with the same bankers and gave them an honest assessment of what I thought we could do to turn it around. Unfamiliar bankers would have walked away because of our problems, but Harris jumped in, confident in my credibility about the opportunities that I also saw.

Jon Huntsman wrote:

> Make it a point to never misrepresent or to take unfair disadvantage of someone. That way, you can count on second and third deals with companies after successfully completing the first one. Have as a goal both sides feeling they achieved their respective objectives.[18]

Similar advice can be found in Leviticus 25:14: "If you sell land to one of your countrymen or buy any from him, do not take advantage of each other."

When I became CEO of Young America, I was troubled by the reputation of our industry. Young America handles consumer response on rebate promotions, which includes processing rebate forms, mailing rebate checks, and providing customer service for consumers with questions about their rebate. The industry had a lousy reputation for slow service and errors. Each Christmas, news reporters would do features on how companies in our industries were "cheating" honest buyers out of their rebates. Some reports suggested that companies in our industry purposely invalidated consumers or withheld payment to pad earnings. Our industry had a bad reputation.

The truth was somewhere in between. Some of our competitors did have practices designed to minimize the number of checks mailed or cashed, and others of us simply made too many errors and provided service that was too slow.

I decided that our core strategy was going to be, "Provide consumer services on rebates that make the promotion experience a positive one." It was a winning strategy for two reasons. First, for our industry to continue down the same path meant the death of rebates as a promotional tool, and second, manufacturing companies who truly cared about their consumer would seek us as the preeminent service provider to protect their reputation.

Our strategy led us to totally change services. We accelerated our data processing standards from four weeks to five days. We added a significant quality control department to do root cause analysis on errors and correct them. We encouraged clients to do rigorous audits. We studied our customer service staffing model and made changes to ensure prompt answering of calls. We also strengthened standards to ensure that consumer advice was more courteous and accurate. We became more active as consultants to our clients to ensure that they designed consumer-friendly rebates, even though poorly designed programs could result in larger billing revenues for us. Our organization was also instructed to proactively own up to mistakes. When we made one, we called the client, reimbursed him for the error, and took steps to correct it with consumers at our own cost.

It was a strategy rooted in integrity, and it was successful. Between 2000 and 2004 we more than doubled the units processed. A reputation of integrity and honesty can be powerful.

For a Christian, honesty and integrity is the only path. It may seem at times that those practicing dishonest methods have an advantage in this life, however, strategies and tactics consistently rooted in integrity are often a powerful competitive difference in the long-term. I've found that others want to do business with you when they recognize honesty—even if they themselves are less than honest. The honest person demands the honesty of others, but the dishonest person hopes your honesty will give him or her an advantage. For the latter, Scripture also has good advice:

> To the pure you show yourself pure, but to the crooked you
> show yourself shrewd.
> —2 SAMUEL 22:27; PSALM 18:26

Being shrewd doesn't mean responding with deception or guile; Webster's dictionary defines it as being "marked by clever discerning awareness and hardheaded common sense." Christians need not be naïve and soft dealing with crooked business people. In fact, when they discern this behavior, they should be more resolute in dealing or negotiating with such individuals.

Some say everyone cheats, but Christian leaders don't. In 2 Timothy 2:15 Scripture commands us, "Do your best to present yourself to God as one approved, a workman who does not need to be ashamed and who correctly handles the word of truth." If we do this, we need not be concerned about others, for He will uphold us and punish them, as promised in 2 Peter 2:8–9:

> (For that righteous man, living among them day after day,
> was tormented in his righteous soul by the lawless deeds he
> saw and heard)—if this is so, then the Lord knows how to
> rescue godly men from trials and to hold the unrighteous for
> the day of judgment, while continuing their punishment.

Christian leaders can compete successfully, but they must also keep in mind the most important crown to win. Second Timothy 2:5 says, "If anyone competes as an athlete he does not receive the victor's crown unless he competes according to the rules." Others may seem to succeed in the short race when they cheat, but they will not win the victor's crown. You can win in business and also win the crown.

> The rationale that everyone fudges, or that you have to cheat
> to stay competitive is a powerful lure, to be sure. The path to
> perdition is enticing, slippery, and all downhill. Moral bank-
> ruptcy is the inevitable conclusion.
> —JON HUNTSMAN[19]

Obsession and Burnout

I have labored and toiled and have often gone without sleep.
—2 CORINTHIANS 11:27

As a CEO or a top executive, whether you are at work forty hours or sixty hours, you are probably thinking of work 80 percent of your waking time. This is an extraordinary burden, one that can come into conflict with your family, spiritual life, social world, and your own peace of mind. There were times when I was weary with work issues, when I felt burned out. Douglas LaBier says many executives feel the same:

> The highly successful new breed careerist is often a victim of
> burnout and stress because the combination of high ambition,
> willingness to work hard, and latent ideals make the person
> more vulnerable to impediments in the desire for success and
> fulfillment.[20]

How can leaders handle stress and burnout? Former Chrysler chairman, Lee Iacocca suggested, "In times of great stress or adversity, it is always best to keep busy, to plow your anger and energy into something positive."[21] Wow, I wonder what Mr. Iacocca's blood pressure ran at! Bob Weinstein, former chairman of Miramax Films, seems to disagree with Iacocca's advice, saying, "You can try to cope with the situation by working harder. But that will only make you angrier and eventually lead to burnout."[22] This seems like better advice.

The church might suggest that the way to avoid burnout is to balance your work, family, and spiritual needs. *Balance*, however, implies more of one thing and less of another. Perhaps it is that we should sleep less in order to find more time for family and spiritual needs, but I think the message almost always sent by the church is really that we should work less. It is disappointing to me that one of the few messages I have heard from the church regarding our work lives is not "do it well," but, "do it less."

Working less is sound advice for some leaders, but I've seen leaders who worked sixty hours a week with little stress and others that were burned out despite working only forty hours a week. Cutting back the hours in the office doesn't relieve burnout if the leader worries that there is much yet to be done or is thinking about unsolved problems or crises most of the time while at home. Neither will it help if you are constantly checking work-related E-mails and messages on your computer or Blackberry. Leaving the office doesn't help if you are not mentally leaving work. The key is to put some trust and faith elsewhere. When you leave the office, leave the work there.

Last week I had a question for an investment banking associate with whom I had worked some time ago. It was Saturday evening, but I thought I'd shoot an E-mail to him so he would see it Monday morning. Ten minutes later, I got a heated E-mail response from him, "I'm out having dinner with my wife! Couldn't this wait until Monday?" Of course, I had intended for it to wait until Monday but forgot that he checked his Blackberry constantly, even in the evenings and on weekends. In today's electronic age, leaders often never leave work.

Some leaders, usually Type-A personalities, are more prone to obsession and burnout. Eugene Raudsepp, former president of Princeton Creative Research, Inc., describes such people:

> At the office, Type-A personalities work hard and fast to achieve. They set backbreaking deadlines and frequently bring work home. They are highly competitive, impatient and prone to anger if someone gets in the way of their success. Rarely, if ever, are they able to leave the job at the office.[23]

Leaders who obsess and burn out often feel that everything is up to them. If they don't personally attend to every detail right away, they don't have faith that it will be handled well. They trust few responsibilities and burdens to others.

A balanced leader, however, lets go of some things. He or she depends on the team for some matters and God for others. For matters where more work is likely to be fruitful, a leader needs to pick and choose when and where he or she can add value most. What's left is letting go of the other issues and choosing instead to delegate and place faith in team members entrusted to handle it. To do this requires strong and competent team members.

Colorado governor Bill Owens worked twenty years in consulting with Deloitte Touche before entering politics. As both a consultant and governor, Mr. Owens is very familiar with the stress of long hours. Here is his advice to leaders:

> Leadership is an active role; *lead* is a verb. But the leader who tries to do it all is headed for burnout, and in a powerful hurry.[24]

So, a first key to relieving burnout is to focus on building the strongest team possible. Lack of complete functional competence in any team member makes it impossible to completely let go of many delegated matters. Whenever

I had confidence in all of my team, it seemed easy to let go of certain tasks and pick where I could add most value. When I had areas of weakness in my team, I felt drained by the pull of extra details and decisions.

However, for matters where more work is unlikely to be fruitful, a leader needs to also let go and place trust in God. Christ invites us to share our burdens with Him. In Matthew 11:28–30 He said:

> Come to me, all you who are weary and burdened, and I will give you rest. Take my yoke upon you and learn from me, for I am gentle and humble in heart, and you will find rest for your souls. For my yoke is easy and my burden is light.

A balanced leader is one who delegates certain burdens to competent and trusted team members, so it makes sense that when a Christian leader has done all that can be done, he or she "delegates" the rest to the One who is *most* competent and trusted. Christian evangelist Charles Swindoll observed, "The happiest people I know are the ones who have learned how to hold everything loosely and have given the worrisome, stress-filled, fearful details of their lives into God's keeping."[25]

The chairman of Carlson Companies, Marilyn Carlson Nelson, suggests, "You are not alone, God is with you. There are little messages of hope out there. If you let them they will rekindle your hope and spirit."[26]

Ronald Reagan's accomplishments as president were among the greatest of all presidents. He revitalized the American economy and won the Cold War. Yet, he always seemed relaxed and optimistic. I believe it was because of two factors. He was known for surrounding himself with cabinet members and other key leaders who were highly competent and who shared his philosophy. He delegated much to them and focused on a small but powerful agenda. Second, he was always an optimist, which I believe came from his deep religious beliefs. He did not seem to worry because he had clarity in what was right and he trusted in God's plan to work things out.

A final recommendation for combating burnout is to have a variety of outside interests. I am astonished at how many corporate leaders have no passion for hobbies or recreational interests outside of work. Their whole identity is work-related. Outside interests relax the mind and lessen tension. They provide a diversion that keeps your mind off work for a period of time. Reading, golf, fishing, painting, and any other recreation that holds your concentration are all mini-vacations that can refresh and restore you.

Obsession, burnout, and stress are high-risk diseases for leaders. Leadership and large responsibilities require hard work. Simply working less is not a solution and may make things worse if tasks are left undone and deadlines are unmet. The practical advice is to surround yourself with a strong team and delegate, except for priority items in which you can have the greatest impact. Cultivate outside interests to renew yourself and divert thoughts from the office. And when the work is done but the outcome is uncertain, delegate your concerns to God. The prophet Isaiah said, "He gives strength to the weary and increases the power of the weak" (Isa. 40:29).

> Clearly, the possible risk of work obsession is high. There is a line to be drawn, however, between healthy, ambitious work habits and workaholism.[27]
>
> —EUGENE RAUDSEPP,
> CONTEMPORARY AUTHOR ON CREATIVITY

Family Casualties

> He must manage his own family well and see that his children obey him with proper respect. (If anyone does not know how to manage his own family, how can he take care of God's church?)
>
> —1 TIMOTHY 3:4–5

Young executives who seek greater leadership responsibilities often do so at the expense of their families. Work and ambition are consuming. Career commitment can cause harm to those we love. Doug LaBier describes this:

> Another group of casualties who deal with negative coping in a different form are the nonworking wives of senior executives. Their husbands typically work 60–70 hours per week, and are out of town on business about one week out of every month. The amount of time the executive spends with the family is severely limited. The products of the wives coping are seen, for example, in the findings that, although two-thirds of them say they accept the sacrifices as a requirement of success, they also suffer greatly. While they say they enjoy the material advantage, wealth, prestige, and sharing of excitement and power, they also report feelings of tremendous burden, sacrifice, and physical and emotional strains. In

addition, the wives suffer from damaged self-esteem and an inadequate sense of personal identity.[28]

In 1984 Pepsi transferred me to Singapore as finance director for the Far East region, which included Southeast Asia and Australia. For me, traveling all over Southeast Asia and Australia on business was pure adventure from the start. For my wife, however, my travels meant she was largely alone in a new country with a new baby and no family or friends nearby. After several months she adjusted, finding good friends in the expat community and developing outside interests. It was a bonus to have a live-in maid (called an *amah*) who took care of most household tasks and was also an on-call babysitter for those evenings when I was not on the road. We both grew to enjoy life overseas.

When we returned to the United States, the readjustment was surprisingly harder than our adjustment to going overseas had been, a phenomenon called re-entry syndrome. We had become accustomed to our amah, but suddenly there was no amah to do the laundry or to babysit if we decided to go out. Instead of our modern apartment overlooking the Straits of Malacca, we were back in a small, fifty-year-old suburban home. While overseas, we had forgotten what home or auto maintenance involved. I once again had to stand in long passport lines at JFK instead of having a travel agent who whisked me through a side door at Singapore Changi airport. Instead of frequent two-to-three-day regional trips in Australasia, I was off on lengthier business trips around my new and much larger territory (Canada, South America, and India).

The adjustments caused stress in our marriage that got worse and worse. Our marriage was in trouble. We decided to take a vacation to Disney World with our daughters. The week after this planned vacation I was scheduled to do an important human resource planning (HRP) presentation back at the New York office. These were serious events at Pepsi since we had to make career calls based on the "promotability" of each of our people. It had a big effect on the future of each person.

Two days into the vacation, my boss called. "I've made plans for a trip next week," he said. "So I have moved the HRP presentations with the president to tomorrow. You need to catch a plane tonight." I shared with my boss that we were dealing with some relationship issues that would be hurt if I left my family for three days to fly back up to New York. I reminded him that he had a completed copy of my presentation on his desk and he could do it in my absence. His reply was, "Don't forget that I am also doing *your* HRP review tomorrow.

It's up to you." I was so intimidated that I muttered, "I'll be there." Fortunately, my wife supported me, but that was the night I decided to leave Pepsi.

Corporations put large demands on careerists, and some executives have little regard for family needs. While corporate leadership has financial rewards for the family, it also exacts a toll. The perks of success can provide a beautiful home, nice clothes, expensive vacation trips, and college educations; but it limits time, energy, and attention to family members. In addition to stresses on the spouse, children are also affected. Doug LaBier explains:

> ...a study of children of senior level executives of corpora-
> tions with sales of $70MM or more shows that money and
> the perks of success buy them security and contentment, but
> at the expense of inner fulfillment, independence of thought,
> and a social conscience.... These children feel weighted down
> by their father's ambition and success.[29]

My own daughters went through six relocations in their first eighteen years of life. Some of these were especially hard, as they were forced to leave behind close attachments and find new ones. Dad uprooted them, and then he was off again on long overseas trips and late nights at the office—not there enough to help with the readjustment. When I was there, I was often jet-lagged or just tired from a strenuous workday.

I have known many career executives whose marriages have dissolved or who can't understand why their children had significant problems growing up. It seems especially hard for many families today with both parents who are careerists.

Having a parent in an executive position or any position with large responsibilities can be stressful for the family. A Christian corporate leader has the same job pressure and demands as any other leader. Perhaps your pastor would advise fewer work hours and less travel in order to come home more refreshed and prepared to provide quality family time, but he or she might as well say you shouldn't be an executive. Many vocations require sacrifices: missionaries must often send children to boarding school; military officers are transferred from base to base; CPAs work eighty hours a week for several months straight during year-end audit periods; salesmen must travel extensively; and even some manufacturing workers on night shift are never able to have dinner with the family or tuck their children into bed.

Certainly, the corporate leader needs to do what is possible to ensure that the job does not totally take over. Build a strong team to share the responsibility and workload, let go of things others can do or things that need to be put in God's hands, and carefully plan for some quality family time each week.

The military has long been concerned with the high divorce rate among soldiers who are transferred or deployed overseas. How does a marriage survive when one spouse is absent for a year or more at a time and is deployed multiple times? I believe the answer is commitment. Without commitment to a marriage, it can easily fall apart during absence or times of stress.

A Christian couple has scriptural guidance that helps them work through challenges when other couples may more easily choose separation. First Corinthians 7:10–11 says, "To the married I give this command (not I, but the Lord): A wife must not separate from her husband. . . . And a husband must not divorce his wife." My wife's commitment has made me desire to be a better spouse and father. Commitment made me more determined to work at it. If two people are absolutely committed, it would be irrational not to work hard at maintaining a good relationship.

Regarding the relationship with one's children, Ephesians 6:4 warns, "Fathers, do not exasperate your children," and Colossians 3:21 says, "Fathers, do not embitter your children, or they will become discouraged." It's interesting that the apostle Paul only advised *fathers* in this regard. Although roles are much less distinct today, fathers traditionally tend to be more rigid and mothers more nurturing; hence Paul's advice was only needed for fathers. As leaders, we practice our skills all day in decision-making, problem solving, and goal-setting. A sense of urgency, rather than patience, is more often the trait required at work. When we get home, however, these same skills are often our downfall. We need to remind ourselves that patience, listening, understanding, and encouragement are more often the needed qualities outside of work.

Christians should also be especially conscious of the stress that job responsibilities can have on their employees' families. As such, a Christian leader should ensure that his or her company maintains an attitude of respect for employees' family needs. Hard work should be expected of your employees, but some sensitivity and flexibility at times should be expected, too. Be sensitive to family needs and your people will be more committed to you.

Family casualties are a danger for corporate leaders. It requires mutual commitment and support from both spouses to maintain a marriage, and you must do your best to balance your work life in order to keep your marriage and children a priority. However, if your spouse cannot fully support the commitment and energy an executive role exacts, it will be difficult. To be a successful executive, both spouses need to accept the commitment. Having a successful career and a loving family is wonderful, but be sure the former does not come at the expense of the latter.

> A greedy man brings trouble to his family.
> —Proverbs 15:27

The Price of Success

> The acts of the sinful nature are obvious: sexual immorality, impurity and debauchery; idolatry and witchcraft; hatred, discord, jealousy, fits of rage, selfish ambition, dissensions, factions and envy; drunkenness, orgies, and the like.
> —Galatians 5:19–21

There are thirty-four kings of Israel recorded in 1 and 2 Kings, excluding those that reigned a very short time. Twenty-six out of these thirty-four kings, or 74 percent of them, "did evil in the eyes of the Lord," say the Scriptures. Only eight "did what was right in the eyes of the Lord." Wealth, ambition, and power led most of these kings to turn from God. Some turned to idolatry, others to immorality, drunkenness, envy, rage, or even murder.

It is common to read about sports stars whose lives are ruined by alcohol, drug abuse, infidelity, promiscuity, dishonesty, and violence. The same is quite often true for actors and politicians. What do Thomas Jefferson, Andrew Jackson, Grover Cleveland, William Harding, Wendell Wilkie, Franklin Roosevelt, Dwight Eisenhower, John F. Kennedy, Lyndon Johnson, Gary Hart, Bill Clinton, Rudy Giuliani, and Newt Gingrich have in common? They were all presidents or presidential candidates that were accused of having extra-marital affairs. This list, compiled from multiple sources, includes 40 percent of the presidents in the last fifty years.

Wealth and prestige opens the door to many sinful temptations. The apostle Paul provides a very clear warning:

> People who want to get rich fall into temptation and a trap and into many foolish and harmful desires that plunge men into ruin and destruction.
> —1 Timothy 6:9

The personal lives of corporate executives are not as subject to media scrutiny as those of sport stars, actors, or politicians; but affluence, ambition, and stress result in similar issues for them. Workaholism, egotism, materialism, and depression are common among corporate leaders. Alcoholism, drug abuse, infidelity, or promiscuity are also frequent problems.

Philip J. Burguieres was once the youngest CEO of a Fortune 500 company (Weatherford Industries). At age fifty-three, he abruptly resigned in order to begin a three-month stay in a mental hospital for treatment of severe depression. He recovered and has become a frequent speaker at CEO conferences. He devotes at least one day a week to meeting with suffering CEOs. Based on his observations, he believes more than 25 percent of top-level executives go through severe depression. Burguieres said, "You would be shocked at the number of CEOs, now running big companies, who are suicidally depressed."[30]

Alcohol abuse and addiction are also dangers. A study in 2000 by the Harvard School of Public Health found that upper-level managers are more likely to drink during the workday than first-line supervisors or hourly workers. Business dinners or after-work meetings generally start with a few martinis and follow with wine. Psychologist Alden Cass comments:

> As far as all the professions go, analysts and brokers have one of the highest [rates of alcohol abuse] because it's probably most widely accepted. This is what they use to network. It has become culturally accepted in terms of relaxing and kicking back with your colleagues. They've learned to use it as an acceptable means of solving their problems.[31]

Even drug abuse is surprisingly common in executive ranks. I was surprised in the 1980s by how many of my young management colleagues used cocaine during the workday and at company functions. Douglas LaBier wrote about this in the 1980s:

> Typical, now, among some fast-track careerists is the extensive use of cocaine, particularly among people in high-pressured careers, such as financial areas like securities, commodities, and the financial service industries. In a survey by a national drug treatment service, 75 percent of the workers reported using drugs at work, of whom 83 percent use cocaine. Twenty-five percent reported using drugs every day. The survey also

found that corporate executives and other high-paid professionals use twice as much cocaine as those who make less.[32]

Twenty years later, Dr. Cass had similar comments about these professionals:

> They have grandiosity and...are high risk-takers by nature.
> It also puts them more at risk for drugs and alcohol—a lot of
> people use amphetamines and cocaine to get through a day.
> There are individuals who use cocaine to stay up during the
> day and smoke marijuana to go to sleep at night. You must
> teach them healthier lifestyles.[33]

Infidelity and divorce among business executives is also high. Long work
hours, frequent travel, and job stress result in many divorces among executives.
The Journal of Psychology reported in 2000 that infidelity was greater among
people with a master's degree or higher and 1.5 times higher among employees
making more than $75,000, compared to those making less than $30,000.[34]
I'm still surprised by the number of successful executives who I've worked
with that have been divorced and remarried. In some corporations, it almost
appears that one of the perks of a senior position is a so-called trophy wife.

Depression, alcoholism, drug abuse, infidelity, and divorce all are dangers
for the corporate leader. Christians are not immune to these, as we see many
examples of church and evangelical leaders who have dealt with the same
problems. Christ warns us about such temptations in Matthew 19:23–24:

> I tell you the truth, it is hard for a rich man to enter the
> kingdom of heaven. Again I tell you, it is easier for a camel
> to go through the eye of a needle than for a rich man to enter
> the kingdom of God.

John 16:33, however, offers encouragement, as Christ said, "In this world
you will have trouble. But take heart! I have overcome the world."

Christian corporate leaders need to stay focused on their purposes:

- to develop and use their God-given gifts to the fullest;

- to be a servant leader and steward of the investments of shareholders and the lives of employees;

- to act as a leader with integrity and morality that reflects God's
  character; and

- to give God honor for success or wealth and generously share it.

For some, the price of success is the loss of one's moral and spiritual compass. As Christian leaders, you may be surrounded by people who are victims of this. They may be your peers or your bosses. They may draw you into their fraternity. Stand fast and seek God's strength to focus on the good mission.

> It's good to have money and the things that money can buy,
> but it's good, too, to check up once in a while and make sure
> that you haven't lost the things that money can't buy.[35]
> —George Horace Lorimer
> Editor-in-Chief of the *Saturday Evening Post* (1899–1936)

— Chapter 10 —
EXECUTIVE BLESSINGS

THERE ARE DANGERS and challenges associated with becoming a leader in the corporate world, but there can also be wonderful blessings. We've discussed several of these already. There are blessings, for instance, from being a righteous steward for many people under your authority, prospering from your work, and giving back generously. There are also other blessings of tremendous significance.

Greater Meaning and Fulfillment in Work

The LORD your God has blessed you in all the work of your hands.

—DEUTERONOMY 2:7

When I was appointed CEO of Young America, the company was nearly bankrupt. I felt a tremendous responsibility to the owners and for the several thousand people who worked there. On the day I was appointed to that position, I called my pastor and asked that we meet for lunch. I asked him to pray with me that I would lead righteously and that God would be beside me as my counselor. That was the beginning of the most blessed and significant time in my work career.

I don't mean that all the ensuing times were joyous or that results came easily. And I didn't always act as I should. Far from it! There were many highs and many lows. There were times that we celebrated, and there were times that we worried that everything was falling apart. There were times when we were full of energy and many times that we were terribly exhausted. There were wonderful people to work with and others that distressed me by their behaviors.

However, I felt that God was managing that business with me. He gave me feedback on my behavior, He encouraged me when events were troublesome, and He rejoiced when we met successes. The meaning of work was greater during that time than at any season in my career, and it began to change my life. Sherman and Hendricks describe this experience very well:

> His work. His way. His results. Adopting such a perspective could transform the way you approach your job each day. It could eliminate the chasm between your work and your spiritual life, bringing them back together into a meaningful whole. It could mean working with a sense that you are participating in the highest and noblest thing any man or woman could ever do—God's work.[1]

The sense that I was "participating in the highest and noblest thing any man or woman could ever do—God's work" is what gave my work much greater meaning. I had finally found the most important vocation I could pursue; I was finally doing what God had designed me to do.

Most of my career I had sought selfish ambition. I wanted to rise as high as possible in responsibilities for four reasons:

1. to make money for myself and family,
2. to receive recognition for myself,
3. to validate myself, and
4. to challenge myself.

Everything was built around me, but God began to change that. Eventually, as my life changed, everything began to be rebuilt around Him. He didn't, however, take away my ambition. As I've argued earlier, God designed us and gave us talents, and His wish is that we develop them and use them to their utmost.

After all, why would God give you a gift if He did not intend for you to use it as best as you could and to glorify Him? Remember, God can only be glorified if we use our gifts gloriously and give Him the honor. This, however, is not what many Christians seem to believe. Have you ever heard a Christian say something like this?

> Before I became a Christian, I was driven by ambition. However, since I accepted Christ, I have become content with where I am.

I cringe whenever I hear that! Don't you know that Satan wants to put his followers in high places and keep Christians in places of less influence? Those who do not believe in God have assumed high places in business, the media, entertainment, education, and government. Though they are a minority, their vocal and influential voices have profoundly changed our culture.

Meanwhile, Christians largely sit by the wayside and conclude that this is all part of the end times, preparation for the Rapture. It should not be so. Christ said that He would separate the nations as a shepherd separates the sheep from the goats. (See Matthew 25:32.) As Christians, He wants those of us who are able and anointed to lead and influence our culture in preparation for the days ahead. All of us can be a witness to bring others to Christ, but leaders have a unique opportunity to tip the culture toward influences that prepare the next generation to receive Christ. It is a tremendous opportunity that God gives leaders.

When Christ becomes the center in your work life, He doesn't wish to make you complacent; He wants to magnify your impact. Consider all of the scriptural stories of leaders appointed by God who had limited abilities. God magnified them! God picked a small man to defeat Goliath, and he chose a man who was slow of speech to argue with Pharaoh. He chose Abraham's younger son for the covenant blessing and Jacob's youngest son to be raised up into high places in Egypt, both out-of-the-ordinary choices in a culture that gave priority to the firstborn. He even placed Christ in the humble home of a carpenter. God delights in making us exceed our abilities.

God doesn't just want to use the talents that He gave you, He wants to amplify them! Thus, He wants to see your selfish ambition replaced by a passion to serve in the highest places. When God enables you to perform gloriously and you give Him the glory, God is magnified for others to see. God wants you to rise into high places to glorify Him, to be a shepherd for others, to be a godly influence on our culture, and to bless you.

The blessings that God gives you may take the form of wealth and security for your family and the opportunity to give back generously. I guarantee, however, that one blessing will be the knowledge that you are working in God's will. Whether it is ten employees or ten million that you have leadership over, you can reflect God's righteousness in your life, thereby drawing others to Him. You can help to tip our culture toward the One that will enable a greater harvest in future years.

> For the LORD your God will bless you in all your harvest and
> in all the work of your hands, and your joy will be complete.
> —DEUTERONOMY 16:15

Greater Meaning and Fulfillment Outside of Work

And God is able to make all grace abound to you, so that
in all things at all times, having all that you need, you will
abound in every good work.
—2 CORINTHIANS 9:8

There is a movement today by a number of ministries to help Christians more fully integrate their faith and work. It's important because work can consume 70 percent of our waking hours. How can we be fully in Christ if 70 percent of our life doesn't really include Him? We obviously cannot.

Sometimes, however, we don't speak about how important the integration of work and faith is to your *whole* spiritual life. Finding Christ's purpose in your work will give your workday more meaning and purpose, but it will also increase the blessings in all other areas of your life.

We tend to compartmentalize our Christianity; it's as though we expect that our spiritual life as a parent, a spouse, a neighbor, community member, and as a church congregant might be whole and flourishing, even though our time as a worker is not. The church often speaks to us about being a godly father or spouse and a witness in our community and neighborhood, but we also need to invite God into our work life.

Can we go to church on Sunday and ask Him to fill our life, and then on Monday ask Him to stay home? Can we ask Him to make us a better father or spouse and to help us to be a witness in the community when we don't include Him as equally in our efforts in the workplace? We can't ask God to fill some parts of our life and take a break in other parts. Yet, we try to do that all the time. I think that many of us, if we were honest, would have prayed something like this:

*Dear Lord, come into my life, but only some of the times. Lord, I want
You to live in me, except when I am at work or maybe other times
when it's not so convenient. Help me to be a good husband and parent,*

but I really need to do things on my own at work. I really love You,
but I don't quite trust You in a few areas of my life.

There is no way act shamefully before God for ten hours a day at work and
then come home and expect God to make you a good husband or parent. God
does not come in and out of your life at your beckoning like some servant. We
need to get this straight. He is our Lord, not our servant. He will not accept and
bless only part of us, for He requires *all* of us. He wants to bless all of our lives,
but He cannot fully bless *some* aspects of our lives if other parts shame Him.

That's why it is so important that your work and faith are fully integrated.
By choosing to do that, you'll include Christ in the majority of your waking
time, and the blessings will more easily spill over into the remaining 30 percent
of your day spent on non-work-related matters. When God guides your work
life, He will also bless you in your home and community life.

> Then we will no longer be infants, tossed back and forth by
> the waves, and blown here and there by every wind of teaching
> and by the cunning and craftiness of men in their deceitful
> scheming. Instead, speaking the truth in love, we will in all
> things grow up into him who is the Head, that is, Christ.
> —EPHESIANS 4:14–15

Are You Called?

> We know that in all things God works for the good of those
> who love him, who have been called according to his purpose.
> —ROMANS 8:28

Are you called to be a corporate leader? Has God designed you for this? Do
you have the skills and qualities for leadership?

Perhaps you are already a corporate executive. Do you feel your chosen
career is God's plan for you? Do you lead because God has designed you with
the skills to do so? Do you believe that God wants you to lead well, to be a
good steward for shareholders and a shepherd for your employees, to be honest
with your clients and fair with your vendors?

Perhaps you are a student deciding to start a corporate career or a manager
hoping to become an executive. Are you developing the right skills to be
competent in that role?

If God has called you to be a Christian leader in the corporate world, I hope you answer the call. I pray that more Christians will become leaders in secular corporations. We need strong and competent leaders who have total integrity and a spirit of servanthood.

If He designed you for this, it is *for you*—the most important vocation you could pursue. The corporate mission is not to be greedy and uncompassionate; it is only made that way by some leaders and portrayed that way by the press. Your mission is to be a competent steward for investors and a good shepherd for employees. You motivate your team, as the apostle Paul did, and you set high expectations, as he also did. You are courageous, decisive, bold in your vision, and even understand your responsibility to make judgments about your team! You rejoice and celebrate in the success of team members, and you are respectful to those that fail. You are humble, but not too modest to show charisma and presence. You avoid the dangers of greed, arrogance, and obsession. It matters little to you that "everyone else" cheats. For you, integrity is the most powerful competitive edge.

Your job is demanding, but you are sensitive to the stress it puts on spousal relationships and the development of your children. You are also sensitive to the family needs of your employees.

Your success as a leader brings material affluence, but this is not the primary reason you have an ambition to lead. Your success brings gain to both shareholders and employees. It also gives satisfaction to consumers, clients, and vendors. Your employees have better lives because you respect them and care that the workplace is stimulating, challenging, and rewarding. Your success gives you the privilege to give back generously and to honor God with all His blessings.

If you agree, then you are a Christian leader in a secular corporation! May God bless you.

> His kingdom will be an everlasting kingdom, and all rulers
> will worship and obey him.
> —DANIEL 7:27

> You are the light of the [business] world.
> —MATTHEW 5:14,
> AUTHOR'S PARAPHRASE

THE CHRISTIAN EXECUTIVE'S

STUDY GUIDE

Chapter 1: The Need for Christian Executives

God's First Commandment

1. If God's first command was to work as managers of His creation, am I giving it the best of my abilities and energies?

2. Am I striving to integrate my Christian faith and my time at work as best as I can?

3. How can I get further guidance on integrating work and faith from my church and my Christian brothers/sisters?

The Most Important Vocation

1. What do you feel God has designed you to be? Have you explored an inventory of the gifts that God gave you and sought to understand what these designed you to do?

2. Do you feel you are using God's gifts today in your work? Do you thank God for those specific gifts and the opportunity to put them to work? Example: *Thank You, Lord, for an analytical mind that enables me to help this corporation of families to better succeed, amen.*

3. Are you conscious of the opportunities in work to minister through your actions and to be a caregiver for those under your responsibility? Are you thankful for the blessings from hard labor and doing your best?

The Morality Vacuum

1. What examples have you seen of immoral, dishonest, or unethical conduct in business? How widespread do you feel it is?

2. Have you seen examples of Christians or persons of special integrity who have been successful or effective in their executive jobs?

3. Do you feel you can practice integrity and Christian virtues in business and still be successful?

The Assault on Christianity

1. What have you recently seen or read about relating to the assault on Christianity?

2. If you were to share your belief in Jesus Christ with your boss, do you think this would have a positive or a negative effect on your career?

3. Do you believe that there is a greater need for Christians to enter positions of influence in government, educational institutions, entertainment, media, and businesses?

The Clergy Conundrum

1. Look up any of the following verses: Hebrews 13:17; Proverbs 28:19; 2 Thessalonians 3:11; Ecclesiastes 5:18; Proverbs 14:23; Ephesians 6:5; or Proverbs 18:19. Has your church ever discussed such verses in the context of your business life?

2. What struggles have you had with decisions about unproductive employees, handling dishonest vendors or clients, dealing with business decisions that seem to have no good alternatives, satisfying impatient or unethical owners, or competing successfully with shady competitors? How has your church supported you on these matters?

3. How many people are on the staff of your church? Did any of them have real-world experience in the corporate arena before they entered the ministry? Do you have lay ministers? Are they qualified to minister to laity needs, or are they primarily responsible for getting the laity involved in the church's needs?

4. What can you do to encourage your church to be more active in ministering to the lives of congregants within the business world?

Where Are the Christians?

1. How many Christians in leadership roles have you known at work?

2. Why aren't there more?

3. Do you feel that it is difficult to compete for advancement with non-Christians who are not inhibited in their methods? Why?

4. How can you be an example of Christ's grace when at work, given corporate culture and laws?

5. Can you make a difference?

Chapter 2: Answering the Call

Leadership 101

1. Take an inventory of what you think your own gifts are.

2. Which gifts are overpowering strengths?

3. What particular skills have you developed?

4. What skills that you may have a gift for are undeveloped?

Business Ethics 101

1. At which levels of the ethical hierarchy does your company primarily operate on tough business issues?

2. Does your company have a values statement?

3. Is it largely based on principles that are righteous?

4. What has been the most difficult ethical decision in business (or life) for you? How did you resolve it? Do you wish you had resolved it differently?

It Takes a Lot

1. How many hours out of your waking day are you neither at the office nor elsewhere thinking about work?

2. Are you putting in too much effort, not enough, or about right?

3. As an executive, how are you handling stress or fatigue, related to the demands made on you?

4. Which of the eight recommended practices do you regularly practice? Which ones do you fail to do? Why?

Chapter 3: Understanding the Responsibilities

The Corporate Mission

1. Why do corporations exist? What benefits do they provide to humanity?

2. Without a profit motive, you need either socialism or government-run enterprises. What would the result of this be?

3. Have you seen examples of how the profit motive has been corrupted? In what ways?

4. Investors have entrusted their savings to your corporation. What is your responsibility to them? What limits do you place on this responsibility?

The Christian Executive's Mission

1. Do you feel that your company's mission is acceptable to God?

2. What is your primary mission and obligation when at work?

3. Is this in line with the company's mission?

4. Is it in line with God's will?

The Good Steward

1. When you define your responsibilities at work, does it include stewardship for investors, employees, vendors, and clients?

2. How does an attitude of stewardship differ from defining your job simply in terms of budgets, revenues, and profits?

3. What is the full scope of your stewardship responsibility? Have you tried to quantify it or picture its extent?

4. Does an attitude of stewardship toward investors also encompass the responsibility to grow shareholder wealth?

5. Do you view stewardship as God's gift—an awesome responsibility and a wonderful opportunity?

The Problem of Wealth

1. Do you constantly thank God for what He has blessed you with, whether it is just your basic needs or considerable wealth?

2. Is your focus on doing your best to use God's gifts and trust that He will bless it, or do you yearn to make more money as soon as possible?

3. You don't need to hide wealth, but are you sometimes arrogant in the way you try to show it off?

4. Do you feel your plans for spending, tithing, saving, and passing on wealth are blessed by God?

Giving Back Generously

1. How do you balance your gift to give back generously with righteous responsibilities to provide for your family (and even to leave something for your children)?

2. Should it be the responsibility of the state to provide for the needy, or is it the responsibility of those who are called? What are the differences and effects of each?

3. Have you prayed about what is the right amount of giving? If not, your giving may be done grudgingly with some guilt, instead of being a joy to you.

4. When you tithe or give to a charity, do you imagine what good those funds will do and thank God for your ability to do this? Have you ever thought about taxes in a similar way?

Chapter 4: Corporate Leadership Qualifications

The Right Stuff—Executive Qualities

1. What do you think the most important job performance characteristics are in an executive?

2. Do you think these differ significantly from those characteristics sought in the hiring or selection process?

3. Which characteristics do you feel are your biggest strengths?

4. Are there any areas in which you feel you have less talent or skill?

The Christian Leadership Survey

1. What do you feel are your greatest leadership strengths?

2. Do you have an assessment of your relative weaknesses? What are they?

3. Are any of these relative weaknesses in some part due to your views as a Christian? Why?

4. What ought you do in order to strengthen some of the weaker areas?

Chapter 5: The Christian Advantage

Generosity and Servanthood

1. How does servanthood exhibit itself in your attitudes and management style?

2. Have you worked for someone who was clearly self-promoting and arrogant? How did this effect your motivation and your desire to continue to work for him or her?

3. Have you worked for someone who had clear interest in your development, success, health, and happiness? How did this affect your motivation and your desire to continue to work for him or her?

4. Does your organization value a culture of servanthood? Is it shown by the top executives?

Character and Integrity

1. Does your company consistently embrace high standards of integrity?

2. Have you experienced a struggle with a decision over the question of integrity?

3. Have you ever felt pressure at your job to compromise integrity?

4. Have you ever refused to do something because of your convictions? What happened?

5. Do you feel that having high standards of integrity is an advantage or a liability in the corporate world?

Commitment and Dedication

1. Are you committed to the goals of your organization? Does your team feel your dedication?

2. How do you communicate your commitment to the corporate mission to the organization?

3. If you are in doubt about the corporate objectives, who do you share that with? Your subordinates, your peers, or your boss/board?

4. If you cannot fully embrace the goals or mission, can you commit to them?

5. If you cannot commit, what should you do?

Positive Attitude

1. Do people look to you for encouragement and a positive attitude in tough times?

2. Have you known any great or respected leaders who did not have a positive attitude?

3. Are you drawn to people who exude a positive attitude and optimism? Isn't this a component of charisma?

4. Do you endeavor to show a positive attitude regarding business challenges, even when you are feeling fear or anxiety inside you?

5. How do you moderate or manage your fear and anxiety in order to better display a positive attitude?

Passion

1. Do you have a passion to lead? If so, why?

2. Do you feel that most of the strong leaders you know or have worked for have passion (overmastering conviction) for their business mission?

3. Do you feel most Christian leaders in secular corporations have greater passion for their work than nonbelieving leaders? If so, why?

4. How do passion and obsession differ?

Relationship Skills

1. Do you feel your relationship skills are strong? Have you ever had 360-degree feedback on this area?

2. Have you had a leader who remained aloof and avoided relationships with his or her team? How did you feel about it?

3. Does biblical instruction guide us to be a distant leader or one who has strong relationships with followers?

4. What practices or behaviors do you follow to develop strong relationships with your team or organization?

5. Is it challenging to get your team members to "fly in formation"? How do you encourage them to behave as a team?

Listening Skills and Teachability

1. Do you have a teachable spirit? In what ways do you practice or show this?

2. Do the people working for you feel that you actively seek their counsel and listen to them with interest and respect?

3. Who do you value more, the employee who challenges your thinking or the employee who obediently waits for your instruction?

4. Have you had a boss who you felt did not listen, but was instead arrogant in his belief that his views were always superior? How did that affect your desire to counsel him?

Accountability

1. Do people trust you to have a strong sense of accountability, or do they think you avoid responsibility in tough times?

2. Do you feel that Christians have a greater sense of accountability on the job because of scriptural instruction than nonbelievers?

3. Have you ever worked for a leader who would not take accountability but instead tried to protect himself (or herself) by assigning blame? How did you feel about this?

4. As a leader, are you prepared to be accountable for all that happens in your organization?

5. If you have done your best to manage expectations but the expectations are still beyond what you feel are possible, what should you do?

Focus

1. Are you known for staying focused and being able to identify the important priorities?

2. There are leaders who are immersed in details and those who are focused on priorities: which are more effective? Is there a correct balance?

3. What are your key priorities today at work? How many are there?

4. How do you ensure that your organization is focused on key priorities?

Chapter 6: Perceived Christian Weaknesses

Charisma and Presence

1. Are you perceived as having great charisma and presence?

2. Consider leaders you have known and assess their charisma and presence. Were those with the greatest of these qualities necessarily the ones you wanted to follow?

3. Where would you place charisma and presence in importance for success? What other qualities do you think are more important?

4. Do you feel humility and gentleness may conflict with the qualities of charisma and presence?

5. To be bold in leadership, can charisma and presence be used effectively?

6. How can you develop or project these skills better?

Courage and Risk Taking

1. Are you a risk-taker? Do you have courage to take risks? How?

2. Do you feel that Christians are perceived as risk-averse and less courageous than nonbelievers?

3. Do you feel Scripture instructs Christians to be more risk-averse?

4. As a leader, what situation in your experience most required you to have courage?

5. What were the greatest risks that you took in business? How did they turn out? What learning did you derive from them?

6. If there were a fourth servant in the parable of talents who tried to wisely invest the master's money but experienced a loss, what do you think the master would have said?

Initiative and Innovation

1. Do you think you exhibit strong skills for innovation and initiative? Why?

2. Are you leading competition or following them?

3. What are the key areas in which you are differentiating or innovating compared to the competition?

4. What innovation did you initiate (or drive) that best succeeded? Why?

5. Which one failed the most? Why?

6. Name five things you are planning to change this year.

Decisiveness, Determination, and Security

1. Do you consider decisiveness and determination to be one of your strengths? Why?

2. Have you ever seen a leader with "analysis paralysis"? Was this a good leader?

3. If you ask God for an answer on a business decision, how long should you wait?

4. Is it OK to petition God for what you desire? (See Philippians 4:6.)

5. When you relinquish control to God, what are you asking? (See Matthew 6:10.)

Vision

1. Do you think that vision is one of your strengths? Why?

2. Why do you think that survey respondents felt vision was one of the weakest qualities for Christian leaders? Bias, or does their response have any merit?

3. As a Christian, how would you balance responsibility with vision?

4. Does your company have a vision statement? Does it paint a picture of "the promised land"? Is it one that inspires employees?

Problem-Solving Skills

1. Do you consider problem-solving skills to be one of your strengths? Why?

2. Do you solve problems, or do you look to avoid them unless absolutely necessary?

3. How do you attack problems?

4. Are you the chief problem-solver or do you have a team that is most often able to do this?

Communication Skills

1. When you think of leaders with strong communication skills that you have worked for, is your evaluation based on their presentation skills or their informal communication abilities?

2. Do you consider yourself a good presenter? If not, what instruction or coaching have you sought in order to improve?

3. When communicating with your team, do you consciously practice listening, relate the message to their needs, seek understanding, and ask for acceptance?

4. Which do you feel is more important: that the message is clear or that the listeners are receptive?

5. What lessons from Scripture can assist you in being a better communicator?

Competence

1. In business, how do faith and competence interrelate?

2. Do you feel that God wishes you to develop competence in your vocation to its utmost? Why?

3. As a leader, what is your strongest area of competence? Your weakest?

4. What have you done to assess your competence and address areas of opportunity?

Chapter 7: Motivating the Team

Care and Respect

1. Do people who report to you feel that you care for them, or do they feel that you view them as simply instruments of your own success?

2. Have you had a boss who used you for his or her advancement with no care for your own career or life?

3. Do you show respect for each employee at every level in the organization?

4. How do you feel when you see an executive speaking down to or demeaning a person lower in the organization?

5. Challenge question: How should you show care and respect for a dishonest or disloyal employee?

Encouragement

1. Were any of your business triumphs assisted by people that provided encouragement?

2. One merely overcomes inaction when you say, "If you don't do this the consequences are *X*." On the other hand, he or she overcomes doubt when you say, "I know you can do it." Which kind of boss do you want to be? Why?

3. Have you had a leader who used fear to motivate employees, threatening them with negative consequences? Have you had a leader who was an encourager or even a "cheerleader"? Which did you respond to best?

4. As a servant leader, does God instruct us to motivate with encouragement or with fear?

Coaching and Honest Feedback

1. Do you provide open and honest feedback to your staff on a regular basis?

2. When giving a formal performance review, has the subordinate ever been very surprised and disappointed? Whose fault was this?

3. What is your motivation to provide feedback and coaching? What was the apostle Paul's motivation?

4. Think of your business successes. Do you include on this list the success of people who you helped to develop?

Trust

1. In your career, for whom did you feel the most desire to delight: the leader who invested trust or the boss who scrutinized your work? Explain how both felt.

2. Do you feel all the people on your staff are trustworthy?

3. Do your employees feel that you give them enough trust?

4. A famous Ronald Reagan quote is, "Trust, but verify."[1] How do you balance giving trust with being accountable?

Vulnerability and Humility

1. When employees have shared their fears or concerns with you, are you comfortable validating them by giving them a glimpse of your own apprehension?

2. How have you used vulnerability to help strengthen the confidence of others?

3. Have you had a boss who never seemed to be in doubt and who always barreled straight ahead? Did he practice listening skills often? Were you anxious to follow him or her?

4. Do you have an inner circle at work with whom you feel freer to be vulnerable?

5. How has sharing your vulnerability and fears in prayer helped to strengthen you for leadership?

Rejoice and Celebrate

1. What customs do you follow regarding celebrating accomplishments or events with your staff?

2. What do you feel these celebrations accomplish?

3. Have you ever had a boss who always pushed for more and never called a time out to enjoy a good accomplishment? If so, how did you feel about it?

4. When celebrating, who should you give thanks to? Your staff, God, or both?

Chapter 8: Setting Expectations

Hard Work

1. Paul told Christians to work hard in their secular jobs, but is this still important today?

2. As a leader, you work hard. Do you expect as much from your people?

3. Who complains about hard work the most at your company? The people who work hard, or the people who do not?

4. Are there differences between how you handle employees who are unwilling and those who are unable to do a good job?

5. Have you considered or developed ways in which you can support people who are willing and can be a positive addition, but need some creative support?

Results and Performance

1. Do you clearly set expectations for results and performance?

2. As a Christian, do you struggle with accurately evaluating poor performers?

3. Are you more concerned with giving generously to those who achieve, or are you more concerned that those who do not might be disappointed?

4. Do your employees believe that you will discern greatly between excellent results and unacceptable results?

Team Players

1. Is your staff a team? Are they all team players?

2. What do you do to set expectations for teamwork? What have you done to encourage it?

3. Do you tolerate members who are not team players? Where do you draw a line?

4. Do you think all members of your team are in large part equally important? Does your feeling on this impact how you treat different members?

Total Integrity

1. Do you have a clearly-thought-through strategy and implementation plan to establish a culture of high integrity in your organization or on your team?

2. Do you do enough to ensure that each new hire has solid integrity and character?

3. Have you ever been "burned" by a person who did not have the integrity to always do the right thing? Were there any warning signals that you should have acted on earlier?

4. Are you confident that all members of your team have strong integrity? If not, what are you doing to manage the risk and resolve the issue?

You're Fired

1. Has concern or compassion for an individual caused you to delay or avoid a termination decision, even though you knew it was the right thing for the company? What ended up happening?

2. How might employees view your leadership when they see no action taken over a long period of time with an underperforming employee?

3. Is it compassionate to allow a person to stay in a job for which he or she is not suited?

4. When you have terminated an employee, what were your guiding principles for handling the action? What was your hope or prayer for that employee?

Corporate Layoffs

1. Do you feel that companies who offshore labor needs are bad? What alternatives would you suggest for them to be globally competitive?

2. Your business is unprofitable because competition is more efficient than you. Rather than lay off 10 percent of your people, you come up with a plan to survive by eliminating bonuses, cutting benefits, and putting many of your people on reduced hours, hoping the business soon improves. What will the most valuable and talented employees usually do?

3. Have you ever had to deal with downsizing or a layoff? Did you thoroughly explore alternatives and other solutions before making the best long-term decision?

4. What is the responsibility of a servant leader to employees affected by a layoff?

Chapter 9: Executive Dangers

Power and Greed

1. What are your greatest motivations for seeking corporate leadership?

2. How is longing for power different from seeking responsibility?

3. Does your organizational culture support people who manipulate for power and advancement?

4. Is your energy focused primarily on making the pie bigger for everyone, or do you worry about how you can get the biggest share?

5. In a good year, are you more pleased with opening your own bonus check or handing them out to your staff?

Pride and Arrogance

1. Do you feel that you are superior to your subordinates? Why or why not?

2. Write down a list of the things that each staff member is better than you at.

3. Do you study, discuss, and ask questions on a decision adequately before you offer an opinion? Would your staff agree?

4. To whom do you attribute your success? Is it primarily people that have coached and mentored you, or is it largely due to your own hard work and efforts? Or, is it also because God was generous in giving you certain gifts?

Everyone Else Cheats

1. Do you have competitors who seem to win through unethical or dishonest practices?

2. Are there any unethical, dishonest, or misleading practices in your company? What can you do to correct these and still succeed?

3. How have you considered strategies of integrity to make this a competitive advantage?

4. How do you (or your company) deal with unethical, dishonest, or misleading vendors or clients? Is there a way for both parties to rise up to an honest plane and benefit from it?

Obsession and Burnout

1. Have you felt stressed and burned out at work? Do you now?

2. Do you feel that you need to complete or closely monitor nearly all details and tasks?

3. Do you have a strong enough team to largely let go of all but the priorities you wish to focus on?

4. Do you often bring work home, or are you mentally occupied with work when not at the office?

5. Do you have a variety of outside interests that refresh you and take your thoughts off work?

6. Do you let go of worry on things that you can do little to impact and trust God to handle it?

Family Casualties

1. How is the health of your marriage and your relationships with your children?

2. What strains does your career put on your family?

3. Does your spouse support your career despite the time and emotional commitment required?

4. How do you balance your responsibilities at work and at home?

5. As a corporate leader, are you sensitive and responsive to the family needs of employees?

The Price of Success

1. What examples have you seen of executives that have suffered from depression, wrecked their marriage, or been victims of alcohol and drug abuse?

2. Have any of these problems been a challenge to you in your career?

3. Have you sought spiritual or medical counsel to deal with any of these?

4. How do you effectively partner with those peers or associates in corporate life who are susceptible to such problems without "joining the fraternity"?

5. What guidance have you found from Scripture regarding these topics?

Chapter 10: Executive Blessings

Greater Meaning and Fulfillment in Work

1. What are your motivations to be a business leader?

2. What significance do you feel that you have in your work?

3. How much does God wish to use you in the workplace?

4. How do you invite God into your workplace?

5. How is God blessing you in your work?

Greater Meaning and Fulfillment Outside of Work

1. Are there certain parts of your life that God is more included in than others?

2. When you've "forgotten" God for ten hours of your working/commuting day, how easy is it to reconnect when you arrive at home?

3. How do you stay connected with God in each part of your day?

Are You Called?

1. Has God designed you to be a corporate leader? Is this your calling?

2. Is it His will that you use the talents He created in you and to develop them into skills that will enable you to be a strong and successful leader?

3. Do you feel His purpose in your efforts and challenges at work?

4. Are there still any areas of work, other responsibilities, or decisions that you do not feel God supports you in? If so, where can you seek further guidance?

NOTES

Introduction

1. Laura Nash, *Believers in Business* (Nashville, Tennessee: Thomas Nelson Publishers, 1994), 25.

Chapter 1—The Need for Christian Executives

1. Doug Sherman and William Hendricks, *Your Work Matters to God* (Colorado Springs, Colorado: Navpress, 1987).

2. Dorothy Sayers, *Creed or Chaos? Why Christians Must Choose Either Dogma or Disaster (Or, Why It Really Does Matter What You Believe)* (Manchester: Sophia Institute Press, 1999), 77–78.

3. Sherman and Hendricks, *Your Work Matters to God*.

4. Ibid., 269.

5. Ibid., 135–136.

6. Ibid., 134.

7. Sayers, *Creed or Chaos?*, 77–78.

8. Larry Julian, *God Is My CEO: Following God's Principles in a Bottom-Line World* (Avon, Massachusetts: Adams Press, 2001), 12.

9. Charles Lane, "Justices Overturn Andersen Conviction," *Washington Post,* A01, June 1, 2005.

10. Wayne Grudem, *Business for the Glory of God* (Wheaton, Illinois: Crossway Books, 2003), 11.

11. Jon M. Huntsman, *Winners Never Cheat: Everyday Values We Learned as Children (But May Have Forgotten)* (Upper Saddle River: Wharton School Pub., 2005), 4.

12. Ibid., 7.

13. Ibid., 38.

14. Dennis Prager, "Why Are U.S. Universities Moral Wastelands?" WorldNetDaily (May 21, 2002), http://www.worldnetdaily.com/news/article.asp?ARTICLE_ID=27694 (accessed April 9, 2008).

15. Ghandi quote accessed at http://thinkexist.com/quotation/ghandi-s-seven-sins-wealth -without-work-pleasure/1233166.html (February 1, 2008).

16. Vincent Carroll and David Shiflett, *Christianity on Trial, Arguments Against Anti-Religious Bigotry* (San Francisco, California: Encounter Books, 2002), x.

17. Tammy Bruce, *The Death of Right And Wrong* (New York: Three Rivers Press, 2003), 41.

18. Carroll and Shiflett, *Christianity on Trial*, vii.

19. David Limbaugh, *Persecution: How Liberals are Waging War Against Christianity* (New York: Harper Collins, 2004), 225.

20. Voltaire quote accessed at http://www.valuequotes.net/ (February 1, 2008).

21. Laura Nash and Scotty McLennan, *Church on Sunday, Work on Monday: The Challenge of Fusing Christian Values with Business Life* (San Francisco, California: Jossey-Bass, 2001), xxx.

22. Ibid., xxvii.

23. Karl Barth quote accessed http://www.blogtoplist.com/rss/karl-barth.html (February 1, 2008).

24. J. Michael Straczynski quote accessed at http://thinkexist.com/quotes/j._michael_straczynski/ (February 26, 2008).

Chapter 2—Answering the Call

1. Dean William Willimon, "Christian Leadership 101," Duke University Sermon Archives, August 26, 2002, www.chapel.duke.edu/worship/sunday/viewsermon.aspx?id=69 (accessed February 28, 2008).

2. Vince Lombardi quote accessed at http://www.brainyquote.com/quotes/quotes/v/vincelomba151247.html (February 1, 2008).

3. Joseph L. Badaracco Jr., *Harvard Business Review on Corporate Ethics: We Don't Need Another Hero* (Boston, Massachusetts: Harvard Business School Publishing, 2003), 10.

4. Ibid., 8.

5. Laura L. Nash, *Harvard Business Review on Corporate Ethics: Ethics Without The Sermon* (Boston, Massachusetts: Harvard Business School Publishing, 2003), 22.

6. Lynn Sharp Paine, *Harvard Business Review on Corporate Ethics: Managing for Organizational Integrity* (Boston, Massachusetts: Harvard Business School Publishing, 2003), 85.

7. Thomas Donaldson, *Harvard Business Review on Corporate Ethics: Values in Tension, Ethics Away from Home* (Boston, Massachusetts: Harvard Business School Publishing, 2003), 114.

8. Joseph L. Badaracco Jr., *Harvard Business Review on Corporate Ethics: The Discipline of Building Character*, 163.

9. Charles Colson and Jack Eckerd, *Why America Doesn't Work* (Nashville, Tennessee: W Publishing Group, 1992).

10. Jon M. Huntsman, *Winners Never Cheat* (Upper Saddle River: Wharton School Publishing, 2005), 24.

11. Dennis Prager, "Judeo-Christian Values, Part 11: Moral Absolutes," *WorldNetDaily* (May 3, 2005), http://www.wnd.com/news/article.asp?ARTICLE_ID=44093 (accessed April 9, 2008).

12. Adrian Gostick and Dana Telford, *The Integrity Advantage* (Salt Lake City, Utah: Gibbs Smith, 2003), 29.

13. George Washington quote accessed at http://www.brainyquote.com/quotes/authors/g/george_washington.html (February 29, 2008).

14. Leo Hindery Jr., *It Takes a CEO* (New York: Simon and Schuster, 2005).

15. Michelangelo quote accessed at http://www.brainyquote.com/quotes/authors/m/michelangelo.html (February 29, 2008).

16. John C. Maxwell, *The 21 Indispensable Qualities of a Leader* (Nashville, Tennessee: Thomas Nelson), 15.

17. Ray Kroc quote accessed at http://www.brainyquote.com/quotes/authors/r/ray_kroc.html (February 29, 2008).

Chapter 3—Understanding the Responsibilities

1. PepsiCo's mission statement at the time of writing this book in 2007 is available at "Pepsi Mission Statement," *Samples Help!*, http://www.samples-help.org.uk/mission -statements/pepsi-mission-statement.htm (accessed April 7, 2008).

2. "Our Credo," Johnson & Johnson, http://www.jnj.com/our_company/our_credo/index .htm;jsessionid=D4KUAQCMYNHBOCQPCB3WU3QKB2IIWTT1 (accessed February 29, 2008).

3. "Purpose, Values and Principles," Proctor & Gamble, http://www.pg.com/company/ who_we_are/ppv.jhtml;jsessionid=5YLXABLVSOSPFQFIASJXKZGAVACJG3MK (accessed February 29, 2008).

4. McDonald's mission statement at the time of writing this book in 2007 is available at "Homework for Business Planning," *Entrepreneurship Education and Outreach Program,* Cornell, http://www.eeo.aem.cornell.edu/ag%20food%20series/issues/issue02.htm#combined (accessed April 7, 2008).

5. "General Company Information," Intel, http://www.intel.com/intel/company/corp1 .htm#anchor1 (February 29, 2008).

6. "Mission Statement," Center for Business Planning, http://www.businessplans.org/ mission.html (accessed April 7, 2008).

7. Henry Ford quote accessed at http://www.brainyquote.com/quotes/authors/h/henry_ ford.html (February 29, 2008).

8. Milton Friedman, "The Social Responsibility of Business Is to Increase Its Profits," *The New York Times Magazine*, September 13, 1970.

9. Merriam-Webster's Collegiate Dictionary, 11th Ed., s.v. "stewardship" (Springfield, Massachusetts: Merriam-Webster, Incorporated, 2006).

10. Arnold Glasgow quote accessed at http://www.winston-churchill-leadership.com/ leadership-quote-part4.html (February 29, 2008).

11. Sherman and Hendricks, *Your Work Matters to God.*

12. Manuel L. Jose, "The Development of Taxation in the Bible," *Accounting Historians Journal* (December 1998).

13. Ibid.

14. Jonathan Swift quote accessed at http://www.worldofquotes.com/author/Jonathan -Swift/1/index.html (March 4, 2008).

Chapter 4—Corporate Leadership Qualifications

1. Benjamin Franklin quote accessed at http://en.wikiquote.org/wiki/Benjamin_Franklin (March 5, 2008).

2. Merriam-Webster's Collegiate Dictionary, 11th Ed., s.v. "meek."

Chapter 5—The Christian Advantage

1. Douglas LaBier, *Modern Madness; The Hidden Link Between Work and Emotional Conflict* (Lincoln, Nebraska: iUniverse.com Inc., 2000), 5.

2. Maxwell, *The 21 Indispensable Qualities of a Leader*, 62.

3. Ibid., 138.

4. His Holiness the Dalai Lama, *Ethics for the New Millennium* (New York: Riverhead Books, 1999), 75.

5. Dale Carnegie, *How to Win Friends and Influence People* (New York: Pocket Books, 1998).

6. Gostick and Telford, *The Integrity Advantage*, 2.

7. Gostick and Telford, *The Integrity Advantage*, 37.

8. Martin Luther King Jr. quote accessed at http://www.quotationspage.com/quotes/ Martin_Luther_King_Jr (March 5, 2008).

9. General Norman Schwarzkopf quote accessed at http://www.brainyquote.com/quotes/ authors/n/norman_schwarzkopf.html (March 5, 2008).

10. Sherman and Hendricks, *Your Work Matters to God*, 45.

11. Maxwell, *The 21 Indispensable Qualities of a Leader*, 18.

12. Merlin Olsen quote accessed at http://thinkexist.com/quotes/merlin_olsen/ (March 5, 2008).

13. Frank Lloyd Wright quote accessed at http://thinkexist.com/quotation/the_thing_ always_happens_that_you_really_believe/155539.html (March 5, 2008).

14. Napoleon Bonaparte quote accessed at http://www.brainyquote.com/quotes/quotes/n/ napoleonbo106371.html (March 5, 2008).

15. Winston Churchill quote accessed at http://www.quotationspage.com/quote/3253 .html (March 5, 2008).

16. Peter Kyne quote accessed at http://www.leader-values.com/Content/quotes .asp?Letter=P (March 5, 2008).

17. E. W. Forster quote accessed at [http://www.leadershipnow.com/passionquotes.html] (March 5, 2008).

18. Maxwell, *The 21 Indispensable Qualities of a Leader*, 85.

19. Steve Jobs quote accessed at http://en.wikipedia.org/wiki/John_Sculley (March 5, 2008).

20. "Chip Shots Gallery," *Molecular Expressions*, Michael W. Davidson and Florida State University, http://micro.magnet.fsu.edu/chipshots/index.html (accessed April 8, 2008).

21. Maxwell, *The 21 Indispensable Qualities of a Leader*, 83.

22. Denis Diderot quote accessed at http://www.quotationspage.com/quotes/Denis_ Diderot/ (March 5, 2008).

23. Geoff Colvin, "Steve Jobs' Bad Bet," *Fortune* (March 5, 2007), CNNMoney.com, http://money.cnn.com/magazines/fortune/fortune_archive/2007/03/19/8402325/index .htm?source=yahoo_quote (accessed April 7, 2008).

24. Jeremy Noakes, "Hitler and 'Lebensraum' in the East," *BBC History*, http://www.bbc .co.uk/history/worldwars/wwtwo/hitler_lebensraum_01.shtml (accessed April 7, 2008).

25. Billy Graham quote accessed at http://www.christianitytoday.com/leaders/features/ lesecbgraham.html (March 5, 2008).

26. Michelangelo quote accessed at http://www.quotesandpoem.com/quotes/listquotes/ author/Michelangelo (March 5, 2008).

27. Bob Briner and Ray Pritchard, *Leadership Lessons of Jesus* (New York: Grammercy Books, 1998), 90.

28. Alan Loy McGinnis, *The Friendship Factor* (Minneapolis, MN: Augsburg Fortress Publishers, 2004); Dale Carnegie, *How to Win Friends and Influence People*.

29. Maxwell, *The 21 Indispensable Qualities of a Leader*, 103.

30. William Wrigley Jr. quote accessed at http://www.quotationspage.com/quotes/ William_Wrigley_Jr./ (March 6, 2008).

31. Mary Kay Ash quote accessed at http://thinkexist.com/quotes/mary_kay_ash/2.html (March 6, 2008).

32. Carnegie, *How to Win Friends and Influence People*.

33. William Mizner quote accessed at http://thinkexist.com/quotation/popularity_is_ exhausting-the_life_of_the_party/325761.html (March 6, 2008).

34. Publilius Syrus quote accessed at http://www.giga-usa.com/quotes/topics/interest_t001.htm (March 6, 2008).

35. Sam Walton quote accessed at http://thinkexist.com/quotes/sam_walton/ (March 6, 2008).

36. Jesse Jackson quote accessed at http://www.brainyquote.com/quotes/authors/j/jesse_jackson.html (March 6, 2008).

37. Dale Carnegie, *How to Win Friends and Influence People.*

38. Maxwell, *The 21 Indispensable Qualities of a Leader*, 74.

39. Dean Rusk quote accessed at http://www.brainyquote.com/quotes/authors/d/dean_rusk.html (March 6, 2008).

40. Maxwell, *The 21 Indispensable Qualities of a Leader*, 145.

41. Winston Churchill quote accessed at http://thinkexist.com/quotation/personally-i-m_always_ready_to_learn-although_i/150140.html (March 6, 2008).

42. Harry Truman quote accessed at http://www.trumanlibrary.org/buckstop.htm (March 6, 2008).

43. Jon M. Huntsman, *Winners Never Cheat: Everyday Values We Learned as Children (But May Have Forgotten)* (Upper Saddle River: Wharton School Publishing, 2005), 65.

44. Michael Armstrong quote accessed at http://thinkexist.com/quotation/the_ancient_romans_had_a_tradition-whenever_one/216701.html (March 6, 2008).

45. Dan Zandra quote accessed at http://stonebridgecrossings.blogspot.com/2006/02/accountability.html (March 6, 2008).

46. Maxwell, *The 21 Indispensable Qualities of a Leader*, 53.

47. Robert Shiller quote accessed at http://www.quotationspage.com/quote/25936.html (March 6, 2008).

48. Briner and Pritchard, *Leadership Lessons of Jesus*, 230.

Chapter 6—Perceived Christian Weaknesses

1. Charles Bradlaugh quote found in Rufus K. Noyes, ed., *Views of Religion* (Boston, Massachusetts: L. K. Washburn, 1906), 459; available at http://books.google.com/books?id=KGcSAAAAYAAJ&pg=PA459&lpg=PA459&dq=i+cannot+follow+you+christians+for+you+try+to+crawl+through+life+on+your+knees+while+i+stride+through+mine+on+my+feet&source=web&ots=FcaRsHxFH7&sig=an_yeYw5TDlONBXpYx55KO059mI&hl=en (accessed March 6, 2008).

2. Peter Drucker quote accessed at http://www.quoteland.com/topic.asp?CATEGORY_ID=441 (March 6, 2008).

3. Debra Benton, *Executive Charisma* (New York: McGraw-Hill, 2003).

4. Quote accessed at http://thinkexist.com/quotes/with/keyword/charisma (March 6, 2008).

5. P. J. O'Rourke quote accessed at http://thinkexist.com/quotation/making_fun_of_born-again_christians_is_like/218627.html (March 6, 2008).

6. Maxwell, *The 21 Indispensable Qualities of a Leader*, 41.

7. James Freeman Clarke quote accessed at http://thinkexist.com/quotation/conscience_is_the_root_of_all_true_courage-if_a/151566.html (March 6, 2008).

8. George Patton quote accessed at http://www.quotationspage.com/quotes/George_S._Patton/ (March 6, 2008).

9. Alan Wheelis quote accessed at http://www.positiveatheism.org/hist/quotes/quote-w0.htm (March 6, 2008).

10. Michael Eisner quote accessed at http://thinkexist.com/quotes/michael_eisner/ (March 6, 2008).

11. Mark Galli and Ted Olson, *131 Christians Everyone Should Know* (Nashville, TN: B & H Publishing Group, 2000).

12. Winston Churchill quote accessed at http://thinkexist.com/quotation/i_never_worry_about_action-but_only_about/175245.html (March 6, 2008).

13. Bill Gates quote accessed at http://www.brainyquote.com/quotes/quotes/b/billgates 191255.html (March 6, 2008).

14. Peter Drucker quote accessed at http://www.innovationtools.com/Quotes/Quotes.asp (March 6, 2008).

15. David Ogilvy quote accessed at http://www.cfiae.org/quotesoninnovation.php (March 6, 2008).

16. C. S. Lewis, *Perelandra* (New York: Scribner, 1972), 88.

17. Voltaire quote accessed at http://www.brainyquote.com/quotes/authors/v/voltaire.html (March 6, 2008).

18. Julian, *God Is My CEO*, 219.

19. George Patton quote accessed at http://thinkexist.com/quotation/i-would-rather-have-a-german-division-in-front-of/545684.html (March 7, 2008).

20. Deloitte & Touche survey results accessed at www.fast500.com (March 7, 2008).

21. Lee Iacocca quote accessed at http://thinkexist.com/quotes/lee_iacocca/3.html (March 7, 2008).

22. Will Rogers quote accessed at http://www.quotationspage.com/quote/272.html (March 7, 2008).

23. Benjamin Franklin quote accessed at http://thinkexist.com/quotation/lighthouses_are_more_helpful_than/159913.html (March 7, 2008).

24. Bertrand Russell quote accessed at http://www.brainyquote.com/quotes/authors/b/bertrand_russell.html (March 7, 2008).

25. Maxwell, *The 21 Indispensible Qualities of a Leader*, 153.

26. Antoine de Saint-Euxpéry quote accessed at http://thinkexist.com/quotation/if_you_want_to_build_a_ship-don-t_drum_up_people/170927.html (March 7, 2008).

27. Henry David Thoreau quote accessed at http://www.brainyquote.com/quotes/authors/h/henry_david_thoreau.html (March 7, 2008).

28. Maxwell, *The 21 Indispensible Qualities of a Leader*, 153.

29. Bertrand Russell quote accessed at http://www.quotationspage.com/quotes/Bertrand_Russell (March 7, 2008).

30. Carroll and Shiflett, *Christianity on Trial*, 84.

31. Maxwell, *The 21 Indispensable Qualities of a Leader*, 102.

32. Norman Vincent Peale quote accessed at http://www.motivational-inspirational-corner.com/getquote.html?startrow=11&categoryid=64 (March 7, 2008).

33. Karl A. Menninger quote accessed at http://www.sawyerpartnership.com/quotes.htm (March 7, 2008).

34. Brett Lemoine quote accessed at http://radioatheist.com/ (March 7, 2008).

35. Lowell Thomas quote accessed at http://www.brainyquote.com/quotes/authors/l/lowell_thomas.html (March 7, 2008).

36. Doc Childre and Bruce Cryer, *From Chaos to Coherence* (Boulder Creek: Heartmath LLC, 2004), 7.

37. John Marshall quote accessed at http://www.brainyquote.com/quotes/quotes/j/johnmarsha170190.html (March 7, 2008).

38. Carnegie, *How to Win Friends and Influence People*.

39. Jesse Ventura quote accessed at http://thinkexist.com/quotation/organized_religion_is_a_sham_and_a_crutch_for/210461.html (March 7, 2008).

40. Maxwell, *The 21 Indispensable Qualities of a Leader*, 30.

41. Report by National Merit Scholarship Corporation for the 1999 class.

42. *U.S. News and World Report*, 2001.

43. Franklin and Marshall College rankings report.

Chapter 7—Motivating the Team

1. John C. Maxwell, *There's No Such Thing As Business Ethics* (New York: Warner Business Books, 2003), 34–48.

2. Ibid., 45.

3. Robert Schuman quote accessed at http://thinkexist.com/quotes/robert_a._schumann/ (March 7, 2008).

4. Maxwell, *There's No Such Thing As Business Ethics*.

5. James Howell quote accessed at http://www.quotationspage.com/quote/2691.html (March 7, 2008).

6. Nash, *Believers in Business*, 124.

7. Albert Einstein quote accessed at http://www.brainyquote.com/quotes/authors/a/albert_einstein.html (March 7, 2008).

8. Robert Collier quote accessed at http://www.brainyquote.com/quotes/authors/r/robert_collier.html (March 7, 2008).

9. Maxwell, *There's No Such Thing As Business Ethics*.

10. Benjamin Disraeli quote accessed at http://thinkexist.com/quotes/benjamin_disraeli/ (March 7, 2008).

11. Walter Lippman quote accessed at http://thinkexist.com/quotes/walter_lippman/ (March 7, 2008).

12. W. A. Nance quote accessed at http://thinkexist.com/quotes/rev._w.a._nance/ (March 7, 2008).

13. Harry Gordon Selfridge quote accessed at http://www.motivatingquotes.com/leadership.htm (March 7, 2008).

14. Briner and Pritchard, *Leadership of Jesus*, 77.

15. George MacDonald quote accessed at http://www.brainyquote.com/quotes/quotes/g/georgemacd134599.html (March 10, 2008).

16. Democritus quote accessed at http://www.whatquote.com/quotes/Democritus/13203 -Do-not-trust-all-men.htm (March 10, 2008).

17. Ralph Waldo Emerson quote accessed at http://www.quotationspage.com/quote/2067 .html (March 10, 2008).

18. *The Sands of Iwo Jima*, DVD, directed by Allan Dwan (1949; Santa Monica, California: Lionsgate Home Entertainment, 1998).

19. Huntsman, *Winners Never Cheat*, 62.

20. St. Augustine quote accessed at http://www.quoteopia.com/famous.php?quotesby =saintaugustine (March 10, 2008).

21. Mohandas Ghandi quote accessed at http://www.brainyquote.com/quotes/authors/m/mohandas_gandhi.html (March 10, 2008).

22. *Merriam-Webster's Collegiate Dictionary*, 11th ed., s.v. "rejoice."

23. Ibid., s.v. "celebrate."

24. Briner and Pritchard, *Leadership of Jesus*, 51.

25. Thomas J. Peters quote accessed at http://thinkexist.com/quotes/thomas_j._peters/ (March 10, 2008).

Chapter 8—Setting Expectations

1. Sources: U.S. Department of Interior (1883) and Ethel Jones in the *Review of Economics and Statistics* (1963)

2. "Bureau of Labor Statistics," US Department of Labor, http://www.bls.gov/cps/wlf-table21-2007.pdf (March 10, 2008).

3. Judith M. Bardwick, *Danger in the Comfort Zone: From Boardroom to Mailroom—How to Break the Entitlement Habit That's Killing American Business* (New York: AMACOM, 1991), 10.

4. US Bureau of the Census, *Historical Statistics of the United States, Colonial Times to 1970*, Part 1, Series D 152-66, p. 138.

5. US Department of Labor, Bureau of Labor Statistics, *Women in the Labor Force: A Databook*, May 2005.

6. Peter Drucker quote accessed at http://www.brainyquote.com/quotes/quotes/p/peterdruck131070.html (March 10, 2008).

7. Mitchell Kaplan quote accessed at http://pcexperts.multiply.com/journal (March 10, 2008).

8. Winston Churchill quote accessed at http://www.quoteopia.com/famous.php?quotesby=winstonchurchill (March 10, 2008).

9. Briner and Pritchard, *Leadership of Jesus*, 86.

10. Huntsman, *Winners Never Cheat*, 99.

11. Casey Stengel quote accessed at http://www.heartquotes.net/teamwork-quotes.html (March 10, 2008).

12. Huntsman, 91.

13. Gostick and Telford, *The Integrity Advantage*, 76.

14. Ibid., 3.

15. Albert Einstein quote accessed at http://www.quoteopia.com/famous.php?quotesby=alberteinstein (March 10, 2008).

16. Nash, *Believers in Business,* 155.

17. Briner and Pritchard, *Leadership of Jesus*, 34.

18. Julian, *God Is My CEO*, 186.

19. Ibid., 191.

20. Ibid., 11.

21. Robert Schuller quote accessed at http://www.brainyquote.com/quotes/authors/r/robert_h_schuller.html (March 10, 2008).

Chapter 9—Executive Dangers

1. LaBier, *Modern Madness*, 8.

2. Huntsman, *Winners Never Cheat*, 153.

3. LaBier, *Modern Madness*, 61.

4. Lord Acton quote accessed at http://www.quotationspage.com/quote/27321.html (March 10, 2008).

5. Charles Caleb Colton quote accessed at http://www.notable-quotes.com/p/power_quotes.html (March 10, 2008).

6. LaBier, *Modern Madness*, 81.

7. "Carly May Get 42 Million," CNNMoney.com, February 12, 2005, http://money.cnn.com/2005/02/12/news/newsmakers/fiorina_severance/index.htm (accessed March 10, 2008).

8. Daniel Yankelovich, *Profit With Honor, The New Stage of Market Capitalism* (New Haven, Connecticut: Yale University Press, 2006), 138.

9. Erich Fromm quote accessed at http://www.brainyquote.com/quotes/quotes/e/erichfromm391095.html (March 10, 2008).

10. Huntsman, *Winners Never Cheat*, 63.

11. Bill George quote taken from the synopsis of *True North*, http://www.truenorthleaders.com/book.htm (accessed April 8, 2008).

12. Ralph Waldo Emerson quote accessed at http://en.thinkexist.com/quotation/every_man_i_meet_is_in_some_way_my_superior/11826.html (March 10, 2008).

13. Antoine de Saint-Exupéry quote accessed at http://www.quoteland.com/author.asp?AUTHOR_ID=230 (March 10, 2008).

14. Benjamin Franklin quote accessed at http://www.quoteopia.com/famous.php?quotesby=benjaminfranklin (March 10, 2008).

15. Robert Half quote accessed at http://www.brainyquote.com/quotes/authors/r/robert_half.html (March 10, 2008).

16. H. L. Mencken quote accessed at http://www.quotationspage.com/quotes/H._L._Mencken (March 10, 2008).

17. The Marquis de Sade quote accessed at http://www.josephsoninstitute.org/quotes/quotecrimecheat.htm (February 2008).

18. Huntsman, *Winners Never Cheat*, 40.

19. Ibid., 7.

20. LaBier, *Modern Madness*, 132.

21. Lee Iacocca quote accessed at http://www.finestquotes.com/author_quotes-author-Lee%20Iacocca-page-0.htm (March 11, 2008).

22. Bob Weinstein quote accessed at www.stressdoc.com/news0607_1.htm (March 11, 2008).

23. Eugene Raudsepp, "Are You a Workaholic?" MediaRecruiter.com, http://www.mediarecruiter.com/career/docs/Are%20You%20a%20Workaholic.htm (accessed at April 9, 2008).

24. Bill Owens quote accessed at http://www.brainyquote.com/quotes/authors/b/bill_owens.html (March 11, 2008).

25. Charles Swindoll quote accessed at http://www.stresslesscountry.com/stressquotes/index.html (March 11, 2008).

26. Julian, *God Is My CEO*, 64.

27. Raudsepp, "Are You a Workaholic?"

28. LaBier, *Modern Madness*, 197.

29. Ibid., 149.

30. Hara Estroff Marano, "The Price of Success," *Psychology Today* Magazine (May/June 2003), http://psychologytoday.com/articles/pto-20030725-000001.html (accessed March 11, 2008).

31. Jessi Hempel, "A Drinking Problem on Wall Street," *Business Week* (August 17, 2004), http://www.businessweek.com/bwdaily/dnflash/aug2004/nf20040817_8507_db008.htm (accessed March 11, 2008).

32. LaBier, *Modern Madness*, 35.

33. Hempel, "A Drinking Problem on Wall Street."

34. D. C Atkins, N. S. Jacobsen, and D. H. Bacon, "Understanding Infidelity," *Journal of Psychology* 15: 735–749.

35. George Horace Lorimer quote accessed at http://www.quotegarden.com/money.html (March 11, 2008).

Chapter 10—Executive Blessings

1. Sherman and Hendricks, *Your Work Matters to God*, 129.

The Christian Executive's Study Guide

1. Ronald Reagan quote accessed at http://www.brainyquote.com/quotes/quotes/r/ronaldreag147717.html (March 11, 2008).

ABOUT THE AUTHOR

Roger Andersen received his undergraduate degree in economics from Wheaton College and a master of business administration degree from Oregon State University. He also studied in Europe at Oxford University (Balliol College) and the University of Leiden.

Mr. Andersen worked for PepsiCo from 1976 to 1989. There he held numerous positions in strategic planning and finance, including senior director of finance for Canada and Latin America. Following his career at PepsiCo, Mr. Andersen served as vice president of finance for Tonka/Kenner/Parker International, chief financial officer for Rollerblade, and as senior vice president/CFO for Pepsi General Bottlers. Most recently, he served as president and chief executive officer of Young America Corporation, the largest consumer promotion services company in North America.

Roger lives in Minnesota with his wife and daughter.

To Contact the Author

www.theexecutivecalling.com